THE ARMIES
OF GOD

BOOKS BY PAUL BAILEY

Fiction

FOR TIME AND ALL ETERNITY
THE CLAWS OF THE HAWK
TYPE HIGH
FOR THIS MY GLORY
THE GAY SAINT
SONG EVERLASTING

Mystery Fiction

DELIVER ME FROM EVA

Biography

SAM BRANNAN AND THE CALIFORNIA MORMONS
JACOB HAMBLIN, BUCKSKIN APOSTLE
FABULOUS FARMER (the Story of Walter Knott and
    His Berry Farm) — with Roger Holmes
WALKARA, HAWK OF THE MOUNTAINS
WOVOKA, THE INDIAN MESSIAH
GRANDPA WAS A POLYGAMIST

Editor and Compiler of

THE MORMONS IN CALIFORNIA
    (Pioneer Journal of William Glover)

Non-Fiction

THE ARMIES OF GOD

THE ARMIES OF GOD

OF GOD

PAUL BAILEY

DOUBLEDAY & COMPANY, INC.
GARDEN CITY, NEW YORK
1968

289, 3

To Evelyn . . .
in remembrance
of early summer
in Kirtland and Nauvoo

Contents

Illustrations

THE ARMIES
OF GOD

Zion's Camp

I

THERE is nothing strange or unprecedented about Christians marching off to war. History is replete with incidents and examples of the followers of Jesus taking up the sword, either in defense of Messianic precepts, or to more vigorously ram home the points of Christian doctrine to the unbelievers or the intransigents. The pattern holds for Mormonism. Though distinctly an American religion, its Old World roots are more in keeping with the Judean tradition, rather than the Romanistic model of traditional Christianity. Its martial aspects run close parallel to everything in the European pattern of Christian militance — from the Crusades to the Inquisition — but with the dramatic variance which only America itself can give.

Mormon menfolk have made exceptionally good soldiers, because, zealous in a cause transcending life itself, no sacrifice could ever be too great. Nor was death in its name a thing to be feared. Their shakos were usually only the dim, drab caps and hats of the prairie and western frontier, and their uniforms considerably more bizarre than dazzling. But they needed no outer flash to the garb they wore in service. The undergarment of their priesthood stood as protective cloak to their bodies. An unshakable belief in God and the Prophet Joseph Smith lent motivation and unassailable conviction to their minds.

No longer is militarism a part of the Mormon tradition. The liberation army of Zion's Camp, the Nauvoo Legion, the Mormon Battalion, the military heroics of the the Utah War, are now only faintly remembered as parts of the rich mosaic of Mormon history. But like an echo out of the past, there still remains the fingered shadow of this militance.

Even today, in every Mormon heart remains the conviction and the promise that the cause they espouse will eventually take over and remake the world. Every Latter-day Saint is still a soldier for God and the Prophet — willing and anxious to sacrifice himself for the salvation of the world. And even today this willingness and sacrifice means strict adherence to the will and order of the Church Authorities, actually to the point of paying the cost in time and money for two-year missions to any part of the corld to which they may be "called." Their weapons may be only a scant ecclesiastical training, the *Book of Mormon,* and an unshakable conviction in the cause for which they sacrifice. But they are Christian soldiers, and as eager for the fray as were their grandfathers.

II

Up to the time of the Missouri expulsion of the Latter-day Saints in the fall and winter of 1833, Mormons generally had shown themselves as agrarian and gentle in attitude. While odd indeed to their neighbors on the American frontier, they were meek, pacific, and almost servile in their anxiety and efforts to win friends and converts to their cause. It took the roughing and rubbing of borderland hostility, along with a substantial measure of death and suffering, to stir up the latent strength of numbers which spilled over into resentment at abuse and indignity, and the will to fight back at their oppressors. The strange marching army, known as Zion's Camp, had as its primary objective the raising of the siege of Jackson County, and reinstatement of the expelled Saints to their "inheritances" in the land which God, through the Prophet Joseph Smith, had declared as the New Jerusalem of the imminent millennium.

The beginning of Mormonism, in upstate New York from 1823 to 1830, was wrapped in wonders and miracles. With the personal appearance of God the Father and His Son Jesus Christ to the youthful Joseph Smith, it would appear that with this smile and guidance of beneficent diety, the new sect should have been well led through the bogs and pitfalls of human inequity. But this was not so. From the beginning, the young prophet and his young church ran into the implacable hostility of its "Gentile" neighbors.

In search of more peaceful and fertile soil in which to nourish the revealed and momentous "plan of salvation" which was to save a lost world — that doctrine preached by the Prophet and his disciples as an actual restoration of Galilean Christianity in "the last days" — the church moved itself from New York to northern Ohio. The new seat of Mormondom was the town of Kirtland, sixteen miles east of Cleveland. A beautiful temple was immediately projected by the enterprising "Saints."

Even though Kirtland prospered, and converts to the new religion flowed into it in ever-increasing numbers, the Prophet needed no spiritual nudgings to convince him that additional space was needed away from America's populous centers, if ever the work of the Lord was to properly mature according to plan. Oddly, the Lord's eyes like those of everyone else, were roving westward in those days. In a revelation on September 22, 1832, it was divinely made known to Joseph Smith that Jackson County, in borderland Missouri, not only was diety's choice for the gathering place, but was to be the actual site for the New Jerusalem as biblically predicted for the coming millennium.

The new revelation had instant and dramatic effect upon the Prophet's followers. In spite of the projected temple, and town of Kirtland, in Ohio, there was soon a steady migration of Saints into Missouri — most of them settling in or immediately adjacent to the raw, tough town of Independence. At first the Missouri natives were more curious than angry. But when the Saints staked out twenty acres of the town's south side as the site for the greater temple, and the Saints made no bones of the fact that God had chosen to remake Independence into the New Jerusalem, the natives began having a few revelations of their own. They didn't so much mind new townsfolk, but this clannish breed, who were neither southerners nor westerners, had begun elbowing into Jackson County like a drove of locusts. When they threatened to take over an abnormal amount of real estate, in the name of the Lord, it was a little too much for the old settlers.

The Lord may have chosen Jackson County and Independence as His own, but the natives were not yet ready for any divine surrender. The Mormons seemed never to make any attempt to fraternize with the old settlers. They kept themselves aloof; made no bones about their intentions of transforming the rough little town into the abode of the blessed. They bought land, squatted on vacant acres, nudged relentlessly into the township, and within a space of months possessed a voting majority over the Missouri settlers. These new and sanctimonious land grabbers were a different breed from Missourians. And since there was no mixing, and never could be, a line of battle was not long in forming.

If Jackson County, Missouri, were the Lord's choice for the Mormon holy land, it seems a bizarre one in retrospect. Independence sat like a burly scab on the western border of the state, and Missouri itself, in 1833, was on the western borders of civilization. "Beyond stretched the domain of the savage. The population was composed entirely of frontiersmen, all of whom, little accustomed to the restraints of law, and unschooled in the lesson of its supremacy, were in the habit of correcting fancied grievances in their own way."[1]

These were the times and days of Judge Lynch, and the law of the strong armed, and the strong willed. Justice and injustice were served out with primitive directness and dispatch. "All were rough, many were desperadoes and outlaws. The proximity of the borders, the Indian traffic, the remoteness from effective civilization and laws, combined to make Jackson and its neighboring counties, particularly unfavorable localities for the settlement of a peculiar people."[2]

Probably the greatest peculiarity of the Mormon settlers, other than their thunderous Judaic pronouncements, was their close-knit unity. Their stance wore like a hair shirt on the rough old settlers of western Missouri. Their religion was strange, incomprehensible; they stood aloof in politics and sociality; they were "eastern men," possessing little sympathy, and little understanding of their surroundings; they were exclusive in their worship, exclusive in their friendship; exclusive in their dealings. They wore their inner conviction of God's choice in an outer aura that appeared as though they were looking down their nose at Missourians. And, when they discouraged the attentions of the Gentiles to their daughters, forbade inter-marriage, and on the touchy issue of slavery talked abolition, there could be little left to commend them to popularity.

At a mass meeting of the Jackson County citizens, held at Independence on July 20, 1833, the new peril was spelled out by the speakers, and the problems shaped and hammered into a real determination to turn back the scourge of fanatical locusts who had chosen to make their county over into some Judaic image. "The address was unanimously adopted, which, among other things, declared that the evils which threatened their community, by the Mormons settling among them, were such that no one could have foreseen, and were therefore unprovided for by laws; and the delays incident to legislation would put the mischief beyond all remedy."[3] It was decided then and there that, unless fast action was mounted against the invaders, by sheer force of numbers, all civil government would be in their hands, all public officers would be Mormons, and even the old settlers would be forced to court their favor.

"What would be the fate of our lives and property in the hands of jurors and witnesses who do not blush to declare, and would not, upon occasion, hesitate to swear, that they have wrought miracles, and have been the subjects of miraculous and supernatural cures, have conversed with God and his angels, and possess and exercise the gifts of divination, and of unknown tongues, and fired with the prospects of obtaining inheritances without money and without price — may better be imagined than described."[4]

The *Western Monitor* summed up the rising spirits by its public demand that the Mormons exit themselves from Jackson County without delay, refrain from any more unwanted migrations into western Missouri, put speedy end to the Mormon published *Evening and Morning Star,* and all further Mormon printing and publication in the county and "that those who fail to comply with the above requisitions be referred to those of their brethren who have the gifts of divination, and of unknown tongues, to inform them of the lot that awaits them."[5]

The decisive course was unanimously adopted in the mass meeting that followed, and a committee of twelve appointed to wait on the Mormons for immediate answer. Confronted by a united citizenry, the Mormon leaders asked for three months in which to comply with the demands. This was refused. They pleaded for ten days. Fifteen minutes only were allowed for their decision. The fifteen minutes ran out amidst consternation and frustration; the committee withdrew to the courthouse; and the waiting mob immediately marched in jubilation.

With fiendish shouts the mob first attacked the printing office of the Mormon *Star*, forced its editor, William W. Phelps and his family into the street, threw out the household furniture, pied the type, broke up the presses, and destroyed all printings and partly finished books in the office. After leaving the Phelps home and the printery a mass of ruins, the mob demolished the Mormon mercantile establishment of Gilbert, Whitney & Company.

Before the fury of the mob was spent, they had caught a pair of the leading elders — Bishop Edward Partridge and Charles Allen — dragged them through the streets. When, before the maddened throng they refused to renounce the Prophet Joseph Smith, the *Book of Mormon*, and the church of their humiliation, they were stripped naked, daubed with tar and quick-lime, and copiously feathered. Somehow the resignation and meekness with which these elders bore their inhuman indignity before their tormentors, sobered the mob. They were finally allowed to depart without further cruelty and abuse.

But for the Mormons in Jackson County, this was the beginning of the end. The enraged citizenry, operating as terrorists and mobs, with full approval of city, county, and state officialdom,[6] implacably demanded not only immediate and full retreat of Mormondom from the promised land, but the turning back of every Saint with any intention of settling there. "They rode in every direction in search of the leading elders, making the day hideous with their inhuman yells and wicked oaths. They declared it to be their intention to whip those whom they captured with from fifty to five hundred lashes each, allow their Negroes to destroy their crops, and demolish their dwellings. Said they: 'We will rid Jackson County of the Mormons — peaceably if we can, forcibly if we must. If they will not go without, we will whip and kill the men; we will destroy their children, and ravish their women!"[7]

The Saints appealed to Governor Daniel Dunklin. They tried desperately for delaying action in the city and county courts. There was considerable legal sparring while the night-riding mobs made cogent their threats with whip and fire. The state militia was called out. Mormons have never ceased to claim that the militia itself was a tool of the expulsion.

From October 31 to November 7, 1833, the Mormons were thrust out of Jackson County in a veritable reign of terror. Houses were unroofed and burned, furniture demolished, corn-fields set to the torch, women and children driven from their homes, while their men were tied and horsewhipped. But western Missouri had had enough of the Mormons. They were scourged like rabbits across the prairie. For the Latter-day Saints, who had entered Missouri with the bright hope of building the New Jerusalem at Independence, it became a winter of suffering and horror.

Had it not been for the compassion and generosity of the citizens of neighboring Missouri counties — Clay, Lafayette and Van Buren — the Mormons would have perished. Clay County, especially, became the haven of retreat, though eventually, when the burden became heavy, and the plaguing hates ignited new tinder, it too would become anxious to rid itself of the Saints.

The Latter-day Saints, of course, were deeply conscious that they had been wronged and defrauded. Their demands upon Governor Dunklin for redress for the outrage, and return of the "inheritances" they had purchased and nurtured, could not, in justice go unheeded. The Governor admitted the righteousness of their cause, and even promised the militia's help in their rein-statement. In the end, recourse to law proved hopeless. The citizenry of Jackson County, confident they had excised the chancre, were adamant against any return. Besides, half the militia was made up of the toughies who had laid on the whip and applied the torch as night riders.

While the homeless Saints waited for the Governor to act in their behalf, they just as frantically turned to their Prophet, Joseph Smith, and their brethren back in Kirtland, Ohio and the east. Desperately they pleaded for advice and help through these months of tragedy. The Prophet, stunned by the fact that his great prophecy had gone awry, made solemn appeal to the Mormon congregations eastward for money to buy out every old settler in Jackson County, to back Governor Dunklin's hand in reinstating the Saints, and to make Independence once more available to the Lord for the New Jerusalem of the last days.

Cogency to the appeal was added by a new revelation from the Prophet, which not only spelled out this financial and moral necessity, but ordered the eastern Saints to recruit an army of from one hundred to five hundred men to march to Missouri for direct and tangible aid in the reinstatement.[8]

This first Army of God, unmartial in aspect, hastily recruited, was given the name of "Zion's Camp." It was gathered at Kirtland, Ohio, in the spring of 1834. It was born amid the twin urges of enthusiasm and indignation. But, even though the Prophet himself would personally lead it, the bloom was considerably faded by the time it actually faced the long, hard march westward. At the time of its final departure from Kirtland, Ohio for Jackson County, Missouri, it numbered about one hundred and fifty men. Along the way, it picked up fifty additional Mormon recruits.

The impetus which had blown necessity into a revelation had been the arrival in Kirtland, February 1834, of Parley P. Pratt and Lyman Wight, direct from the scene of the Missouri pogrom. Letters had already acquainted Joseph Smith and the church's leading brethren of the disastrous consequence of trying to make over Independence and Jackson County into the millennial image of the New Jerusalem. It was the personal appearance of Pratt and Wight, and their frantic reporting, that finally drove the Prophet to importune and receive of God not only permission, but the blueprint for this army of deliverance.

Parley P. Pratt, emotional and flamboyant, was already a marked man in the church, and destined to play a profound part in its future. Among the Saints, prone to label their leaders with descriptive titles measured to their prowess and repute, Parley was known as "The Archer of Paradise." Lyman Wight, on the other hand, was a convert of the rough-and-tumble school of zealotry. He was tough, hard, and fanatically anxious to do battle with anyone or anything that stood in the way of the grand concept of the gospel. Among the brethren, he was known as "The Wild Ram of the Mountains."

The two men had brought news that the Missouri militia had totally disarmed the western Saints, leaving them defenseless while they sacked their homes and outraged them physically. The only good tidings the men carried out of the west was that Governor Dunklin appeared to be sympathetic to the Mormon cause, and had given the vague promise that he would do all in his power to seek justice for the homeless Saints, including return of their lands, and redress of their wrongs.

It was in the hopes of strengthening the Mormon cause, and sustaining Governor Dunklin in his promise of help, that this citizen's army was hastily mobilized. To Joseph Smith, and the leading elders of the church, "Zion's Camp" would be redemption's column marching in triumph into Missouri, to right the wrongs of his beloved Saints so brutally defrauded and betrayed. "Behold I say unto you, the redemption of Zion must needs come by power," the Lord of Hosts spoke in this new revelation. "Therefore, I will raise up unto my people a man, who shall lead them like Moses led the children of Israel. For ye are the children of Israel, and the seed of Abraham, and ye must needs be let out of bondage by power, and with stretched-out arm."[9] As leader, of course, the Prophet envisioned himself.

Joseph Smith, emboldened by his heavenly declaration, which he immediately published, had expected an enlistment of at least five hundred Mormon males for so noble and desperate a cause. Parley P. Pratt, fresh from the Missouri ferment, and other equally persuasive brethren, were "set apart" to a mission of recruitment among the local and eastern churches. For so immense a challenge, both men and dollars were needed in equal measure. But, after two months of zealous persuasion, only one hundred dollars had been raised in Kirtland, two hundred and fifty dollars from the eastern churches, and less than two hundred brethren were showing up for army drill on the Kirtland green.

To raise the additional desperately needed cash, Joseph was accommodated by another revelation. This time the Lord gave him permission to mortgage the church property.[10] All this time, ringing above the discouragement and delay of preparation, came fresh and disheartening reports out of Missouri. So far Dunklin had failed in reinstating a single Saint to the lost lands and possessions in Jackson County. And every Mormon who had the temerity to return as claimant to his own, was quick to feel the clubs and whips of the old settlers — who had not the least intention of allowing the Lord *or* His Saints to fashion Independence into the New Jerusalem. The Prophet concluded that, small and ill-equipped as it was, it was high time that Zion's Camp marched westward.

III

ON SUNDAY, MAY 4, 1834, the army assembled in Kirtland for final review. Here it received the personal blessing of the Prophet, and the eloquent forensics of Sidney Rigdon, the former Campbellite preacher who had risen to second in command of the church. With cadence and apocalyptic fury Rigdon urged the men on to the intrepid task of redeeming Zion; promised them that their foes would melt away before the sword of righteousness; that they would stand before God and men as heroes and martyrs for a cause transcending the grave.

It was a motley-looking corps. The men carried every weapon imaginable. There had not been enough money raised to put the two hundred heroes into uniform. But at crack of dawn the next morning, Zion's Camp was on the march. At the head, a single soldier carried a white guidon, lettered with the single word *Peace*. Behind him followed the men and the wagons.

Strange and ill-equipped as it was, Zion's Camp contained the present and future elite of the church, commanded by the Prophet himself, and seconded by the Biblically verbose Sidney Rigdon. Under the Prophet's orders, the army was divided into companies of twelve men each — every man assigned to some particular and necessary task. Each twelve-man squad was ruled by a "captain," who received his orders in turn from the heirarchy of the priesthood, governed temporally and militarily by the Prophet himself.

Strict orders had been issued governing personal conduct in camp, with the admonition that complete secrecy was to prevail when passing through settlements, and under no conditions, even when asked, were they to reveal their destination, or the reasons for their journey westward. When towns were reached, the army was to break up, the men were to pass leisurely and inconspicuously through it, and by different routes. When safely beyond the settlement, they were to reassemble at some designated spot far beyond the eyes of the curious.

Joseph Smith went to elaborate, almost laughable pains to conceal his identity in Zion's Camp. Lyman Wight, who already had stood up to the Jackson County mobs, had been given the weighty title of General, and as such, could not be outranked by any man in the walking camp. Actually, with finger and mind on deity and the heavens, the Prophet remained spiritual and temporal leader of everything pertaining to Mormondom — including Zion's Camp. He carried the best rifle and sword, an elegant brace of pistols, and, although he had not yet effected the brilliant and ornate uniforms which in later years would characterize him, Joseph Smith was already showing a definite taste for military pomp and ceremony.

For some obscure reason, he insisted on hiding identity under his heavenly title of "Baurak Ale," or the more earthy pseudonym of "Captain Cook." He democratically set his tent in the ranks with his brethren. But he kept his quarters guarded with an immense and savage bulldog — whom the brethren universally detested. As the little army moved nearer enemy country, he kept a special bodyguard of twenty men alerted to the necessity of constant protection to his sacrosanct presence.

His brethren were astonished and overjoyed to discover that besides being endowed with the special gift of seership, Joseph Smith was a superb horseman and a crack shot with rifle and pistols. He revealed to them a sure and working knowledge of military tactics and drill. Lyman Wight might be General, but "Captain Cook" was soon bossing the camp.

Every night, with a robust blast from his sacred ram's horn, the entire camp knelt with Joseph in prayer. Every morning, the day's march began with the sound of the sacred trumpet. Minor miracles were of daily occurrence. Joseph expounded on the sacred doctrine he was revealing to a lost and groping world. The army, he asserted, was marching to deliverance under the afflatus of heavenly sanction and protection.

In the humble circles of Zion's Camp no less than in the Messianic center of Kirtland, Ohio or Independence, Missouri, Joseph Smith radiated the confidence and power that drew men to him. Outwardly, and especially to his enemies, this brash

young man from New York looked like no prophet — ancient or
modern. But to his followers, Joseph's bucolic and rustic attri-
butes shrank nothing from this mystery, persuasiveness, or power
to move men. Instead, this virility and roughness were factors
that endeared him to them. The Prophet was as likeable as he
was persuasive.

"Joseph Smith was a most extraordinary man;" was John D.
Lee's estimate of him. "He was rather large in stature, some
six feet two inches in height, well built, though a little stoop-
shouldered, prominent and well-developed features, a Roman
nose, light chestnut hair, upper lip full and rather protruding,
chin broad and square, an eagle eye, and on the whole there
was something in his manner and appearance that was bewitch-
ing and winning; his countenance was that of a plain, honest
man, full of benevolence and philanthropy and void of deceit
or hypocrisy. He was resolute and firm of purpose, strong as most
men in physical power, and all who saw were forced to admire
him, as he then looked and existed.

"In the sports of the day, such as wrestling, etc., he was over
an average. Very few of the Saints had the strength needed to
throw the Prophet in a fair tussle; in every gathering he was a
welcome guest, and always added to the amusement of the
people, instead of dampening their ardor."[11] The Saints saw
nothing anachronistic in the fact that this tall, lean young man,
tough as hickory, could talk face to face with God, and still
find amusement in the rought-and-tumble mayhem that went for
wrestling on the frontier.

A scene described by Lee, though it occurred later in the Missouri campaign, is still typical of many another which broke the
monotony of the sodden march of Zion's Camp westward. "The
Prophet came up while the brethren were moping around, and
caught first one and then another and shook them up, and said,
'Get out of here, and wrestle, jump, run, do anything but mope

around; warm yourselves up; this inactivity will not do for soldiers.' The words of the Prophet put life and energy into the men. A ring was soon formed, according to the custom of the people. The Prophet stepped into the ring, ready for a tussle with any comer. Several went into the ring to try their strength, but each was thrown by the Prophet, until he had thrown several of the stoutest men present. Then he stepped out of the ring and took a man by the arm and led him to take his place, and so it continued — the men who were thrown retiring in favor of the successful one. A man would keep the ring so long as he threw his adversary. The style of wrestling varied with the desires of the parties. The Eastern men, or Yankees, used square hold, or collar and elbow; those from the Middle States side hold, and the Southern and Western men used breeches hold and old Indian hug or back hold. If a man was hurt he stood it without a murmur; it was considered cowardly and childish to whine when thrown down or hurt in the fall."[12]

In spite of physical prowess and horseplay, Joseph Smith never allowed Zion's Camp to forget that he was oracle, and spiritual leader of the march. While the long and arduous journey spawned no written revelations to add to Mormon scripture, there were many occurrences indicative to the brethren that the aura of the supernatural traveled with their leader, and that his power of spiritual discernment ran high. Problems were solved with the wisdom of Solomon. Advice was delivered with scriptural redundancy. Exhortations were constantly made for prayer, contemplation, clean thoughts and Godliness.

Discovering an Indian mound on the margins of the Illinois River, the Prophet feverishly dug into it. The quest was rewarded by discovery of a skeleton. The revelation Joseph received immediately matched the find. "This man in mortal life was a white Lamanite," the Prophet declared with instant prescience, "a large, thick-set man, and a man of God. His name

was Zelf. He was a warrior and chieftain under the great prophet
Onandagus, who was known from the eastern sea to the Rocky
Mountains. The curse of the red skin was taken from him, or,
at least in part."[13]

The Prophet went on to describe in detail the great battle that
had wiped out Zelf and his righteous warriors, and, plucking
out a thigh bone, anciently fractured, and pointing to the arrowhead still lodged in Zelf's ribs, he vividly described to the
astonished brethren the vision of this mighty man's last hours.
Brigham Young, who was present to witness this supernatural
moment, pocketed the arrowhead. Others carried west with them
to Missouri, and on into the future annals of Mormondom, Zelf's
thigh bones and femur.

In accord with the pattern of primitive Christianity, miracles
and "signs" were not the sole province of the leader. Although
less spectacular in manifestation, and certainly less spectacular
in acceptance, other brethren reported incidences indicative that
the spirit of God was marching with the army. Parley P. Pratt,
whose job was to range far and wide in search of recruits was,
on one of those lonely excursions away from camp, awakened
one morning by an angel, whose voice and presence not only
warned him of danger, but urged him to get up and about the
Lord's business. Martin Harris, to test the power of faith, offered
his naked toe to a huge black snake. When the serpent backed
away from human flesh, Martin jubilantly called attention to
the Biblical promises which followed the true believer. Farther
along the march, he again tested his faith with another snake.
This serpent bit him without hesitation. The brethren laughed
it off as an uproarious joke, indicative of Martin's failure in the
"gifts." But the Prophet publicly rebuked the whole performance
as a mockery of God's holy promises.

But as the long journey began to wear on the men, when the
dust of the trail choked in lungs and nostrils, when sudden

storms turned the trail into puddings of mud that sank wagons to the hubs, and wore out man and beast, there came a greater testing of spirituality and brotherhood. The Prophet had badly planned the commissary needs of two hundred men, and when the army was reduced to a diet of corn porridge and johnnycake, there were grumblings through the camp. When the Prophet purchased from one of the villages a supply of hams that had been improperly cured and partially spoiled, the brethren dumped the hams at his tent door with the unbrotherly complaint that "We don't eat stinking meat!"

Many of the brethren were convinced that, while their leader was unquestionably a Prophet of God, he was inept at managing and providing for the basic needs of an army marching off to war. The men themselves were forced, along the thousand mile trek, to forage for their own food and necessities. Brigham Young kept his own little command adequately fed by sending two men ahead to buy bread. Long before Zion's Camp reached Missouri, it was torn with enough dissension and bickering to try the godliness and patience of even a lesser prophet.

Loudest complaint came from Sylvester Smith, no kin of the Prophet, but a thorn in his flesh. Not only did Smith openly criticize the leader for his management of the camp, but was contemptuous of his spiritual pretensions — and that was about as mutinous as any Saint dared go. One day when Sylvester flaunted camp rule by refusing to share his bread with Parley P. Pratt, and the contention threatened to embroil the whole camp, the Prophet's patience ran thin. Bitterly he castigated the two men for their childishness, and promised that their lack of respect for the Gospel would bring upon the whole camp the wrath of God. Next morning, as though in answer to prophecy, came the grim news that every horse belonging to Zion's Camp had foundered.

All day long the brethren looked at the groaning, bloated animals, and were reminded of last night's bickerings, and the verbal crisping by Joseph Smith. Not a man doubted but what their ill-fortune was a sign of divine disapproval. "Humble yourselves in prayer," the Prophet solemnly admonished. "Ask for forgiveness. Only those who do so will find their animals restored to health."

That only one horse died — and that horse belonging to Sylvester Smith — was answer enough to the brethren as to the prophetic gifts of Joseph Smith. And for a few hundred miles, Sylvester Smith kept his silence. However, the cruncher came when, after crossing the Mississippi River, the Prophet's bulldog made one too many savage lunges at the malcontent. Not only did Sylvester give fresh vent to his wrath against the Prophet, but promised death to the dog the next time the animal showed his teeth.

Joseph in turn pledged Sylvester a public whipping in the name of the Lord. Along with it was the cogent promise that unless Sylvester repented of his ways, the dog would eat the flesh off his bones, and it would be useless to resist.

No man among them took lightly such public resistance to the Prophet, but some of them resented any idea of whippings even "in the name of the Lord." Furthermore, most of the camp had endured quite enough of the Prophet's snarling bulldog. This time there was a chorus of complaints joining those of Sylvester Smith.

For once the Prophet backed down. For a Prophet, he defended himself rather feebly with the statement that "a spirit of dissension pervades the whole camp. I descended to it purposely to show you how base and ignoble your attitude has become. It was the spirit of a dog, and men ought never to place themselves on a level with beasts. Are you not ashamed of such a spirit? I am."[14]

Before Zion's Camp, the Prophet had ignobly retreated. It would not be the last time he would do so.

By now the whole army had grown weary of the trail; weary of the transparent masquerade as casual travelers as they passed through the western settlements; weary of the religious fervor troweled on by the Prophet and enforced by his windbag of the revivalist circuit, Sidney Rigdon. Actually, in spirit, and as they neared the borders of Missouri, they favored the bellowing militance of "General" Lyman Wight, "the wild ram of the mountains." The Prophet himself, knowing the savage temper of the Jackson mobs, was not discounting the solemn and dangerous task Zion's Camp had assumed in reinstating the Saints to the promised land. The Missouri Mormons, as Wight had revealed, had been totally disarmed by the militia. Without fighting tools, they would be useless as troops and allies in the great battle ahead.

Joseph was counting desperately on the promise of Governor Dunklin to pacify the old settlers, and to aid and allow the dispossessed Saints to return to their "inheritances." With the Missouri Saints destitute and disarmed, to pitch Zion's Camp into lone battle with the fighting Missourians would be as one-sided as it was dangerous.

Born of this apprehension, Joseph Smith had sent Parley Pratt and Orson Hyde on ahead, for special conference with Governor Dunklin, and to cheer the homeless Saints with the news that help was coming. The tidings they brought back was as gall and wormwood. Dunklin, true to his promise, had ordered Colonel Samuel D. Lucas of the militia to restore the Mormon arms that had been unlawfully seized and impounded in the Independence jail. Before Lucas could carry out the order, however, the news that Zion's Camp was nearing the border had exploded the settlers into new fury. They had stormed the jail, appropriated every fighting weapon the Mormons had possessed, and unhesitatingly, and while Dunklin and the state's officers looked helplessly on, had put the torch to every remaining Mormon house in Jackson County.

Bitterest tale brought back by Pratt and Hyde was that the imminent arrival of Zion's Camp had done more harm to the Mormon cause than good. It had placed all of western Missouri on war footing. It had inestimably imperiled the already destitute and impoverished Saints. It had canceled out any help Dunklin might possibly have given to the Mormon cause. Dunklin had told the Prophet's emissaries that a peaceful restoration now was not only impossible, but that Missourians, to a man, were ready and anxious to do battle with the Mormon army the moment it entered their state.

For weeks the Missourians had been in full knowledge that Zion's Camp was on its way. Joseph's elaborate ruses and artifices had not fooled the runners who had followed and reported on the march westward. Knowledge that a well-equipped army, small as it might be, was headed westward to do battle had steeled the determination of the Missourians not only to meet it, and annihilate it, but to herd every Mormon forever out of Jackson County. From four counties, militiamen had assembled, without even waiting to be called up. Zion's Camp, no matter how just its cause, was coming face-to-face with a real war.

Up in Clay County, where the Missourians had driven them, the pitiful and frightened Saints fully expected massacre. Now completely disarmed and helpless, they had established a crude arsenal. Men were fashioning primitive knives, dirks, and swords. Women were molding bullets to fit the home-made pistols the Saints were frantically and crudely forging. They respected their Prophet, and appreciated his teachings, but his visit to Missouri was neither timely or an occasion of great joy. They were fully cognizant that war and massacre was certain, the moment the Prophet and his army crossed the Missouri River.

The news and portents were just as sobering to Joseph Smith as he, now more slowly, moved his bucolic soldiery along the north bank of the Missouri, hesitant about crossing over into the certainty of bloodshed and battle. Gone now was his personal buoyancy and eagerness for the fray. Grave and frustrating was the disclosure that there would be no allies to join ranks; that no longer could there be any likelihood the state's governor and militia would aid the Mormon cause, no matter how just. With the Saints in Missouri stripped of their weapons, and rendered useless for any military campaign, Zion's Camp had brought added jeopardy, rather than help.

It was a worried prophet who, after rafting his troops and supplies across the Wakenda River, learned that the enemy, bivouacked on the south bank of the Missouri, was already awaiting them. A quick reconnaissance by a few of the brethren brought the disturbing news that the Missourians, instead of waiting for Mormons, were planning to cross the river for an all-out attack on Zion's Camp. This was contrary to all hope, expectation, and revelation.

For once Joseph Smith was completely frustrated. His prayers were ascending to a heaven that was brass and impenetrable. The men, nurtured on Lyman Wight's jingoistic boastings and trumpeted bravado, were spoiling for the fight. From Joseph Smith's and Sidney Rigdon's confident predictions and assurances, no man doubted but what angels themselves would join in the fray. Against the hell-inspired mobs of Missouri, they would be invincible. The hour when justice would triumph was here. Let the Missourians come. They were ready.

But the Prophet not only was unready, but he was frightened. Tonight Zion's Camp had planned to bivouac on the river's wooded shore, where there would be shelter, fuel and water. The other choice was out on the prairie, where they might be safer from ambush, but far from water and conveniences. Chas-tended and cautious, Joseph now ordered the army to the prairie.

General Lyman Wight, the wild ram, had no such fright and caution. Brashly, without hesitance, he ordered the men to set up camp in the wooded area of the river bank. Sylvester Smith, still smarting from his previous humiliating confrontation with the Prophet, was quick to apply the rasp to this divisive breach of authority between the camp's leaders. Loudly he urged the men to follow Wight into setting up camp.

But the Prophet, fearing ambush by the Missourians, argued for the prairie retreat. Exasperated by the adamancy of Wight, he finally shouted to the men, "Thus saith the Lord God — march on!"[15] Wight defiantly went about setting up camp on the river. Sylvester loudly urged the men to follow the General, in preference to the bungling and timid Joseph. Most of the men, though preferring the shelter of the trees and river, were still in awe of the supernatural. Dutifully they followed the Prophet to the dry and uncomfortable camp on the prairie.

Neither camp was molested by the Missourians that night, but the next morning a furious scene erupted between the leaders of Zion's Camp. Facing Joseph's blazing fury, Lyman Wight, even though General, was contrite and apologetic. Not so Sylvester Smith. Sylvester claimed that the Prophet was autocratic, unjust, and had stamped out freedom of speech. He made the open accusation that though Joseph had the temerity to prophesy in the name of the Lord, his heart was as corrupt as hell. The Prophet, goaded beyond endurance, angrily hurled the holy trumpet at the recalcitrant brother with force enough to knock off his gabbling head. Fortunately the trumpet missed its mark, and was shattered into uselessness when it landed on the ground. But the brethren were stunned and shaken. It was an hour of evil portent.[16]

Gone now was any chance of triumphant entry into Missouri. Instead of the clanging cymbals of joy and liberation, Zion's

Camp would be lucky if it saved its own collective skin. For three more days the Prophet allowed his troops to temerously skirt the outer margins of the once bright promised land — finally coming to camp on the bank of Fishing River, on the upper line of Clay County, where most of the Saints were in uneasy sanctuary following the expulsion. As if there were not woes enough bedeviling the little army, sickness had entered camp, and several of the men had been struck down by a strange and unexpected malady.

While Zion's Camp had been reconnoitering and shadow-boxing with the foe, those Missourians who preferred some sort of peaceful settlement in preference to open battle and blood-shed had been feverishly at work toward some sort of amicable settlement of the crisis. Headed by Judge Ryland, a committee of Jackson County citizens had badgered out of the old settlers a list of proposals of minimum necessity to avert the coming war. These proposals were read to the homeless Mormons in Clay County.

Jackson County citizenry, under the offer, would buy up all land claimed by the Mormons, at double the appraised value — the value to be determined by a committee of three disinterested arbitrators. The arbitrators would be persons agreed on by both parties, with the Mormons being allowed twelve of their members to advise and assist the committee in its appraisal. Jackson County citizenry would pay the agreed-on price within thirty days — providing the Mormons would promise never again to settle in the county. The alternative was for the Mormons to buy out the settlers, on the same terms.

While Zion's Camp chafed with inactivity and frustration, the Saints in Clay County, under the leadership of W. W. Phelps, ex-editor of the defunct and demolished *Star,* pondered the Jackson County proposal. There was nothing they could do but reject it. God Himself had designated Jackson County as the New Jerusalem of the last days, and had set His Saints to accomplishment of the mighty purpose. Unless the great edict were set aside by direct revelation, Mormons were still bound to the promise, with no moral right to abandon all claims, now and forever, to their "inheritances," or to scuttle the obligation to raise the great and holy temple on land already consecrated for that purpose. And the Prophet, sick and silent in Zion's Camp, had tendered them no release from their vows.

Impoverished and destitute though they were, Phelps and his Saints turned bitterly away from the offer. Generous as it sounded, the proposal was larded with tricks and deception. With most of the Mormon homes already burned and destroyed, the only consideration left would be the naked land, probably set back to its original valuation of a few dollars an acre. And, in their penury, to buy out the fat and unmolested estates of their persecutors, at double the appraised value, was as ridiculous as it was impossible. The Prophet, instead of wealth, had brought with him only another hornet's nest. Zion's Camp had tragically compounded the problem.

Phelps, knowing that the Mormon cause in Missouri would be forever lost the moment the army entered, added a counter-proposal to his rejection of the Jackson County offer. Sparring for time, and desperately hoping to avert a massacre, he promised that Zion's Camp would remain bivouacked at Fishing River until an acceptable agreement might be worked out.

The more militant factions in the Missouri impasse openly scoffed at such wordy overtures toward peace. The Mormon problem could be ended in only one decisive manner — strip the Mormons from the state, like one would the offal from a sausage gut. Get the Prophet. Wipe out his army.

Zion's Camp, poised in dilemma at Fishing River, its men sickening one by one, its Prophet moodily staring into the heavens for answer, its militant ones chafing at the delay, and anxious for war, was a threat the Missourians had no intention of tolerating. While the peace-minded citizenry attempted arbitration, the impatient and scoffing warring factions moved toward opening hostilities with the army across the river.

One group, under leadership of a wild ruffian by the name of James Campbell, attempted a Missouri crossing to draw the blood of Zion's Camp. Campbell had publicly sworn that the buzzards would eat either his flesh or the Prophet's within two days. However fortuitous it may have been, the daring raid by Campbell and his companions, on the night of June 17, was aborted when the ferry boat they had commandeered for the crossing capsized midstream. Seven of the party were drowned. The Prophet, ever ready to translate an act of fate into an act of God, pointed a lesson at his brethren when Campbell's body was later found downstream. His wicked flesh had been picked clean by the carrion hunters of the skies.

Two nights after Campbell's assault, a larger raiding party came nearer success. Two hundred well-armed Missourians gathered at Williams Ferry on June 19. Two scows had been commandeered for the crossing. The first scow load, forty men, had not even reached mid-river when a howling twister hit the river bottoms. The shrieking wind, driving rain and hail, and the thunder and lightning, added handicap to decision. In spite of it, however, the Missourians eventually managed to get across and form ranks for the attack. But the storm persisted.

The men finally got within shooting distance of Zion's Camp, and some sporadic gunfire was exchanged. But the rain had already wet down the Missouri ammunition, and hailstones the size of pigeon eggs finally forced the militant attackers to seek whatever shelter they could find from a storm that was more lethal than the Mormon defense.

As for the Prophet and his brethren, their retreat from the storm had been to the shelter of a Baptist church. When morning brought surcease from the weather and the enemy, the Prophet stentoriously made notice that even God and the elements were on the side of righteousness.

Cornelius Gilliam, the sheriff of Clay County, made his own crossing two days later. His was not to make war, but to deliver to Joseph Smith and Zion's Camp an ultimatum. Cornelius, already known to Missouri as the greatest wolf hunter in the state, laid the matter before the Prophet with frontier brusqueness. Any crossing of the river by an armed body of Mormon soldiery would be construed as invasion and insurrection, and would be met with force by the state's militia, already mobilized and ready. To maintain the camp on Fishing River, or any other spot along the borders would be open invitation to conflict by an aroused citizenry ready and anxious to do battle.

In no uncertain manner Gilliam reiterated the terms of the peace committee — to relinquish all Mormon lands to the Jackson County citizenry, demobilize Zion's Camp on the spot and march it back to Kirtland, or to buy out the old settlers at double the appraised value of their holdings. In this confrontation with Gilliam, the Prophet knew he was whipped.

To save face Joseph Smith agreed that Zion's Camp would not cross the river, nor invade Jackson County, providing the county's rabid anti-Mormons would sell their property to the Saints on the proposed terms, but allow them one year to pay off the indebtedness — less the cost of the loss already suffered by the Saints in the expulsion. It was indeed a sick bargain, and he knew it.

In the redemption of Zion, Zion's Camp had been an absolute failure. As a military unit, it had been rendered impotent before it could fire a shot or draw a sword. In strategy, it had been a blunder of the most flagrant sort. Had its two hundred men traveled in pairs, and quietly infiltrated Clay County to join the destitute Saints, it might have accomplished its objective, without blatantly giving the mobsters the chance to mobilize against them. General Wight, and the obstreperous brethren, chafing for action, would never understand this ignoble surrender — but surrender they must. The war was over before it could even begin. Mormons must wait their day for the revenge against Jackson County. Stealth and secrecy must be a part of future planning. When next they came up against Missourians, their strategy must be different, and more telling.

After Gilliam had departed, Joseph Smith allowed God to announce the surrender in a brand new and appropriate revelation, which Joseph read aloud to the dismayed and startled brethren. "It is expedient in me that mine elders should wait for a little season for the redemption of Zion," the revelation solemly declared. "For behold, I do not require at their hands to fight the battles of Zion; for, as I said in a former commandment ... I will fight your battles. Behold, the destroyer I have sent forth to destroy and lay waste mine enemies; and not many years hence they shall not be left to pollute mine heritage, and to blaspheme my name upon the lands which I have consecrated for the gathering together of my saints ...

"For it is my will that these lands should be purchased ... And after these lands are purchased, I will hold the armies of Israel guiltless in taking possession of their own lands, which they have previously purchased with their moneys, and of throwing down the towers of mine enemies that may be upon them, and scattering their watchmen, and avenging me of mine enemies unto the third and fourth generation of them that hate me ... And again I say unto you, sue for peace, not only to the people that have smitten you, but also to all people."[17]

The revelation promised a greater army, and postponed vengeance. It reminded also that God had seen it "expedient in me that they should be brought thus far for a trial of their faith," and for those who had no families in Missouri, to return to

Kirtland to "receive their endowment from on high in my house, which I have commanded to be built unto my name in the land of Kirtland."[18]

Firebrands like Lyman Wight and Parley Pratt, who had witnessed the expulsion of the Jackson County Saints, and who had expected to avenge the rape of Zion, could see nothing "expedient" in triple-trailing back to Kirtland like a pack of whipped dogs. The capitulation to the Missouri mobsters brought howls of disgust and anger from many of the men. Lyman Wight's demand for the army to advance, rather than retreat, was quieted only when the Prophet showed him the revelation, and set the actual date for the future redemption of Zion as September 11, 1836.[19]

However, a much more tragic defeat for Zion's Camp already was upon them. More and more of the men were sickening; a few of them already were dead. The great cholera epidemic of that year, which in five weeks killed seven thousand people in St. Louis, and was sweeping the west like wildfire, had already fastened its grisly tentacles on Zion's Camp. Within another week, nearly half the brethren of the camp were stricken. Before the Fishing River camp broke up in panic, fourteen Mormon men were dead.

When even the "laying on of hands" of the Prophet failed to heal the men, or stay the onslaughts of the murderous epidemic, the frontier prescription of whiskey, thickened with flour, and heavy dousings of cold water, were hopefully tried. But still the brethren sickened and died. Nor did the plague show any respect for friend or foe, righteous or unrighteous. It traveled with lethal effect through the camps of the homeless Saints in Clay County with the same speed and finality that it mowed down the Missouri mobsters and their kin. For a time it appeared that divine vengeance might sweep Missouri clean of both friend *and* foe.

Abandoning any further attempt at divine healings in the stricken camp, Joseph Smith, and a few trusted brethren, slipped quietly into Clay County. There the Prophet filled the ears of his destitute followers with the comforting promise that he was returning to Ohio to raise funds enough to buy out all of Jackson County, and, in line with his latest revelation, that the redemption of Zion, and the restitution of all Saints, was not only a promise but a certainty.

On July 9, with a cadre of the most faithful and dependable of Zion's Camp, and with the promise of "endowments" for these loyal brethren, Joseph Smith wiped heels on Missouri, and started the long return journey back to Kirtland. Militarily, Zion's Camp had been a fiasco. For the Prophet, the lesson in border warfare had been a hard one.

NOTES – ZION'S CAMP

1. *The Contributor,* IX, No. 1, p. 2.
2. *Ibid.*
3. *Ibid.,* p. 3.
4. *Western Monitor,* August 2, 1833.
5. *Ibid.*
6. Lilburn W. Boggs, Missouri lieutenant-governor, resided in Jackson County, and witnessed the expulsion. Mormons have never ceased to claim that he aided in directing it. Walking among the ruins of the printing office and the Phelps home, Boggs is reputed to have told the horror-stricken Mormons: "You now know what our Jackson boys can do, and you must leave the county!" See *History of the Church,* Period I, vol. I, pp. 391-392.
7. *Comprehensive History of the Church,* vol. I, p. 337.
8. *Doctrine and Covenants,* Sec. 103.
9. *Ibid.,* Sec. 103.
10. *Ibid.,* Sec. 104; v. 84-85.
11. John D. Lee, *Mormonism Unveiled,* p. 76. 1880 edition.
12. *Ibid.,* pp. 76-77.
13. *History of the Church,* II, pp. 79-80.
14. For this, and the later trial of Sylvester Smith, before the Kirtland High Council, for misconduct, see *History of the Church,* II, pp. 150-160.
15. See *History of the Church,* II, pp. 100-101, 154, 159.
16. *Ibid.*
17. *Doctrine and Covenants,* Section 105. See verses 14, 15, 29, 30, 38.
18. *Ibid.,* Sections 19, 20, 33.
19. *History of the Church,* II, p. 145.

THE KIRTLAND TEMPLE

The Sons of Dan

I

NEARLY four full years were to elapse before Joseph Smith would return to Missouri, and the return would not be at all like plan or prophecy. First there was an accounting to be made in Kirtland for the dismal failure of Zion's Camp. Sylvester Smith had preceded him, and had verbally done his worst in heaping blame and censure on the Prophet. Worst of all there was the grief and heartache to assuage of those who had lost sons and husbands to the cholera plague of the abortive march.

In Kirtland "I was met with a catalogue of charges as black as the author of lies himself," Joseph recorded in his journal, "and the cry was Tyrant — Pope — Usurper — Abuser of Men — Angel — False Prophet — Prophesying lies in the name of the Lord — Taking consecrated monies — and every other lie to fill up and complete the catalogue."[1] With a smoothness born of experience he weathered his trial before the Council, and by the time it was over had turned back the barbs of his accusers, to the extent that even his worst critic, Sylvester Smith, made public apology. With the crisis safely behind him, Joseph Smith went deftly and determinedly to work patching up dissension, and shoring up the collapsing timbers of his church.

The Missouri revelation, while binding heaven and earth to the eventual redemption of Zion, had also been rich in promise to the brethren who had survived Zion's Camp, and who had shown and proven their integrity toward the Prophet and the gospel through the time of testing inherent in the long march.

An "endowment" from on high had been promised the faithful, and this, the Prophet explained, could only be given in a temple of the Lord. Feverishly now he bent his energy and goaded his people in the necessity for earliest possible completion of the great edifice in Kirtland. And, while the Saints in Missouri suffered on in homeless discomfort, the Kirtland Mormons raised not only a spiritual home to diety, but provided, through these peaceful years, an equal comfort for themselves.

For the first time in Mormondon, twelve apostles were chosen to stand with the Prophet at the head of the church, and most of these men were either tried and true survivors of Zion's Camp, or brethren who had humbly and successfully tended house, either in Ohio or Missouri, during the Prophet's absence. The actual choosing, however, in line with previous revelation,[2] was the special prerogative of the three witnesses to the *Book of Mormon*. At least two of the witnesses, Oliver Cowdery and David Whitmer, were on hand for this promised "searching out" of the Twelve.

The church's initial "Quorum of the Twelve," as announced to the world on February 14, 1835, contained names that would ring with persistent familiarity down through the annals of Mormondom — Thomas B. Marsh, David W. Patten, Brigham Young, Heber C. Kimball, Orson Hyde, William E. McLellin, Parley P. Pratt, Luke S. Johnson, Orson Pratt, John F. Boynton, and Lyman E. Johnson. Added to this illustrious roster, as one of the Twelve, was the Prophet's maverick and undependable younger brother, William Smith.

This 1835 beginning of the complex priesthood of Mormondom was further expanded to a special deliberative quorum of
seventy men — all of them, incidentally, tried and true members
of Zion's Camp. With the church now governed by five councils
— the Presidency, the Apostles, Seventies, and the two High
Councils of Kirtland and Missouri — all with equal authority —
the Prophet almost went too far in sidelining himself. He had
wanted to democratically spread the honors and responsibilities,
but soon found himself in the center of an internecine battle for
power — with the nod in strength going to the tough and able
men he had "set apart" as the Twelve.

In these, the fighting days of Mormondom, and unlike its
modern counterpart which is presently governed by a body of
senile old men, the church in Kirtland and Missouri was officered
by as young, brash and arrogant a cadre of zealots as it would
be possible to assemble. Few of them were over thirty years
of age. Most of them, like the Prophet, were in their twenties.
And, given heady responsibility and power, were prone to run
away with the bit. With each "quorum" equal in power, the
Prophet suddenly saw his church splintered and negated by a
whirling storm of brawling factions.

Again it took a revelation to restore harmony, authority, and
quiet the voices of dissension. This time the Prophet used his
unique specialty as amenuensis from heaven to write down a
complete and specific definition of every office and body under
the Mormon priesthood; retaining for himself the headship and
authority he had come so dangerously close to losing. "The duty
of the President of the office of the High Priesthood is to preside over the whole church, and to be like unto Moses . . . yea,
to be a seer, a revelator, a translator, and a prophet, having all
the gifts of God which he bestows upon the head of the church."[3]

By this he had made certain of a return to the previous prerogative, that to himself and his two counselors went every im-

portant officerial choice. This autocratic and monolithic power structure was given a democratic facade by allowing the assembled membership in conference to vote publicly, yes or no, for the single candidate already chosen. This custom, still time-honored by more than a century, was and is known under the rather ironic label of "sustaining the authorities." But the revelation had returned Joseph to power, and by winning and holding the loyalty and goodwill of the strong young men with whom he was surrounded, the church at Kirtland was rapidly hammered into a force potent and vital enough to change lives and make history.

The great temple was finished in March of 1836, and dedicated amid heavenly signs and wonders. To Joseph, and others of the Twelve and High Councils, appeared in vision the Biblical figures of Christendom. "The Savior appeared and proclaimed his acceptance of the temple and of the saints as his people; Moses appeared and restored the keys of the gathering of Israel; Elias appeared and committed the dispensation of the gospel of Abraham; Elijah came in fulfillment of the words of Malachi 'to turn the hearts of the fathers to the children, and the hearts of the children to their fathers,' preparatory to the coming of the great and dreadful day of the Lord."[4] This Kirtland temple visit of the Prophet Elijah marked the great revealment of Mormondom's vicarious baptisms and temple ordinances for the unsaved dead – a unique and singular custom among Christian sects.

The temple completion was an exciting experience for the Prophet and his people, and a new sign of opulence, mystery and strength in the church. With converts from abroad moving into northern Ohio again, rather than to strife-torn Missouri, Kirtland grew and prospered. It was during these years of peace and prosperity that the Prophet emerged from a presumptive country bumpkin preacher into a dynamic and eloquent voice that could weld a diversity of people into a religious movement of power and consequence.

He and his young and eager associates were studying Greek and Hebrew under hired tutors. Joseph Smith, unique of all men of his time, now claimed that his gift of translation had encompassed the so far unreadable Egyptian from the hieroglyphics. As proof, he had procured a supply of mummies that had come out of Thebes, purchasing them outright from an itinerant showman and lecturer, Michael Chandler. Wrapped in with one of the mummies, written in the sealed language of the Egyptians, Joseph now found a lost and pivotal piece of scripture — *The Book of Abraham.* After hopelessly attempting to decipher the papyri with his home-made Egyptian alphabet, Joseph Smith returned to the system he previously had used in bringing to fruition the *Book of Mormon* — by spiritual divination, and vocal dictation to a scribe.

The new scripture, later published as *The Pearl of Great Price,* proved as great a sensation as the Prophet's peculiar views on matrimony. The stellar find, illustrated with reproductions from the original papyrus, was not only as readable as a novel, but was majestic in spiritual concept. In this work, unlike the Bible, Abraham emerges as an accomplished astronomer. For the first time, scripture was proving that the ancients not only had modern knowledge of the solar system, but gave scope and habitation to "worlds without end." The status of the Negro and his antecedents were settled as far as Mormons were concerned, by this ancient piece out of Egypt. All Negroes, it explained, came under the curse of the son of Ham. Pharaoh, first ruler of Egypt, was the son of Egyptus, daughter of Ham. All Egyptians, therefore, came under the curse of the black skin. With this onus went endless denial of the holy priesthood. It settled the matter of the Negro in the Mormon Church. From that time on, Joseph Smith, and most of the brethren around him, became anti-abolitionists. But even this pronouncement was of small help to the still-beleagured brethren in Missouri.

The Prophet's prediction that Zion would be redeemed within two years, and the wrongs of the Missouri Saints righted with wealth and manpower from the east, was now postponed to the indefinite future while the church at Kirtland grew in spiritual power and wealth. By now Clay County had begun to regret the asylum they had given to the dispossessed brethren, and movements among their old settlers were stirring the scene into a likely repetition of the calamitous events at Jackson County.

While the Missouri Saints struggled on in poverty and neglect, Kirtland took on the sheen and opulence that once had been promised for the still ethereal New Jerusalem in Jackson County. The Saints, emigrating westward, from New England and Europe, and who had anticipated their promised land as Missouri, now stopped a thousand miles short of their journey, and swelled the population congregated about the Prophet and the bright new temple at Kirtland.

It was a period of prosperity — and endless speculation on continued prosperity. The leading brethren of the church, from the Prophet down, were living in ease — many of them in opulence. Great tracts of land were purchased, at high prices, and on easy credit, laid out into town lots and sold and resold for profit. Joseph Smith and his church had set the pattern now, and for later years, by entering the temporal kingdom of the world for the purpose of making money. A steam sawmill and printing plant had been established, mercantile establishments had been set up in Kirtland and surrounding Ohio communities, and heavily stocked on easy credit.

In November of 1836 the Prophet and leading elders organized a bank, to be operated by and for the church. Buoyant in anticipated success for the "Kirtland Safety Society Bank," application for a charter was made before the Ohio legislature. And Oliver Cowdery, second elder of the church, was dispatched to Philadelphia as agent for the proposed Mormon financial institution. There he had plates engraved, and currency printed for issuance by the bank.

But, as in Missouri, Ohioans had begun to look in suspicion and fright on the mushrooming population and power of the Mormon world within the borders of their state. When the Ohio legislature turned thumbs down on granting a charter for the bank, the Prophet was shaken, but only slightly delayed in the great plan. Refused the right to operate a bank, the Saints now organized a mutual "Stock Industrial Company" with the defiant and heretical name of "Kirtland Safety Society *Anti*-Bank-*ing* Company," under which they "proposed the management of their respective occupations . . . agriculture, mechanical arts and merchandising." Under the society's articles, each of its subscribing members and directors bound themselves to the redemption of all notes given by it in proportion to their individual holdings of its stock.[5] By striking in "Anti" and "ing," the bales of currency printed at heavy expense in Philadelphia at the direction of Oliver Cowdery were made to do, even at law's defiance, as Mormon money, hopefully utilizing the ornate green-backs struck from the plates engraved for the proposed Kirtland Safety Society Bank.

The new institution, however, soon found itself in grave difficulties. Lacking a state charter, the currency and notes of the Society were rejected in New York, Cleveland and Pittsburgh as legal tender for the heavy stocks of store merchandise, and the mechanical equipment for the church industries. The cause for this disaster was aggravated by the calamitous financial panic which swept the entire nation in 1837. The Kirtland Safety Society was only one of hundreds of wildcat banks wiped into oblivion by the great panic, which that year had dumped the entire nation into poverty and stagnation.

The national panic, of course, had nothing to do with the Prophet and his elders. The Kirtland Society were only doing what every big bank in the nation was doing — papering the known world with enough privately issued currency to insure wealth for its every citizen. When alarmed establishments, and even the government itself, demanded payment of obligations in specie, the bubble burst, the currency became worthless, banks across the land collapsed, and the roseate real estate and industrial boom vanished into history.

The Kirtland Bank, which Joseph had predicted would "grow and flourish, and spread from the rivers to the ends of the earth, and survive when all others should be laid in ruins,"[6] suddenly found itself bankrupt, its ornate currency worthless, and the brethren who had joined it with such goodwill saddled with enough suddenly called debts to send the institution and themselves over the brink.

Worse, the institution, defiantly operating without a charter, had been an illegal operation from the start. It took only a few disgruntled holders of its now worthless money to swear out a complaint against the Prophet. He was hauled into court, and fined a thousand dollars. Among the Saints, to build up confidence in Kirtland's tottering structure, he begged them to keep faith in the bank and its money, and predicted that they would again see the time when every bill would be worth its face value. This is one prediction of the Prophet which eventually came true. Today's collectors of the unique and ornate money issued by The Kirtland Safety Society *Anti*-Bank-*ing Company* are willing and happy to pay for its ownership many times its face value.

But with the bank closed, the Prophet and his church foundering in a sea of debt, the end of Kirtland's great dream came fast.

Beset by an hundred acrimonious accusations, the storm blew in on the Prophet, from Mormons and non-Mormons alike. The great temple, scene of supernatural wonders, and the showplace of the church, was, for debt and unamortized mortgage, wrested away from the Saints by the unbaptized and unfeeling Gentiles. Many of Joseph's most trusted disciples — apostles and seventies included — turned in bitter anger upon him, sued him in the courts, and openly accused him not only of being a false prophet, but publicly branded him as a thief and lecher.

The once peaceful and prosperous Kirtland was suddenly become a hornet's nest of vituperation and hate. The doctrine of "spiritual wives," which the Prophet had made known only in secret and to his intimates, for the first time became a public revelation to the world. Suit after suit for damages were brought against the Prophet, and apostasy was so widespread that Heber C. Kimball, in later years describing the scene in a sermon, confessed that at that time "there were not twenty persons on earth that would declare that Joseph Smith was a prophet of God."[7]

The last meeting with the brethren in the temple, a meeting which Joseph had hoped would excise the ulcers of discontent, ended in denunciation and verbal brawls enough to put heavy strain on the consecrated edifice. To tumble from ethereal seership to that of fallen prophet, to be dinned in the ears with enough charges and counter-charges to damn him forever, he walked out of the temple, never again to return. That night, he and Sidney Rigdon fled Kirtland by horseback, for Missouri. A few nights later the Mormon printing plant was burned to the ground. Following after the fleeing Prophet, in dribbling contrast to the march of Zion's Camp, were those of his faithful followers who still believed in him.

But the great apostasy had done its worst. Kirtland, Ohio, no longer was America's seat of Mormondom. The beautiful city

went back to the Gentiles. The temple eventually was used as
shelter for a hog farm. Those Latter-day Saints who did not
follow the Prophet into Missouri drifted away from the church,
many of them in bitterness and disillusionment. But there were
still steadfast and believing men in the church. One by one they
showed up in Missouri.

II

UNFORTUNATELY, the Prophet and the loyal brethren had escaped
one disaster, only to move on to troubles afresh. Much had
happened since the debacle of Zion's Camp, and little of it was
good or fortuitous. Clay and Van Buren Counties, had long since
regretted their generous offers of sanctuary to the homeless
Saints after the bloody and dramatic expulsion from Jackson
County. It had been expected that the Mormon stay would only
be temporary, but when the Saints, with characteristic enterprise and industry began "digging in," the patience of the old
settlers had worn thin, and the now familiar hue and cry began
again to be heard in the land.

On June 26, 1836, a mass meeting had been held at the court
house in Liberty, in which Missouri's worries were again given
vent. Out of this meeting had come not only public declaration
of attitude toward the Clay County Saints, but the resolution
of what to do about it. The old settlers claimed of the Saints
"that their rapid emigration, their large purchases and offers to
purchase land, the remarks of the ignorant and imprudent portion of them that this country is destined to be theirs, — are
received and looked upon, by a large portion of this community
as strong and convincing proofs that they intend to make this
country their permanent home, the center and general rendezvous of their people."[8]

At the meeting the reasons why Mormons had become objectionable to Clay County had been succinctly stated, and made a matter of record:

1. Their religious tenets were so different from the present churches of the age, that this always had and always would excite deep prejudice against them in any populous country where they might locate.

2. They were eastern men whose manners, habits, customs, and even dialect were essentially different from the Missourians.

3. They were non-slave holders, and opposed slavery, which excited deep and abiding prejudices in a community which tolerated and protected slavery.

4. Common report had it that they kept up a constant communication with the Indian tribes on the frontier; and declared from the pulpit that the Indians were a part of God's chosen people, destined by heaven to inherit with them the land of Missouri.[9]

These accusations were mild as compared to the furious charges which eventually forced the Prophet to flee Kirtland. But in the resolution drafted by the Clay County citizenry was an implacable determination that could not be ignored or side-stepped.

Resolved, that it is the fixed and settled conviction of this meeting, that unless the people commonly called "Mormons," will agree to stop immediately the immigration of their people to this country, and take measures to remove themselves from it, a civil war is inevitable.

We do not contend that we have the least right under the constitution and laws of the country to expel them by force. But we would indeed be blind, if we did not foresee that the first blow that is struck at this moment of deep excitement, must and will speedily involve every individual in a war, bearing ruin, woe, and desolation in its course. It matters but little how, where, or by whom the war may begin, when the work of destruction commences, we must all be borne onward by the storm, or crushed beneath its fury.[10]

In a mass meeting of their own, the Mormons had denied the open accusation, including the charges of anti-slavery or overt dealings with the Indians. But they had been no more anxious than were the Missouri citizenry to bring down upon themselves a repetition of the outrage they had suffered in Jackson County. Willingly had they accepted the offer of the Clay County citizenry for a peaceful removal into some area relatively free of the abrasive elements that seemed to forever spell their downfall.

Fortunately, the northern reaches of Missouri were but sparsely settled, and few counties there had been organized. Acting in concert with the Clay County citizenry, a petition was made to the governor and legislature for the setting aside of a new county for Mormon settlement. Governor Dunklin was only too happy to throw his influence toward this fortuitous settling of the pernicious Mormon problem. Out of it, in December of 1836, had come Caldwell County, and soon the Mormons had begun moving into this more desolate and unwanted part of the state. Soon the first Mormon settlement was going up on Shoal Creek, a tributary of the Grand River, north and east of Liberty, in Clay County.

Another county, Daviess, was carved out, and made eligible to the Saints, and, with permission of its residents, Mormons were acceptable to the town of DeWitt, in Carroll County.

The redemption of Zion, as revealed by the Prophet for September 11, 1836, came and went, with the Missouri Mormons again as homeless as the day they had been expelled from Jackson County. The New Jerusalem, and the promised millennium, seemed farther than ever away. Little of the wealth promised to buy out the Missouri settlers had trickled in from Ohio and the east, and no sign of the Mormon army that would avenge the outrages, and reinstate the faithful to their lost homes and farms.

Joseph Smith, in fleeing Kirtland, had left a church debt-ridden, in the throes of rebellion and anarchy, and with the accusations of "false prophet" dinning in his ears from many of those who had been his closest associates. If pessimism, frustration and heartbreak were his mental companions as he fled westward, they were quickly dispelled by the faithful Saints who joyfully greeted him in Missouri. Many of them were the church's earliest converts, and had weathered persecution's storms since their first arrival in 1831. All of Missouri Mormondom, saddened and piqued by years of inattention and neglect, turned out to greet the Prophet and to make him welcome.

Mormon accomplishment, in the face of overwhelming odds, cheered and delighted the Prophet. Poverty-stricken though the Saints were, already twice ousted and driven, they had nevertheless, within one year, built another city. With a population of fifteen hundred, Far West had been hewed out of the wilderness of the new counties. Like the still ephemeral New Jerusalem, it was laid out in the Prophet's own revealed plan of the ideal city, with wide streets, symmetrical lots, and airy squares. Schools had been erected, Far West's temple square had been surveyed and measured, and cavernous excavations already had been made for a House of the Lord, to take the place of the lovely building now lost forever at Kirtland.

Touched by what he saw at the hands of his faithful, Joseph dismissed the Ohio debacle as a bad dream. With renewed spirit, and fresh determination he set heart and strength once again to the rebuilding of Zion. While he could not erase from the books God's own statement that Jackson County not only would be the millennial center of the "last days," but that in the world's pristine beginnings it was the actual geographical site of the Garden of Eden, he looked out upon this new world of northern Missouri with prophetic fervor. He explored it with delight. Once more the spirit of the gathering was upon him.

By boat he went up the Grand River, crossed over the north bank into Daviess County. The possibilities of what he saw more than satisfied him. On a towering bluff, overlooking an immensity of green and rolling earth, as yet unmarked by man, Joseph and the brethren of the exploring party discovered a pile of stones in the form of an altar. Joseph not only assured the brethren that they were on holy ground, but that they stood in the very Valley of God, where Adam had blessed his own children. On this very altar, preserved from the earth's beginnings, Adam himself had offered up sacrifice to Jehovah God.

Known as Spring Hill, or Tower Hill, Joseph Smith, in the ecstatic grip of prophecy, gave the place its true name. "Adam-ondi-Ahman, because, said he, it is the place where Adam shall come to visit his people, or the Ancient of Days shall sit, as spoken of by Daniel the prophet."[11] And that, of course, meant that on this hallowed spot would the world be judged. For here, according to Daniel, "The Ancient of Days did sit, whose garment was white as snow, and the hair of his head like the pure wool: his throne was like the fiery flame, and his wheels as burning fire ... thousand thousands ministered unto him and ten thousand times ten thousand stood before him; the judgment was set, and the books were opened ... and, behold, one like the Son of Man came with the clouds of heaven, and came to the Ancient of Days, and they brought him near unto him. And there was given him dominion, and glory, and a kingdom, that all people, nations, and languages, should serve him: his dominion is an everlasting dominion, which shall not pass away..."[12]

The Ancient of Days, mentioned by Daniel, and reiterated in the new revelation, was, the Prophet explained, none other than Father Adam. Here, at Adam-ondi-Ahman, was the land where Adam had lived after his expulsion from the Garden of Eden, where, with Mother Eve he begat his numerous progeny, and where, probably in this very valley, Cain had slain Abel. The vision was a heady one. The Saints had been thwarted in their plans for the great Zion in Jackson County. But Far West, a reality, was alive and growing. And now, Adam-ondi-Ahman, the holy place, would see another great city pledged to the redemption.

The Prophet, too, was cheered by the continued arrival of Saints straggling in from Kirtland. Back in Ohio, with the Prophet no longer on hand to lend confidence and direction, some of the most bitter dissenters had wearied of the apostate brawlings in the temple and town meetings. Even though their claims to having been victimized held validity, Joseph's fleeing westward had left a vacuum that no other person or persons could fill. It was better to be with him, for good or ill, than without him. And it is a tribute to the magnetic powers of Joseph Smith that one of the largest wagon trains ever seen in Ohio was gathered together by the once bitter Saints of Kirtland, to follow their "fallen" Prophet into the new adventures in Missouri.

The Prophet, of course, was gratified to see these contrite and apologetic brethren rejoin the ranks. As for himself, completely obsessed with the new vision, Kirtland was a thing of the past, a closed door, a bad dream to be discounted and forgotten. Kirtland, like Jackson County, had repudiated and rejected the Kingdom of God on earth. Now, suddenly free of duress, with the endless acres of northern Missouri to be filled up with an equally endless flow of converts from Europe and America, here was an empire and a kingdom to be built.

The buffetings he had received from the Gentiles had hardened him, and had made him perceptive and calculating. The speed with which the loyal and warm-hearted brethren, even when illuminated and indoctrinated with the mysteries, could turn upon one with the snarling viciousness of a pack of dogs, had taught him the frailty of the human soul, and weariness for even their professions of friendship and loyalty. This time the kingdom would be shored up with stronger timbers. This time there would be no mistakes.

This time the seer stone was trained on the mysteries of Missouri's old settlers. He needed no prophetic perception to know that, since Mormonism drew its strength in numbers out of the eastern states and Europe, in settling and populating a slave state, they would be viewed as abolitionists by the Missourians, and probably rightly. It mattered not that the *Book of Abraham,* so miraculously translated from the papyri, made clear that, doctrinally at least, God, and therefore Mormonism, acknowledged the inferiority of a race accursed to blackness. The rough Missourians were not interested in doctrinal niceties. Mormons tilled their own fields with their own hands. They neither bought, sold, nor worked slaves. Mormonism had flowered in the land of the abolitionists, its adherents were peculiar and aloof. They bred and multiplied like flies wherever they sunk their plows. Give them two years in Caldwell and Daviess Counties, and they would control the politics and destinies of the state.

Conversely, Joseph Smith knew this to be true, and he cultivated the idea as a virtue rather than a vice. Because of past cruelties, Mormons would hate Missourians to their dying days. Missourians would just as forever hate and mistrust Mormons. The lines were drawn between these people. Never could there be anything but a temporary rapprochement. Conflict was ahead, and inevitable. This time the Prophet would be a Mahomet with the sword.

This time Joseph Smith bypassed the meek and the humble. Into leadership in this new dispensation, he placed men who were as handy with guns, knives and fists, as they were with Mormonism's portfolio. Lyman Wight, the wild ram of the mountains, was made president of the new center stake of Zion at Adam-ondi-Ahman. Sampson Avard, a convert, had brought into the church a new and secret plan for its defense. The Prophet listened willingly to Avard's counsel, and made him a part of the intimate circle. Knowing the possibility of assassination, he surrounded himself with zealots, quick of trigger, and of unquestioned obedience, such as Orrin Porter Rockwell and John D. Lee.

David Whitmer, Oliver Cowdery, and Sidney Rigdon had been considerably less than loyal in the Kirtland debacle, even though they had shared the very top leadership with the Prophet. All three of them could not quite cut the bonds of affection for their strange and erratic seer, and were now in Missouri. Whitmer and Cowdery still nursed grudges, and were coy and aloof, but the bond of brotherhood remained and they could not break it. Unlike these two, who were slow to bring themselves back into full trust of the Prophet, Sidney Rigdon was soon sharing the work with fanatical zeal.

Cowdery, Whitmer, and some of the apostles loathed the narrow-minded bigotry of Rigdon, blamed him for most of the church's woes, and would willingly have entered into full fellowship once again had it not been for the bungling and vindictive Rigdon, who blocked their path. But Sidney Rigdon hated Missourians as much as he hated Mormon turncoats. Because he represented the strength and fierce loyalty the Prophet felt he needed to cope with the coming crisis, Sidney Rigdon was back in favor, and was soon again closest to the Prophet's ear.

Rigdon was wildly enthusiastic about the silent and secret army Sampson Avard was proposing. It would be made up of only the most tried and trusted of the brethren, recruited into companies of tens and fifties, and bound to secrecy by the most solemn of oaths. The power of this silent and obedient corps would be two-pronged and two-fold. It would be directed against any and all Missourians who raised hand or voice against the Saints; it would be dedicated to rooting out apostates and traitors before they could hurt the church. And this pleased Sidney Rigdon mightily.

It also pleased the Prophet. Abetted by Rigdon, Joseph Smith placed in the hands of Sampson Avard, a border physician of questionable medical ability, and equally questionable anteced-ents, the command and responsibility of recruiting the secret band of fighters. Avard bound them by fraternal oaths, tied them with sacred signs and passwords, pledged them to the death in protecting the lives of the Prophet and their brethren, in fighting any hostilities among their Missouri neighbors, and scourging from the ranks any Mormons guilty of the black taint of dissent.

Dr. Avard went at his task with fanatical dispatch and thoroughness. By early summer of 1838 Far West and Adam-ondi-Ahman were aware that some sort of movement was afoot. No one knew for sure, and there were whispers. But Sampson Avard, Sidney Rigdon, and probably Joseph Smith knew about this meticulously recruited secret army. The Prophet, wise from past buffetings, and more aware now of the necessity of remain-ing circumspect in his role as spiritual leader, kept himself aloof from the proceedings. This time he did not make the mistake of personally drumming up a military force, as with Zion's Camp. Nor would he allow himself to be personally identifiable and responsible as to police-state leadership. To the close-mouthed and devious Avard, he handed the reins, and granted full power.

At first the secret military society was given the name of the Brothers of Gideon. Later it became known as the Daughter of Zion. "Arise and thresh, O daughter of Zion; for I will make thine horn iron, and I will make thy hoofs brass; and thou shalt beat in pieces many people; and I will consecrate their gain unto the Lord, and their substance unto the Lord of the whole earth."[13] In spite of the impressive scriptural premise, with its spelled-out definition of the army's secret purpose, the name,

Daughter of Zion, still sounded too effeminate for so solemn an undertaking. Later it became known as The Sons of Dan,[14] and its oath-bound soldiery as the Danites.

The Prophet himself would later repudiate the Danites, disclaim having anything to do with its organization, and blame it entirely upon Sampson Avard. He still has given the best extant description of its plan and function. This is Avard's instructions to the Danite captains, as quoted by the Prophet:

Know ye not, brethren, that it will soon be your privilege to take your prospective companies and go out on a scout to the borders of the settlements, and take to yourselves spoils of the goods of the ungodly Gentiles? for it is written, the riches of the Gentiles shall be consecrated to my people, the house of Israel; and thus you will waste away the Gentiles by robbing and plundering them of their property; and in this way we will build the kingdom of God, and roll forth the little stone that Daniel saw cut out of the mountain without hands, and roll forth until it filled the whole earth. For this is the very way that God destines to build up His kingdom in the last days. If any of us should be recognized, who can harm us? for we will stand by each other and defend one another in all things ... in this way we will consecrate much unto the Lord ... And if one of this Danite society reveals any of these things, I will put him where the dogs cannot bite him.[15]

If Avard moved wraithfully as the Danite captain in arms, Sidney Rigdon soon became its public mouthpiece. This fanatical ex-Cambellite minister, who saw sin in every pleasure, apostasy in every dissent, and persecution in the heart of every Gentile, now became the ranting voice of the church in upper Missouri. Through his insistence, Oliver Cowdery, and the Whitmer brothers, David and John, were excommunicated. Every Saint who refused to be tamped into the narrow mold of bigotry, was either cut off from the church or publicly rebuked. By now, out of the original eleven witnesses to the divine origin of the *Book of Mormon,* only the fathers and brothers of Joseph Smith were left to the church.

Sidney Rigdon, because he was noisily loyal to the Prophet, and had elevated criticism and heresy to the stature of capital crimes, was in turn given free rein and support by the Prophet. And, having purged the priesthood of every rival for power, he now stood majestically alone with the Prophet. With most of the twelve apostles away on missions to Europe or the east, Rigdon went unchallenged in his increasing fury against apostates and Gentiles. Of the apostles, Brigham Young alone remained in Missouri. Although he was president of the Quorum of the Twelve, Brigham was not yet ready to draw the sword of Peter against this Jeremiah in the wilderness. Too, in the shadowy background was the sinister figure of Sampson Avard — a man whom no Saint in their right mind dared challenge.

The former high elders, like Oliver Cowdery and the Whitmers, owning homes and property in and about Far West, refused, even after excommunication, to flee Missouri on the crest of Rigdon's storm of wrath. They remained, to mock, taunt, and embarrass Mormondom's highest authority. For Sidney Rigdon, at least, the situation was intolerable.

On June 17, Rigdon publicly delivered the sermon that was to blow the lid off Caldwell County. Historically it was to become known as his "salt sermon," because, for its text, he had chosen the scriptural challenge: "Ye are the salt of the earth: but if the salt have lost its savor, wherewith shall it be salted? It is thenceforth good for nothing, but to be cast out, and to be trodden under foot of men."[16] The dissenters were quick to catch the veiled threat in Rigdon's sermon, and the public meeting was a stormy one.

But Rigdon was not yet finished with the Mormon "traitors" of Far West. It was shortly followed by a resolution directed at Oliver Cowdery, David and John Whitmer, William W. Phelps and Lyman Johnson, and others, unnamed, allowing them three days to get out of Caldwell County, under the penalty of a "more fatal calamity." It was signed by eighty-four of the highest and most responsible Mormons. Though the Prophet and Sidney Rigdon considered it politic not to attach their signatures to the explosive document, it stood almost as a manifesto of the Danite organization against their fallen brethren.[17]

... Whereas the citizens of Caldwell county have borne with the abuse received from you at different times, and on different occasions, until it is no longer to be endured ... out of the county you shall go, and no power shall save you. And you shall have three days after you receive this communication, including twenty-four hours in each day, for you to depart with your families peaceable; which you may do undisturbed by any person; but in that time, if you do not depart, we will use the means in our power to cause you to depart, for go you shall ...[18]

The ultimatum, as bald, cruel and threatening as the one the Saints had once received in Jackson County, shook the excommunicated Mormons so deeply that Oliver Cowdery, the Whitmer brothers, and Lyman Johnson hurried to Liberty, in Clay County, for a lawyer to defend them before the threatened violence descended. On the way back from Liberty, they were met by their families, destitute and frightened. While the men were away, the Danites had forcibly expelled the wives and children from their homes. The women had been allowed to keep only their bedding, with the admonition that they get out of Caldwell County, with death promised to any of them returning to Far West. Everything else, including their homes and furniture, had been forcibly taken from them.

But purging Caldwell County of the dissenters was not enough for the Danites. Years of abuse and harassment by the Missourians had built up a vast reservoir of hate. Whipped up by the fanaticism of Sidney Rigdon, directed and channeled by the calculated and cold machinations of Sampson Avard, the holy war was soon extended toward the source of those ever-present hurts — the Missouri persecutors.

Because of the solemn oath, which bound each member in secrecy to his death, the full size of the Danite army will never be known. But enough has been told by those who participated to indicate that many, if not most of the Mormon militia of Caldwell County had accepted the oath and responsibility of the Brothers of Dan under the coercive urgings of Dr. Avard, and the example of what had happened to those Saints who made light of their obligations.

The preachings by Sidney Rigdon, Lyman Wight, and the Prophet were now ringing with venom against the old settlers who, in the past, had so fearfully used them. That Lyman Wight and Sampson Avard were chafingly anxious to spread the gospel at the point of the sword was understandable, in light of their violent natures. But that the Prophet himself should fall into the trap of the conquering Mahomet can be understood only in his own insatiable yearning to ride in pomp and splendor at the head of the column.

III

THE FIRST real indication to the Missouri citizenry that they faced an army, indoctrinated against them, ten time the size of Zion's Camp, came on the morning of July 4, 1838. This Independence Day celebration, called by the Prophet, at Far West, brought thousands of Saints together in a united display of pomp and solidarity. This was the day the Prophet had chosen to lay the cornerstone of the great Far West temple. This was the day of true independence for the Latter-day Saints of Missouri. This display made pale shadow of the similar ceremony, held years before at Independence, Jackson County.

Every Mormon male, of military age, each armed to the ready, participated in the gigantic parade to the temple site. The "infantry," in Avard's order of tens and fifties, came first, followed by the church leaders. Companies of Mormon cavalry brought up the rear. The whole parade, with bands and music, swung down Far West's main street under the watchful eyes of Sampson Avard, chief of Danites, and Lyman Wight the wild commander of God's legions. Waiting, at the deep temple excavation were the Mormon women and children, and the hundreds of Missourians who had dropped into Far West to view the excitement. What they saw and heard was a sobering experience.

After the cornerstone ceremony, the eloquent and dramatic Sidney Rigdon was given the honor of delivering the day's oration. The "declaration of independence" he trumpeted that day has never been forgotten by Mormons, or Missourians. Its keynote was "Better, far better to sleep with the dead, than to be oppressed among the living."

. . . But from this day and hour we will suffer it no more. We take God and all his holy angels to witness, this day, that we warn all men, in the name of Jesus Christ to come on us no more for ever, for from this hour we will bear it no more; our rights shall no more be trampled on with impunity; the man, or the set of men who attempt it, do it at the expense of their lives.

And that mob that comes on us to disturb us, it shall be between us and them a war of extermination; for we will follow them until the last drop of their blood is spilled; or else they will have to exterminate us, for we will carry the seat of war to their own houses and their own families, and one party or the other shall be utterly destroyed. Remember it then, all men! We will never be the aggressors; we will infringe on the rights of no people, but shall stand for our own until death.

. . . We this day then proclaim ourselves free, with a purpose and a determination that never can be broken — No, never! No, never!! No, never!!![19]

The Mormons, sensing vindication of their cause, and victory over their old enemies, cheered themselves hoarse. In unison they chanted "Hosanna, hosanna to God and the Lamb!"

The Missouri Gentiles, astonished by the martial performance, and with the aggressive tumult dinning in their ears, recognized the battle lines. What they saw was an open and unmistakable challenge to civil war.

NOTES – THE SONS OF DAN

1. *History of the Church*, II, p. 144.

2. *Doctrine and Covenants*, Section 18, verse 37.

3. *Ibid.*, Section 107, verses 91-92.

4. *Comprehensive History of the Church*, I, p. 389.

5. Articles of Agreement were published in *Messenger and Advocate*, Kirtland, July 1837, p. 535. See *History of the Church*, I, vol. ii, chapter 32.

6. *Zion's Watchman*, March 24, 1838.

7. *Journal of Discourses*, IV, p. 105.

8. Minutes of the meeting, June 29, 1836. See *History of the Church*, Period I, vol. II, p. 449.

9. *Ibid.* See also *Comprehensive History of the Church*, I, p. 414.

10. Minutes of the meeting. *Op. cit.*

11. *Doctrine and Covenants*, Section 116.

12. *Daniel*, chapter 7.

13. *Micah*, 4:13.

14. "Dan shall be a serpent by the way, an adder in the path, that biteth the horse heels, so that his rider shall fall backward." Genesis 49:17.

15. *History of the Church*, III, pp. 180-181.

16. *Matthew* 5:13.

17. Published at length in *Documents, Correspondence, Orders, etc. in Relation to the Disturbances with the Mormons*, published by order of the Missouri legislature, Fayette, Missouri, 1841, p. 103 *et seq.*

18. *Ibid.*

19. See *Church History* (Lamoni, Iowa), Vol. II, pp. 157-165. *Comprehensive History of the Church*, I, pp. 440-441.

The Missouri War

I

IT STARTED with a skirmish, one month after Sidney Rigdon's "declaration of independence." Election day at Gallatin, in Daviess County, was August 6, 1838. The Mormons throughout Missouri, emboldened by the presence of the Prophet, and strengthened in spirit by the new militance, had entered politics for the first time since the Jackson County debacle. The first Mormon who attempted to vote at the polls, a man by the name of Stewart, was challenged. Negroes and Mormons were not considered voting citizenry. When the Mormon argued, he was viciously felled by one of the poll-watching Missourians.

There were only thirty Mormons present at Gallatin that day, against a force of three hundred Missourians, determined to deny suffrage to the Saints. But those Mormons, witnessing the Danite sign of distress as one of their number went down, acquitted themselves well. As John D. Lee describes it:

... Close to the polls, there was a lot of oak timber, which had been brought there to be riven into shakes or shingles, leaving the heart, taken from each shingle-block, lying there on the ground. These hearts were three square, four feet long, weighed about seven pounds, and made a very dangerous, yet handy weapon; and when used by an enraged man they were truly a class of instrument to be dreaded. When Stewart fell, the Mormons sprang to the pile of oak hearts, and each man, taking one for use, rushed into the crowd.

The Mormons were yelling, "Save him!" and the settlers yelled, "Kill him; d - - n him!" The sign of distress was given by the Danites, and all rushed forward, determined to save Stewart, or die with him. One of the mob stabbed Stewart in the shoulder. He rose and ran, trying to escape, but was again surrounded and attacked by a large number of foes. The Danite sign of distress was again given by John L. Butler, one of the captains of the Host of Israel . . .

Capt. Butler was attacked from all sides, but, being a powerful man, he used his oak club with effect and knocked a man down with each blow that he struck . . . In the battle, which was spirited, but short in duration, nine men had their skulls broken, and many others were seriously injured in other ways. The severe treatment of the mob by the Danites, soon ended the battle. Three hundred men were present at this difficulty, only thirty of whom were Mormons, and only eight Mormons took part in the fight.

I was an entire stranger to all who were engaged in the affray, except Stewart, but I had seen the *sign*, and, like Sampson, when leaning against the pillar, I felt the power of God nerve my arm for the fray. It helps a man a great deal in a fight to know that God is on his side . . .[1]

The Mormons, all thirty of them, voted at Gallatin that day, but they carried their oak clubs with them, and threatened their free use again on any old settlers who dared challenge them. No one was killed at this altercation, but it ended forever the peace in Missouri.

Witnessing the blood and carnage, a rider had galloped into Far West with the hasty news that two of the Mormons had been slain at Gallatin, and that the town's justice of the peace, Adam Black, was gathering the Missourians to lay waste to Adamondi-Ahman, and to drive the Mormons out of Daviess County.

Avard immediately mobilized the Mormon fighting men at Far West. Sidney Rigdon, never at a loss for words, stood before them, sword upraised, and swore they would avenge Mormons against Missourians, or die in the attempt. With the Prophet in the lead, the little army headed for Daviess County.

At Adam-ondi-Ahman there was as yet no sign of vengeance or destruction on the part of the Missourians, and the Prophet soon learned that the story of the Gallatin battle had been somewhat exaggerated. But, as so often happens when history becomes unhinged by a single small act, Joseph Smith made the mistake of moving into Gallatin with his army. There the Mormons surrounded the house of Adam Black, while the Prophet, Avard and Rigdon entered. There they demanded that Black execute an agreement that, so far as Mormons were concerned, he would keep the peace.

Black argued vociferously against this stark display of intimidation and threat, but in the end, confronted with the angry Prophet and his Danite chief, Black acquiesced with a tepid and ambiguous statement that he would refrain from mob acts, and support the American Constitution. The Mormons retired back to Far West, but it proved a thin and hollow victory.

News of the "Battle of Gallatin," and the use of Mormon armed forces for the purpose of intimidation and coercion sped all the way to Jefferson City. Austin A. King, a judge of the circuit court, immediately issued a warrant for the arrest of Joseph Smith. Judge King, whose brother had been killed in the Jackson County turmoil and expulsion, was a rabid Mormon-hater.

Knowing the temper of the Gallatin citizenry, and convinced that he would be lynched, Joseph Smith refused to surrender himself, unless he could be tried in Caldwell County. Lilburn Boggs, now Governor of Missouri, answered the Prophet's defiance by ordering out six companies of state militia to lend force and cogency to Judge King's warrant. The Prophet sought the legal advice and aid of attorneys Alexander W. Doniphan and David Atchison. Through them he surrendered — under the stipulation that his trial, if held in Daviess County, would be well inside the borders of the county and a maneuverable distance away from Gallatin. With Avard and the army stationed handily along the county line, the Prophet went on trial. Doniphan and Atchison succeeded in freeing him on a five hundred dollar bond to keep the peace.

The Missourians were furious at the outcome of the trial, and the visible presence of Mormon armed might. Once more the tide of hate was rising. Gentile merchants refused to sell to the Mormons, the old settlers refused to mill Mormon corn and grain. Under this deliberate embargo, the Saints soon were feeling the pinch of want. Armed night riders now began firing Mormon barns, haystacks and houses. Cattle and horses were stolen, Mormon men, caught singly or in small groups, were savagely beaten. By intimidation and terror, the Mormons in Carroll and Daviess counties were given to understand that they were unwanted, and nothing short of removal would satisfy their Missouri neighbors.

Caldwell County, being predominantly Mormon, was comparatively quiet, and Far West, for a time became a rendezvous and gathering place for those Saints who were taking to flight under this new Missouri roust. DeWitt, the river port in Carroll County, whose citizenry had once welcomed the homeless Saints, was now just as rabidly anxious to expel them. And Adam-ondi-Ahman, in Daviess County, was already under virtual siege. Land agents, who once so willingly had sold to the Mormons, were seeking now to foreclose, buy back, or pre-empt the acres which Mormon industry had so attractively improved with houses, gardens and tillable fields. The angry chorus heard on every hand, had the familiar and deadly ring of the Jackson County expulsion.

II

UNDER THREAT and duress, the Prophet expanded Avard's Danite band into the "Army of Israel," and Far West took on the appearance of an armed camp. Drill and discipline became a daily necessity to every Mormon male who served either as militiaman, or under the more secret oaths of the Sons of Dan. This time, the Prophet had vowed, there would be no drivings without a fight.

Atchison and Doniphan, the legal aids hired by the Prophet, though both Gentile lawyers, were serving the church wisely in this crisis. While they attempted, by law, to head off the conflagration, the Army of Israel and the Danites carefully avoided any overt moves that might fan the flames. Such restraint was not an easy thing, with whippings and burnings an almost every night occurrence. But the policy was bearing fruit. Doniphan, with diplomacy and tact, had come very close to solving the troubles in Daviess County. Under his urging, and in the name of common sense and peace, the old settlers had almost agreed to sell out to the Mormons at a high and attractive price.

Doniphan, like his law partner Atchison, was a general in the Missouri State Militia. As an additional move toward keeping the peace, he arranged for the Mormon soldiery to be commissioned as a regiment of the state's militia, under command of Colonel George M. Hinkle, a Mormon convert. Though this meant moving Avard, Wight and Rigdon out of the militant forefront, the Prophet agreed to the new and conciliatory plan.

But even while these happy and promising arrangements were being worked out, the Gentiles of Carroll County shattered the uneasy truce by summarily ordering every Mormon person out of DeWitt. This sudden and drastic proclamation allowed them only until October 1 to comply. Reminded anew of the tragic ultimatum of Jackson County, the Prophet now stepped boldly to the front again. Disregarding the advice and caution of Doniphan, and throwing patience to the winds, he dispatched troops to the river city. As gesture of defiance for the DeWitt ultimatum, he sent along two hundred Saints, newly arrived from Canada, as additional Mormon settlers for the DeWitt area. It was a calculated answer to Carroll County's demand for Mormon evacuation. The Missourians quickly countered this defiance by laying siege to DeWitt. The war was on.

Shaken by the savagery of the Missourians, and their quickness and willingness to turn guns upon the Mormons, Joseph Smith made a secret night trip to his embattled brethren at DeWitt. He found them half starved, frightened, and demoralized. Seeing that they were hopelessly outnumbered, with no chance of victory against their enemies, he advised capitulation. Under flag of truce, DeWitt was abandoned as a Mormon community, and the bitter and unhappy Saints retreated to Far West by wagon train.

Far West now seethed with anger and frustration, with demands upon the Prophet for unleashment of military might against the enemy. When the citizenry of Daviess County saw how decisively Carroll County had answered the Prophet, and solved its Mormon problem, they rejected the Doniphan plan for buying out the Saints, and made ready for a repeat performance at Adam-ondi-Ahman. By driving the Mormons out of Daviess County, they, like their Carroll County compatriots, would get their lands back without the necessity of paying a dollar for it.

Within a week Adam-ondi-Ahman was under siege by an angry mob of over eight hundred Missourians. In the public square of Far West, on October 14, Joseph Smith dropped all semblance of pacification toward the natives. The Saints had been outraged enough. It was senseless and unavailing to turn the other cheek. This time they would fight.

Two hundred and fifty men were dispatched at once to Adam-ondi-Ahman, to augment the command of Lyman Wight, whose home there was under the threat of the mob's guns. A few days later over one hundred other Mormon infantrymen marched, from Far West, into the beleaguered town. Before starting his now substantial army on the offensive, Wight — the hairy and picturesque wild ram of the mountains — addressed his assembled troops with the words they wanted to hear. God had ordered this as a just war. The hosts of heaven were on their side. The sword was now drawn, and would not again be sheathed until every wrong was righted, and every bit of Missouri plunder returned to the Saints.

III

THIS NEW and alarming belligerence coming out of the Mormon settlements spread a thousand rumors across the state. Mormon effective fighting strength was multiplied with every telling, until it became generally estimated that the Prophet stood as a new and fighting Mahomet leading fifteen thousand Danites into anarchy and civil war. Especially was the shock felt in Daviess County. The threatening mob of settlers melted away from Adam-ondi-Ahman, and the citizenry took to their heels to avoid an expected massacre by the fanatical hordes sworn to plunder and destruction.

But the offensive *was* on, and the Daviess County citizenry had reason enough for fright. When a company of Mormon soldiery, under command of Apostle David Patten, stormed into

Gallatin to right the Mormon wrongs in that village, they found it all but deserted. Captain Patten, besides being one of the church's twelve apostles, was a Danite of reckless courage and dedication. In that elite and secret organization he was known by the equally elite and secret name of Captain Fear Not. His Danites promptly looted Gallatin's houses, and Jacob Stolling's store. After dispatching the Gentile war booty by wagons and teams toward Adam-ondi-Ahman, Captain Fear Not and his men put torch to the sacked town.

While Patten and his men were avenging themselves on Gallatin, Lyman Wight was leading a raid on Millport, and Seymour Brunson was mounting an attack on the Missouri settlement of Grindstone Fork. While they refrained from burning out the Gentiles in these forays, they did gather much loot, including herds of horses, cattle, and hogs which, as prizes of war, went as "consecrated property" into Far West and Adam-ondi-Ahman.

To the Prophet, Sidney Rigdon, and Sampson Avard, it was a great day for the Lord. But to the Missourians across the state it was the trumpet call to battle. And, to the more peaceful Saints, viewing the mounting stacks of Gentile plunder, it had become a thing of fright and horror. Some of them, appalled by what they were seeing, the frenzied warlike rantings they were hearing from Sidney Rigdon, and the approval and acquiescence of the Prophet, slipped out of Far West. Those unfortunate enough to be caught in the flight, were brought back and handed over to the Danites for the "traitor's blessing."

The Gentiles answered the depredations by burnings and lootings of their own. Within a week every outlying Mormon home was a pile of ashes, with the promise, born in fury, that Far West and Adam-ondi-Ahman were calendared to the same inglorious fate. Express riders were dispatched to Governor Boggs, with the frightening news and wild claims that the Mor-

mons had gathered an army of fifteen thousand men, pledged
to lay waste to all of northern Missouri. Rumors and alarms
were now flying everywhere. One report in particular went to
Boggs, that the Mormons had massacred a militia company of
fifty men, and that Richmond expected attack at any moment.
"We know not the hour and minute we will be laid in ashes —
our country ruined," cried a Richmond correspondent. "For
God's sake give us assistance as quick as possible."[2]

The "massacre" had blown up out of one of the more vicious
and decisive battles fought in the uprising. It began when one
of the militia companies, captained by a Methodist minister by
the name of Bogart, in patrolling the border of Caldwell County,
had crossed the line and nabbed for themselves three Mormon
prisoners. Hearing of it, and convinced that the enraged Missourians would lynch the prisoners, the Prophet immediately
dispatched a trusted band of sixty Danites, under the command
of Captain "Fear Not" Patten. Their job was to save the Mormon brethren at all costs.

Bogart's men were entrenched at Crooked River, in the oaks
behind one of its sloughs. The ridge above, with its hickory
trees, not only gave them effective cover, but made conspicuous
targets of anyone coming over it. This the Mormons quickly
learned as they rode in from the east, at dawn. The rising light
behind silhouetted them into perfect targets, and the militia
guards took careful aim. The blast killed one Mormon, and
wounded others.

The surprise and confusion among the Mormons gave Bogart's men time to regroup and prepare for the fight. Captain
Patten, shouting courage to his men, led the charge down the
hill. "God and Liberty!" he called out. But clad in a white
blanket overcoat, Captain Fear Not was an even more conspicuous target than his Danites, as their horses galloped down-
ward into the Gentile camp. The next volley rooted four more

Danites out of their saddles, but they never paused until, with drawn swords, they had cleared the slough bank and were in the enemy camp.

All of Bogart's men but one fled before the savage onslaught. This single rifleman, hiding behind a tree, took careful aim at Patten's white coat. With his pull of the trigger, the church was minus one of its most brave and promising apostles. Patten died on the way to Far West. The skirmish had cost the Mormons three dead, and many wounded. One man had been killed in Bogart's camp. But with the roust, and the rescue of the prisoners, it was a decisive Mormon victory.

Patten's death, and the thickening shades of an attritious war, turned Far West from its heady joy of victory into the sobering necessity of preparing for a battle in which they now could expect no quarter. News of the Gallatin attack, the "Battle of Crooked River" now rumor-inflated into a Mormon massacre, and the panicked evacuation of Richmond by its frightened citizenry, had all reached the ear of Governor Lilburn Boggs. The Prophet, and every Saint, knew that Boggs who, for years, had condoned the Missouri citizenry in trampling over the rights of their Mormon neighbors, would move — and fast — in the face of this new determination to fight back.

Some of the excommunicated and rejected Mormons, confidants, leaders and apostles like Oliver Cowdery, David and John Whitmer, William W. Phelps, Thomas B. Marsh, and Orson Hyde, were now siding with the Gentiles, and giving testimony under oath as to the secret machinations of the Danite organization, and the Prophet's public declaration of war against the Missourians. The apostates and fallen angels swore that the Mormons planned to sack and burn Richmond and Liberty, and to poison the water and food of their hostile neighbors.

Alexander Doniphan, in the face of this new belligerence, and the affairs at Gallatin and Crooked River, washed hands of any further attempt to amicably settle the problem by legal means. Both he and his partner, David R. Atchison, held commissions as generals in the Missouri militia, and with the state's mobilization against the sect, their services as barristers to the Saints now ended forthwith. The once friendly Atchison, sped his own conviction, in indignant letters to Governor Boggs, that civil war was inevitable.

Amidst this deluge of alarm and terror out of northern Missouri, Governor Boggs quickly moved to action. On October 27, 1838, he tendered to Militia General John B. Clark the order that has lived both in history, and in Mormon recollection of infamy. "Your orders are to hasten your operations and endeavor to reach Richmond, in Ray County, with all possible speed. The Mormons must be treated as enemies and must be exterminated or driven from the state, if necessary for the public good. Their outrages are beyond all description."[3]

Frantically the Prophet set every available man to the task of strengthening Far West as the center of Mormon defense. Adam-ondi-Ahman and the outlying settlements were ordered to fall back to this fortified and defendable center at the first sign of hostilities. Every Saint in northern Missouri knew now that a decisive struggle with their old enemies was inescapable.

Log-and-earth bastions and traps were constructed around the Far West perimeter, formidable enough to discourage any cavalry charge. Women heated lead in their open hearths, and poured bullets in home-made molds. Powder was ample, but guns were in short supply. Under urgings of Rigdon and Avard, the town blacksmiths worked night and day hammering out crude swords, knives and pikes, from every available source of iron or steel.

In the feverish preparation for siege, the Prophet went among his people cheering the faint hearted, encouraging them in their defensive preparation, and promising them total victory in the name of the Lord. His people were in dire need of something to flag their sagging morale. The late October weather was cold, wet and gloomy. Apostasy, excommunications, and open flight, had thinned the ranks of the leaders. Everyone seemed to sense that crisis was in the air.

IV

It was October 29 before the outlying communities were evacuated, and their families moved into the already over-burdened town of Far West. Jacob Haun, owner of a flour mill which he had just completed, and in which he took immense pride, refused to abandon his possessions to the avaricious claws of the Gentiles. Against the advice and urgings of the Prophet, he, his family, and his neighbors spurned the safety of Far West, and decided to muddle through the war in their own way.

On October 30 Mormon guards and pickets rode frantically into Far West with the news that a company of militia was on its way for the assault. Colonel George M. Hinkle, the defensive commander of Mormon troops at Far West, had been riding patrol with the pickets, and had made first contact with the advancing enemy. Some of the brethren, noting that Hinkle turned his coat inside out when pursued by the Gentile cavalry, reported this suspicious fact to the Prophet on their arrival in the fortified town. From that moment, the Prophet was certain that he had another vacillating and "fair weather" Saint in the circles where he had demanded and expected loyalty.

But Hinkle and the scouts were not wrong about the Gentile troops. When the militia hove into sight, the Mormons manned their defensive positions and grimly waited for the first assault.

But just outside gun range, while the Mormons cautiously watched, the militia halted. Warily the opposing forces eyed one another, and tension mounted. The Mormons of Far West had not yet been apprised of the "extermination order" of Governor Boggs, and the Prophet, in spite of Hinkle's report on the chasing of the patrols, was still hopeful that the militia had come for the purpose of defending the Saints against the rapacious mobs. So, when an emissary, under flag-of-truce, rode out on the plain before the town, he was met by a flag-of-truce emissary from the Mormon forces.

The intelligence, as passed, was a note from General Alexander Doniphan to his erstwhile legal client, Joseph Smith. With it was a copy of the Boggs "extermination order." The note indicated that the troops before Far West were only a fraction of the soldiery advancing on the Mormons. Samuel Lucas, universally detested by the Mormons, was on his way, with General Clark, at the head of six thousand men. Their orders were to ruthlessly enforce the Governor's edict.

The Prophet kept the bad news from his people, and the day passed without exchange of shots between the two wary camps. During the night Lyman Wight brought a portion of his Adam-ondi-Ahman command into Far West without the knowledge of the encamped militia. These added men helped, but the Prophet knew even this was small gain against the Lucas-Clark force of six thousand state soldiers.

What the Saints might expect from the militia was made cogently clear by the wounded Mormon who staggered into Far West that night. Haun's Mill had been attacked by two hundred Missourians — probably part of the Lucas-Clark command. The Mormons at the little settlement had fled for safety into the blacksmith shop, thinking it would be the best possible place to mount a defense. The carnage that had followed was unspeakable. The militia, safe behind trees, firing through the wide log gaps in the shop, had picked the Mormons off as leisurely and surely as bottles on a fence. When the Mormon defenders, and the women, in last desperation, tried fleeing to the brush, they were shot like running rabbits.

Joyous in victory, the Missourians had charged the blacksmith shop. Inside they had found a scene of blood and carnage. One of the Mormons, the venerable Thomas McBride, Esq., himself a veteran of the American Revolution, was lying wounded, his gun at his side. One of the militiamen had demanded the weapon. "Take it," the old man had said. The militiaman did, and, finding it loaded, discharged it into the breast of the helpless old veteran. Then he had calmly hacked up the quivering body with a corn knife.

They had found ten-year-old Sardius Smith hiding in terror under the shop's bellows. "What shall we do with the boy?" one of the men had asked. "I'll show you," another said, and calmly blew out the boy's brains. "Nits will make lice. If he had lived, he would have become a Mormon."[4]

After dark, those of the women and men who had gained the safety of the woods, returned to the scene of butchery and carnage. There had been thirty-eight men and boys at the Haun's Mill colony. Seventeen had been killed outright; fifteen more had been wounded. It had been up to the women to bury the dead — which they did by dumping them into an unfinished well. The helplessly wounded had been dragged into the woods for safety, after the citizen soldiers had sacked the settlement, and had carried off everything movable.

With the telling of the Haun's Mill tragedy, the Prophet was under no doubt as to the temper of the Missourians, and how sure and relentless they would act in carrying out Boggs' orders. The defenders of Far West, incensed to fever pitch, were howling for action to avenge this latest of atrocities. But, against the thousands upon thousands marching against them, undisciplined by their officers, acting more like a bloodthirsty mob than responsible state's troops, Joseph Smith knew that Far West was doomed. Outnumbered, outgunned, defeat was inevitable. Far West would be another Haun's Mill — an hundred times multiplied.

Secretly he sought out Reed Peck and John Corrill, suspected dissenters both, but for that very reason respected and accepted by the Gentiles. They, too, were known personally to General Doniphan. Joseph Smith sent them out into the night. They were to contact Doniphan in the militia camp. They were to use every overture to beg for peace.

But the Prophet was not blind to the possibility that any hint of Far West's surrender might panic the already worried defenders, and bring the militia swarming upon them, rapaciously drunk with victory; their flesh itching for the spoils of war. So, outwardly and grandiosely, he went through the masquerade of the warrior prophet, confident of victory, serenely promising that heaven itself was on the side of the Saints. Inwardly, he knew that the Far West defenders were outnumbered five to one. He knew that their chances of coming out of the struggle alive were slender indeed.

His worst fears were confirmed with the dawning. The assault camp had grown by the arrival of the Lucas-Clark army. And, as morning progressed, they watched the vast camp continuously augmented by the arrival of hundreds more — including Neil Gilliam's forces from western Missouri, painted and garbed like Indians, and as wild and drunken as savages. Nervously, trigger-anxious, both sides waited for the killing to start.

The Prophet tried, with a bravado he did not feel, to whip up courage and bolster the morale of the town's vastly outnumbered defenders, by personal visits to the men dug in at the salients. The remaining army, and the women and children, were

gathered at the square, and there he addressed them. Soberly
he recounted the long series of outrages the Saints had suffered
at the hands of Missourians. Step by step he reviewed the events
which had led to the present impasse. Everything about Mormonism, he reminded them, brought rage and resentment from
the old settlers. If they lived together as communities, Missourians protested; if they scattered as individuals, they were burned
out and massacred. They had no other choice then to fight.

In the coming battle, he told them, their bravery would be
enhanced by the hosts of heaven. Angels themselves would join
ranks in such numbers as to even up the defenders as match to
the raging "mob" confronting them. The Lord would send an
avenging angel to stand in fight alongside every man. Such histrionics, he knew to be a defiant, reckless stance, delivered with
an outward valor scarcely matching his inward trepidation. It
was with profound relief when Corrill and Peck returned from
the militia camp.

The news they brought was anything but encouraging. There
would be no dealing with the fair-minded and once friendly
Doniphan. The troops confronting Far West were under direct
command of Major General Samuel D. Lucas, who hated Mormons with a vehemence equal to that of Lilburn Boggs. But if
Mormons were willing to talk, Lucas would meet them — between the lines — under flag-of-truce.

The Prophet, dismayed at not being able to treat with Doniphan, nevertheless assembled a party for the talk. Purposely he
chose men of questionable loyalty to himself personally, and
thus favorably acceptable to the Missourians. Honorable, or not,
unless a compromise were somehow obtained, Mormonism was
finished in Missouri. Colonel Hinkle headed the delegation,
which included Peck and Corrill, W. W. Phelps, and John Clem-
inson.

They were duly met by Lucas and his command, midway between the lines. The Prophet and his Saints did not squirm in anxiety too long. When the men returned, the Prophet was made quickly cognizant of the price Mormons must pay to avoid bloodshed. (1) The Prophet and his leaders must immediately surrender, and face trial for treason. (2) All Mormon property was to be confiscated to pay off Mormon debts, and to indemnify the Missouri citizens who had suffered loss because of the hostilities. (3) Immediate removal of all Mormons from the State. (4) The surrender of all Mormon arms and weaponry. The price of refusal of the terms was annihilation.

Hinkle, because of the harshness of the demands, had begged Lucas for a twelve-hour delay. Lucas would acquiesce only if Joseph Smith, Sidney Rigdon, Lyman Wight, Parley P. Pratt, and George Robinson would immediately surrender themselves as hostages. The promise was given that, if by morning, the Mormons were still in a mood to fight, the prisoners would be released to join their comrades for whatever it would be worth.

It was an ignoble step down for the Prophet, with massacre of the loyal Saints the only alternative. His counsel for the leading brethren — especially those who had taken any part in the Gallatin and Crooked River incidents — was immediate flight out of the state. He insisted that all Gentile plunder housed in Far West be gathered under one roof, so that if, and when, the Missourians entered the town no Mormon individuals might face lynching for possession of stolen property. His last talk to the assembled troops was couched in defeat and sorrow:

"Joseph Smith called all of his remaining troops together, and told them they were a lot of good fellows, but they were not perfect enough to withstand so large an army as the one now before them," was John D. Lee's recollection of the farewell. "That they had stood by him, and were willing to die for and with him, for the sake of the Kingdom of Heaven; that he

wished them to be comforted, for God had accepted their offering; that he intended to, and was going to offer himself up as a
sacrifice, to save their lives and to save the Church ... He then
blessed his people in the name of the Lord ..."5

Lucas, impatient of delay, and probably reminded of the fact
that some of his Mormon prizes were already taking flight from
Far West, moved his troops to within six hundred yards of the
beleaguered city. Then the Prophet, and the other Mormon
hostages listed on the demand, stepped forward under flag-of-
truce. At sight of them, the Missourians broke into wild and
howling shouts of triumph.

Speaking of Lucas and the surrender, Apostle Parley P. Pratt
wrote: "We had no confidence in the word of a murderer and
robber, but there was no alternative but to put ourselves in the
hands of such monsters, or to have the city attacked, and men,
women and children massacred. We, therefore, commended ourselves to the Lord, and voluntarily surrendered as sheep into
the hands of wolves."

As we approached the camp of the enemy General Lucas
rode out to meet us with a guard of several hundred men. The
haughty general rode up, and, without speaking to us, instantly
ordered his guards to surround us. They did so very abruptly,
and we were marched into camp surrounded by thousands of
savage looking beings, many of whom were dressed and painted
like Indian warriors. These all set up a constant yell, like so
many bloodhounds let loose upon their prey, as if they had
achieved one of the most miraculous victories that ever graced
the annals of the world. If the vision of the infernal regions
could suddenly open to the mind, with thousands of malicious
fiends, all clamoring, exulting, deriding, blaspheming, mocking,
railing, raging and foaming like a troubled sea, then could some
idea be formed of the hell we had entered.6

The Prophet had hoped to spare his people by his own abject
surrender to Lucas, but he soon had reason enough to regret it.

That they were to be considered as "hostages" was a myth instantly dispelled when the five leading men of Mormonism were herded at bayonet point into an open field, and forced to lay all night in the rain, surrounded by their taunting and insulting captors. In the tent of Lucas, the commanding officers argued through a noisy court-martial, while their prisoners, instead of being present while their fate was decided, shivered in the mud and the rain.

At midnight the verdict had been reached. The five men were to be shot by a firing squad, the next morning, in the public square of Far West. When Lucas delivered this news to the prisoners in the night, Lyman Wight spat contemptuously. "Shoot and be damned!" he answered. The Prophet and Parley P. Pratt knelt in prayer. Sidney Rigdon suffered a catalyptic seizure.

At dawn the men were herded out before the troop lines. To General Doniphan and his command had been given the job of shooting the Prophet and his brethren. But Lucas had chosen the wrong man for the job. Doniphan utterly refused to have any part in it. "It is cold blooded murder," he protested, "and I wash my hands of it."[7] Furthermore, if Lucas persisted in carrying out the decree, Doniphan threatened to withdraw his entire corps, and march them back to Liberty. General Achison was just as vociferous in his protest. Faced with insubordination, and himself having second thoughts in so drastic a matter, Lucas postponed the executions. But he did treat himself and his men to the pleasure of Mormon humiliation by marching into Far West with the prisoners before hauling them off to Independence where the Jackson County citizenry could deal in their own way with the Mormon prizes of war.

After the Far West parade of the captives before the Saints, they were taken in heavily guarded wagons and teams to Independence, where Joseph Smith was exhibited to the Mormon-haters like some zoological rarity and freak. Again they were spared death, only to face the long months of imprisonment and trial which the months ahead held in store for Joseph and the brethren so crassly betrayed as "hostages."

V

IN FAR WEST, and the Mormon communities, after the leaders had been taken away by the militia, or, in the case of those luckier ones, had escaped over the border into Illinois, the grinding out of Mormonism in Missouri went on with cold-blooded dispatch by Lilburn Boggs and the dedicated martinets who commanded the state's troops. With removal of the Prophet, Sidney Rigdon, Lyman Wight, Parley P. Pratt — and the ducking out to safety of Sampson Avard — Lucas and Clark made public spectacle of the surrender of the Mormon troops in Far West. Sadly, reluctantly, and with the shock of bewilderment, the men stacked their arms in the public square, and lined up to sign the document which confiscated all Mormon properties as payment toward the costs of the war that had been waged against them.

With all Mormon resistance now crushed and humbled, with the army that was to fight with angels in righting all wrongs now blotted out of existence, Clark and Lucas turned their men loose on Far West and Adam-ondi-Ahman. In one week, six thousand men went through the cities. On pretext of search and seizure the Mormon dwellings were ransacked again and again. The men who were fleeing for safety were hunted down like animals by mounted units in pursuit. The women of Far West and Adam-ondi-Ahman were brutally raped by men gone mad with victory. Some of Far West's younger girls, bound to benches in the school house, were repeatedly ravished by scores of men.

After the Mormon animals and livestock had been driven off, or shot in target practice by the militiamen, and the frightened Saints reduced to subsistence on parched corn, the Missourians gradually sobered up from their erotic binge. The armed might of Mormonism had been destroyed, Mormon wealth confiscated, and with fifty-six of the fleeing church dignitaries captured and sent to Richmond for jailing and trial, only death or expulsion remained the last and final reprisals that could be exacted from the populace. General Clark, after one orgiastic week, at last wound up the show by his Far West declamation:

... The charter of this state has suffered almost beyond re-demption, from the character, conduct, and influence that you have exerted, and we deem it an act of justice to restore her character to its former standing among the states, by every proper means. The orders of the governor to me were, that you should be exterminated, and not allowed to remain in the state, and had your leaders not been given up, and the terms of the treaty complied with, before this, you and your families would have been destroyed ...
... You must not think of staying here another season, or of putting in crops, for the moment you do this the citizens will be upon you ... As for your leaders ... their doom is sealed ... You have always been the aggressors — you have brought upon yourselves these difficulties by being disaffected and not being subject to rule ... [8]

The holy war had come to an ignominious end.

Joseph Smith was hauled back to Richmond, and thrown into the jail already stuffed to capacity with Mormonism's elite. There he and his brethren were arraigned before Judge Austin King on an idictment which just about blanketed every crime in the category — "treason, murder, arson, burglary, robbery, larceny, and perjury." By request Alexander Doniphan stepped out of the military to defend his former Mormon clients. But even this astute barrister's efforts were confounded into a frustrative travesty.

Every man who could have raised voice in the Prophet's defense was already a prisoner of the state. Of the apostles, only Brigham Young, Heber C. Kimball and Edward Partridge had escaped. And to have testified would have opened the prison doors for them. The state's star witnesses were the turncoats — Phelps, Peck, Corrill, Hinkle, and the Whitmers. But the greatest surprise of all was Dr. Sampson Avard who, with devastating treachery, blandly testified against the Prophet and Rigdon. They, he said, had intended conquering not only Missouri in the name of God, but the United States as well. To clinch the case of treason against the Prophet, Avard produced the Danite constitution, its official charter, and the hidden oaths and signs which Avard himself had concocted.

The affair at Richmond, while only an arraignment of the prisoners, was a great show and circus for Missouri at large. But, against the heaviest kind of odds, Doniphan proved an astute and enterprising defender. Through his efforts all but ten of the Mormons were either released from custody, or admitted to bail. The Prophet and his nine brethren, however, were kept securely incarcerated for four more months, before final trial date was set.

While Joseph Smith languished in the cramped and dungeonlike jail at Liberty, in Clay County, all of Missouri, from the legislature down to the old settlers, had time to joust with its collective conscience. During these months, Apostle Brigham Young quietly and efficiently arranged and directed the mass exodus of Mormondom out of Missouri, into the more friendly state of Illinois. The Mormons petitioned their grievances, time watered down the hates, there were legal hassles, and changes of venue. One night, while the prisoners were being transported into Boone County, where it was hoped a less prejudiced jury could be impaneled, Joseph Smith and his brethren escaped.

He is reported to have bribed the guard with eight hundred dollars and a jug of whiskey, but there are historians of the opinion that he gained his freedom through the connivance of the Missourians themselves who, now that the state had successfully shaken its skirts free of the irritating Mormon pests, had grown a little weary of the legal battle to publicly hang or shoot its leaders. In time, Joseph Smith reached his people, whom Brigham Young had successfully gathered in Illinois.

But the armies of God had melted before the Philistines. Twice now the martialed forces of Mormondom had been outwitted and defeated by the Missourians. The next army Joseph would raise must be free of traitors. It must be dedicated. The mistakes, which had cost Mormons their promised land, must never again be repeated.

NOTES — THE MISSOURI WAR

1. John D. Lee, *Mormonism Unveiled,* pp. 59-60.

2. The appeal was also published in *The Missouri Argus,* St. Louis, November 1, 1838.

3. For Atchison's communication, the statements of the Mormon malcontents, and the "extermination order" of Governor Boggs, see *Correspondence, Orders, etc., in Relation to the Disturbances with the Mormons,* Fayette, Missouri, 1841, pp. 57-62, 76. Full text of Boggs' order, with his signature as "Commander-in-Chief," is also printed in *Comprehensive History of the Church,* I, p. 479.

4. See *History of Caldwell County,* p. 149. St. Louis, 1886, National Historical Company. Report of Haun's Mill atrocity quoted *extenso, Comprehensive History of the Church,* I pp. 480-483.

5. John D. Lee, *Mormonism Unveiled,* p. 82.

6. Parley P. Pratt, *Life and Travels,* pp. 186-187. 1938 ed.

7. *Ibid.*

8. *History of Caldwell and Livingston Counties,* St. Louis, 1866, p. 140.

LIEUTENANT GENERAL JOSEPH SMITH

— Contemporary portrait, published in
John C. Bennett's *History of the Saints* (1842).

The Nauvoo Legion

I

THE CITY OF Nauvoo, in Illinois, is still conceded to be one of the greater miracles of Mormonism. Midway down the western rim of the state, the Mississippi River makes one of its tortuous bends. The bluff at this point is cut so high that one can look down on the great circle of water wrapping itself around the point, and westerly across the wide and silvery stream to Iowa, with Keokuk only slightly south of a direct crossing. When Joseph Smith, sick and emaciated from the long months of his Missouri imprisonment, stood, in 1839, on this wooded bluff, only a prophet could have had prescience and imagination enough to have seen promise in the scene spread out before his eyes.

Tapering down the bluff's edges, and southward and eastward of the great bend were the lowlands — miasmic swamps, poisoned with the malaria that already had all but choked the life out of the village of Commerce. The town, with its ramshackle cabins and steamer landing, was the best deal the impoverished Saints could make toward a new start, in a new state. Had it not been for Brigham Young, not even this would have been possible. While Joseph Smith and other leaders languished in

Missouri prisons, this tireless and enterprising apostle had brought the destitute Saints northward out of the land of despair; in the dead of winter.

It had been Brigham Young who had channeled the aid of Quincy and other southern Illinois communities to the best advantage of the fleeing Saints, so that some semblance of order and organization could trade panic for survival in this winter of suffering. As it was, the death toll had been appalling. In Joseph's absence, Brigham Young had been the Saints' source of strength, and their staff of survival. But now the Prophet was free of durance. He had escaped his captors. But he was as penniless as his homeless Saints.

Still Joseph well knew that the source of all wealth and power was tied to people. And thanks to Brigham Young and the loyal ones, he still had a devoted and dedicated following, numbering into thousands. Enterprising land speculators, like Isaac Galland, had deeded the Commerce townsite, and extensive "half-breed" lands on the Iowa side of the river, in exchange for Mormon land claims in Missouri, and some fantastic sums in promissory notes signed by Joseph and Hyrum Smith, and Sidney Rigdon, on behalf of the church.

This was no promising start for Mormonism in the west — but it was a start. With the experiences of Kirtland, Independence, Far West and Adam-ondi-Ahman behind him, Joseph Smith knew that he and his people could make a city grow anywhere they willed. With the bitterness of memory upon him, he had every intention of making Missouri pay not only for this new effort, but for every wicked act of perfidy and abuse that had been heaped upon the Saints they had expelled. His clerks were drawing up meticulous lists of the Missouri losses. These claims he intended presenting to the President of the United States and the American Congress. In the meantime the Saints must be housed; started anew. A city must be built. Commerce, on the

Mississippi River, would, under the brawn and will of the Saints, and the ever-present help of God, become the Mormon metropolis of the west.

With him, as he stood upon the bluff looking outward to the site of his future challenge and hope, were a few of the stalwarts — the wan and thin Sidney Rigdon, bombast drained from him by the coughs and fevers brought on by Missouri's dungeons; the Prophet's loyal and dependable brother Hyrum; Parley P. Pratt and Lyman Wight, who had known with him the dank stone prisons of Richmond and Liberty; Brigham Young who, in the absence of the Prophet and fellow apostles, had carried the brunt of the exodus. What they saw in future for the ague-ridden Commerce was hidden in their own thoughts; certainly none of the overplay of exuberance which the lonely vision brought forth from the Prophet. "It is a place of great beauty and promise," the Prophet declared. "The temple shall rise on the very spot where we stand. Our city shall spread out to the river's edge. It shall be called Nauvoo — which, in Hebrew, means beautiful."

Nauvoo was not exactly Hebrew, nor was there any precise definition as to its meaning. But to the Prophet and his Saints, it *meant* beautiful — it had beauty in sound; there was lilt to it; it possessed beauty in concept. The Prophet had spoken. He had signed the notes with Isaac Galland, who had joined the church to cinch the deal. The Galland agreement deeded the old townsite to the Prophet as trustee-in-trust. And, with Mormon enterprise, the city would be built. Spring was dawning. Time was short. After a prayer of dedication upon the land, the building of Nauvoo would commence.

Again it was the Prophet's master plan — a city four-square, with wide streets, trees, flowers, the temple upon the high rise, the great square where a new Army of God could parade the defensive strength and hold Nauvoo secure forever against the cruel and avaricious Gentiles.

II

THE NEW CITY plan, and the new streets, practically wiped out the claptrap houses and rickety dwellings of old Commerce. The swamps were next drained of thair malarial bogs, and every usable foot of soil — high ground and reclaimed acreage — divided into building lots. These the Prophet began selling to his faithful Saints at five hundred dollars apiece — notes and whatever cash available in payment. Every brother in the faith who had suffered wounds in the Missouri war, received his lot free of charge — in gratitude for having bled for the cause.

Spreading backward from the river, other lands were cleared of scrub timber and marsh brush for the productive fan of farmland that would grow the food for the new city. Across the river, on the Iowa side, the Galland purchase had given the Prophet possession of immense tracts of arable land, which hundreds of agriculturally-minded Mormon families, in turn, bought on long-term credit from the Prophet. Before the year was out Nauvoo could boast of two hundred and fifty completed dwellings, an hundred more in the process of building, a sizable business district, and the cornerstone laid for the new temple.

Shallows and rapids of the great bend were navigational handicaps laid upon the new colony. The fact that the larger Mississippi River steamers could not make it above Warsaw was one of the reasons for the blight of Commerce, and the reason that Mormons could buy in so cheaply. But this was no pause or daunt to Joseph Smith. He visioned a wing dam for the river, with the higher water rise a source of power for Nauvoo's industry, and the depth necessary for the heavy draft steamboats. Pending the time this dream would take to come into fruition, the Prophet bought heavily into the town of Warren, slightly downriver from Warsaw, and with a better and deeper landing. Warren would be Nauvoo's temporary river port, with a railroad envisioned to vitally connect the two communities.

Mormonism — wounded almost to death in the Missouri expulsion — had again come dramatically and dynamically alive in Illinois. But the boldness and industry was not without its price. Epidemics of typhoid and malaria took a fearful toll of life upon the families already weakened and ill from the hunger and exposure they had suffered in the midwinter exodus. Faith healings by the Prophet and his apostles were no match for the hundreds of faithful Saints who sickened and died. Discouragement went hand in hand with vision. Many a Saint would have fled fever-ridden Nauvoo, had there been any other place to flee. But, in spite of discouragements, the Prophet kept his followers doggedly on course. By will, determination, and a faith that would accept no defeat, Nauvoo, by 1844, was a city matching Chicago in size, with a promise from the Prophet that it would eventually become the largest metropolis west of the Appalachians.

But the Iowa side of the river had not fared so well. Title to the land proved faulty. The deeds which Galland had used in the sale to the Prophet were proven forgeries in court, and Galland, like other fair weather Saints in the Prophet's immediate past, had not only betrayed the cause, but had absconded with a large chunk of the church's desperately needed cash. Those Saints who had bought Iowa land in good faith, now in fresh poverty, had to give up their promising farms and cross the river into Nauvoo.

Also, in midst of Nauvoo's unprecedented growth, the church was beset with inner murmurings against its Prophet. There were those who claimed that Joseph Smith was getting rich at the expense of his followers. But by now the Prophet had become somewhat accustomed to criticism and backbiting. Kirtland, Independence, and Far West had taught some bitter lessons. He had found that his Saints, like the world at large, would condone any crime in the category except failure. This time, let them criticize until hell swallowed. There would be no failure.

This time he would build a western empire that would endure. And the answer was to populate this empire. A flow of converts into Illinois was the overpowering necessity. The "gathering" must be preached throughout the world. Every apostle, seventy, high priest and elder who could be spared was sent on missions. From eastern America and Europe must be gathered the honest in heart for the building up of the new Zion. And, too, with the ambitious ones far away preaching the gospel, there would be no power struggle for leadership within the church.

Most of the apostles were sent overseas. Even the loyal and enterprising Brigham Young, who had miraculously held the church together while its Prophet languished in jail, was ordered to England — leaving a sick wife, and an half-finished house in Nauvoo. Parley P. Pratt and his brother Orson were to head up the eastern states mission. Heber C. Kimball and other apostles bolstered the European mission. And, while Nauvoo rose to a city, the Prophet grew mighty and strong again in Zion. Only Sidney Rigdon, ill, crochety, but still the zealot, remained on with the Prophet in Nauvoo. And Sampson Avard, having fastened the Danite curse upon the church, was left among the Gentiles in Missouri.

III

SECURE IN POWER, driven by a singleness of purpose, Joseph Smith built well in Illinois. To consolidate in strength, one needed not only undeviating fealty in the ranks, but support and friendship outside the church. Remembering the Missouri disaster, he especially desired the people of Illinois to turn friendly eyes upon the newly arrived Mormons and their massive colonization along the Mississippi. With the exception of Warsaw — alarmed by the possibility of Mormon population snatching from them the reins of political power in Hancock County, and jealous and worried over Mormon development of the river port of Warren — Illinois citizenry were sympathetic and hospitable toward the establishment of Nauvoo and the state's heavy gain in Mormon population.

Determined that Missouri should still be brought to account for her inhuman treatment of the Saints, the Prophet set his new Nauvoo newspaper, *The Times and Seasons,* to the task of publishing, in complete detail the tragic story of Mormonism in the sister state of Missouri. Every frightful episode, from Jackson County to Haun's Mill, was publicly recorded, and copies of the newspaper sent to influential editors throughout America. Since the stories were told as personal, eye-witness accounts, they were republished, commented on, and won a friendly and sympathetic press all the way to Gordon Bennett and his *New York Herald.* The eyes of America were turning with interest upon the Mormons as they unitedly lifted themselves from defeat in Missouri to success and respectability in Illinois.

One of the very first moves, as Nauvoo was only commencing to rise, was Joseph Smith's direct petition to Congress. With a portfolio stuffed with hundreds of statements and affidavits detailing the legal wrongs of Missouri against its Mormon citizenry, Joseph Smith went to Washington, D. C. During the winter months of 1839-40 the Prophet made personal visits upon President Van Buren, and laid before Congress the Mormon demands for redress against Missouri; asking, as damages, the sum of two million dollars. To his petition and demands, he received friendly reception and sympathetic ear. But in actual help, the trip proved fruitless.

It was the Prophet's first experience at running headlong into the sensitive area of state's rights. Worse, he had picked an election year, with everyone from the President down, so vote-conscious that paralysis on any controversial measure could never be less than a certainty. Van Buren candidly told the Prophet, "I can do nothing for you. If I do anything, I shall come in contact with the whole state of Missouri."[1] Equally friendly were the congressmen, who listened to the Prophet, promised help, and promptly postponed any thought of aid during an election year. Joseph finally, with the most strenuous effort, managed to get the Mormon claims and petitions before the Senate Judiciary Committee.

But any hope of governmental redress was doomed from the start. The Missouri Congressmen, stirred to battle by the Mormon demands for two million dollars against their state, quickly martialed their forces of opposition. Transcripts of the Richmond trials, including the damning testimonies of mobsters, military men, and every apostate and turncoat from Oliver Cowdery to Sampson Avard, were entered into the Senate documents. The result was that when Henry Clay, and the friendly Senator from Illinois, John T. Stuart, attempted a hearing of the Mormon claims, they were voted down. Joseph Smith returned to Nauvoo considerably wiser in the sphere of politics.

Simultaneous with the growth of Nauvoo came the flood of converts to the cause. The apostles overseas were reaping a harvest among the peoples of the British Isles. Idle, impoverished, and made desperate by the Industrial Revolution, a new religion, promising a new start, in a new world, made sense. Many Americans too, of standing and importance, impressed by the journalistic wave of sympathy and goodwill toward the Saints, were joining the ranks of the church. One of the strangest of this new crop of notables, was Dr. John Cook Bennett. Joseph baptized Bennett into the church immediately after his return from Washington.

He claimed to have been, at one time, an assistant surgeon in the United States Army, was a physician, who had a respectable practice in several western States, and was at the time of joining the Church, Brigadier-General of the Invincible Dragoons, in the counties of White, Edmunds and Wabash, and, also, the quartermaster-general of the State, on the staff of Governor Carlin. Bennett had written to the Church authorities in the days of their deepest distress in Missouri, describing how his heart swelled with indignation at the treatment accorded the Saints by the cowardly Missourians, and expressing his desire to march with all the forces he could raise. He was a man of considerable acquirements, enterprising, of great experience in the world and, for those reasons was regarded by Joseph as an individual, who could be of inestimable use to the people.[2]

In Dr. Bennett, the Prophet was certain the net of the gospel had brought in an important catch. And, from the standpoint of Nauvoo and the military aspects of Mormonism, this was so. Besides the martial and political connections claimed by Bennett, he had taught the science of midwifery in an Ohio college, and was now secretary of the Illinois Medical Society. There were rumors that Dr. Bennett was also an accomplished and busy abortionist, but the Prophet was not looking for faults in the light of Bennett's petition for membership, and his impressive dossier of accomplishments.

Bennett was thirty-five years of age, as was the Prophet. He was a dapper, persuasive, handsome man; short and swarthy, as against the Prophet's blond and impressively handsome stature. They were as brothers from the start. From the day Bennett stepped from the waters of Mormon baptism, his progress and destiny in the church was secure.

Joseph immediately enlisted the new convert to his assistance in drawing up the charter for Nauvoo. And, to the credit of the pair of them, they brought forth a city's blueprint unmatched in America to this day. Its provisions included complete autonomy of government; a university; and an army, to be called the Nauvoo Legion.

Among many other things, the charter guaranteed: "The City Council [Nauvoo] shall have power and authority to make, ordain, establish and execute, all such ordinances, not repugnant to the Constitution of the United States, or of this State, as they may deem necessary for the peace, benefit, good order, regulation, convenience, and cleanliness of said city, etc."[3]

The most extraordinary provision of the charter, besides granting Nauvoo the power and authority usually reserved to state and national governments, was its public right to a private army: "The City Council may organize the inhabitants of said City, subject to military duty, into a body of independent military men to be called the 'Nauvoo Legion,' the Court-Martial of which shall be composed of the commissioned officers of said legion and constitute the law making department with full powers and authority to make, ordain, establish and execute, all such laws and ordinances as may be considered necessary for the benefit, government, and regulation of said Legion ... The said Legion shall perform the same amount of military duty as is now or may be hereafter required of the regular militia of the State, and shall be at the disposal of the mayor in executing the laws and ordinances of the City corporation, and the laws of the State and at the disposal of the governor for the public defense and the execution of the laws of the State or of the United States, and shall be entitled to their proportion of the public arms; and provided that said Legion shall be exempt from all other duty."[4]

Dr. Bennett carried the document, the most liberal charter ever drawn for an American city, to the Illinois legislature. With the wily know-how of the most accomplished politician and lobbyist who ever lived, he pushed it through both state houses at Springfield, by a voice vote. So anxious were the legislators to pass the measure, and so completely were they under the spell of the persuasive Bennett, that even the reading of the charter was waived in session.

Bennett had picked a most auspicious time for Mormon governmental favor. The election of August 1840 had indicated how sour the Saints were with the vacillating and timid Van Buren. Except for one single candidate, they had voted the straight Whig ticket in preference to the Democrats, who seemed to care little for the Mormons and their problems. The single exception to Mormon Whig preference, was James H. Ralston, a Democrat who had shown sympathy toward the Prophet and his people. The name scratched for the Ralston preference was that of an obscure young Illinois politician by the name of Abraham Lincoln.

With this display of political solidarity not lost on the Springfield legislators, Bennett had lobbied with the leaders of both political parties, giving hearty promises of Mormon favor. With every politician hungry for Mormon votes, the charter passage was swift and simple. "Every power we asked has been granted, every request gratified, every desire fulfilled,"[5] Bennett happily wrote the Prophet in Nauvoo. Even Lincoln had voted in favor of its passage. Forgiving the Mormon election snub, Lincoln met Bennett after the day's session, and congratulated him on his victory.

After this unprecedented political accomplishment for Mormonism, Joseph Smith repaid the obligation and the gratitude he felt toward Dr. John C. Bennett in a manner commensurate with the hopes of the dapper young entrepreneur. Within a year

Bennett became mayor of Nauvoo, chancellor of the University of Nauvoo, and the Prophet made him assistant president of the church — notwithstanding the fact that Sidney Rigdon was still its first counselor. The difficulty with Rigdon was that the Missouri imprisonment had left him ill and bedridden. Sidney was simply in no physical condition to howl down in wrath from the pulpit, or take the measure of the cocky young adversary who now challenged him.

With every obstacle removed, the Nauvoo Legion became the city's most important single endeavor. Interpreting the charter in its broadest sense, military service became obligatory on every Mormon male over eighteen years of age. The Prophet made the request of Governor Carlin to be commissioned lieutenant general of the new corps. The request for John C. Bennett was only a shade less — that of brigadier general. Carlin, anxious to court political favor from the Mormons, granted both requests.

It pleased Joseph Smith that he now outranked every military officer in the United States, and his preference for the title "General" even over "President" was apparent to his followers from that day on. He enlisted the best Nauvoo tailor in the work of fashioning his military uniforms — blue coat, buff trousers, high polished boots, and enough gold braid to dazzle the eye. His shako was topped with an ostrich plume. With matched pistols, sword, and his own blond magnificence, General Joseph Smith made a dashing and impressive soldier. General Bennett could never hope to match his immediate superior in physical stature, but in sartorial splendor, and the flare with which he wore his own gaudy uniform, he kept par with the Prophet.

And, as usual, whatever the Prophet approved, Jehovah God approved. A new revelation, commending the church's faithful disciples, and pointing out new duties, was by no means slightful of John C. Bennett. "I have seen the work which he hath done," spoke the Lord, "which I accept if he continue, and will

LIEUTENANT GENERAL JOSEPH SMITH
ON HIS BLACK STALLION "CHARLEY"

— From *Contributor*, Vol. IX.

crown him with blessings and great glory."[6] No man could have asked for more.

As the Nauvoo Legion, under the stern discipline of the Missouri-hardened lesser officers, was hammered into martial strength and splendor, the two generals took increasing delight in mustering it for parade and drill. Every holiday or public observance became an excuse for parading the Legion — with Joseph Smith at the head, magnificently astride his black stallion Charlie. Only a few horse steps behind him rode General Bennett, gaudy as a peacock.

With the new military fervor that infected Nauvoo, the Prophet welcomed even the younger boys into a corps of their own. Half a thousand of them marched and drilled on the Nauvoo green with the same zest and precision as did their fathers.

Naturally an army the size of the Nauvoo Legion, trained and on the ready, could not long go undetected or unnoticed. An artillery officer of the regular army, visiting in Nauvoo, wrote his unsigned observation and evaluation of the army to the New York *Herald.* His communication, dated city of Nauvoo, May 8, 1842, was published in the east on June 17:

Yesterday was a great day among the Mormons. Their Legion, to the number of two thousand men, was paraded by Generals Smith, Bennett and others, and certainly made a very noble and imposing appearance. The volunteers of the troops, directed by Mayor-General Bennett, would do honor to any body of armed militia in any of the States, and approximates very closely to our regular forces.

What does all this mean? Why this exact discipline of the Mormon corps? Do they intend to conquer Missouri, Illinois, Mexico? It is true that they are part of the militia of Illinois by the charter of their Legion, but then there are no troops in the States like them in point of enthusiasm and warlike aspect, yea, warlike character. Before many years this Legion will be twenty, and perhaps fifty thousand strong, and still augmenting. A fear-

ful host filled with religious enthusiasm, and led on by ambitious
and talented officers, what may not be effected by them? . . .

These Mormons are accumulating like a snowball rolling
down an inclined plane, which in the end becomes an avalanche.
They are enrolling among their officers some of the first talent
in the country, by titles or bribes . . . They have appointed your
namesake, Capt. Bennett, late of the army of the United States,
inspector-general of their Legion, and he is commissioned as
such by Gov. Carlin. This gentleman is known to be well skilled
in fortification, gunnery, ordnance, castramentation and military
engineering generally, and I am assured he is now under pay
derived from the tithings of this warlike people. I have seen his
plans for fortifying Nauvoo, which are equal to any of Vau-
ban's . . .

A western empire is certain. Ecclesiastical history presents no
parallel to this people . . . The Mormons, it is true, are now
peaceable, but the lion is asleep. Take care, and don't arouse
him.[7]

The Latter-day Saints have always contended that formation
of the Nauvoo Legion was a measure of defense, to insure inso-
far as possible, that the outrages perpetrated upon them in
Missouri would not find duplication in their new sanctuary
within the state of Illinois. And it is true that, other than over-
awing and intimidating Nauvoo's neighbors, its major role was
defensive.

But there can scarcely be wonder at the new anxiety that was
rising throughout Illinois, and spilling out to the nation at large
in dispatches from Nauvoo. It is true that the Nauvoo Legion
was fantastically top-heavy with officers of such titular rank
that its muster roll reads like a lodge hall parade. But no one
can deny that it also had plenty of seasoned muscle within its
ranks. Organized with only six companies of riflemen and
mounted, it had grown to an aggregate of one thousand four
hundred and ninety men by the summer of 1841. A year later, it
numbered two thousand men. By 1844, the year Illinois finally

lynched the Prophet, the Nauvoo Legion carried a muster roll of five thousand men.

Its first cohort was of horse troops, commanded by Brigadier General Wilson Law. First regiment of this cohort was commanded by Colonel George Millert; second regiment, Colonel George Coulson.

Second cohort, of infantry, was commanded by Don Carlos Smith, younger brother of the Prophet, with rank of brigadier general. Its three regiments were headed up by Colonel Charles C. Rich, Colonel F. M. Higbee and Colonel Samuel Bent. A year later another regiment was added to the second cohort, and was commanded by Lieutenant Colonel James Brown.

Expansion of the foot soldiery continued through the years into regiments of light infantry, with such Mormon stalwarts heading up the ranks as Colonel Hosea Stout, Lieutenant-Colonel Theodore Turley, and Major Jesse H. Hunter. When General Don Carlos Smith died in August of 1841, Colonel Charles C. Rich was promoted to the command of the second cohort.

The Prophet's brother Hyrum, besides being patriarch to the Church was, by brevet, a major general — as was also Lyman Wight, Lieutenant General Brigham Young took jaundiced interest in Nauvoo's military histrionics, as did most of the other members of the Quorum of the Twelve. He, like the other apostles, could scarcely stomach General John C. Bennett, who had dropped like a meteor into Nauvoo, and who so quickly and easily had captured the Prophet's interest and affection. Those apostles, holding themselves aloof from Nauvoo's mighty company of generals, colonels, majors and captains, grudgingly served the new and martial cause as chaplains.

There could be no such coyness, or holding out from service for the noncommissioned Mormon males who filled the ranks. "It was very early prescribed that no resident of the City of

Nauvoo, not otherwise exempted by law should be exempt from military duty. Absence from general parades was punishable by fines varying from twenty-five dollars for generals to five dollars for privates, and absence from company parades from five to two dollars respectively."[8]

The Nauvoo Legion, with its top heavy coterie of pomp and peacock feathers, came out of the imaginative efforts of John C. Bennett. The Prophet, whose military background from Kirtland to Far West had been rustic to say the least, now deferred entirely to the more worldly and militarily-experienced Bennett. The Prophet could not fail to be pleased and dazzled with what Bennett achieved.

To Joseph Smith, as lieutenant general, was provided a staff of an inspector general, with the rank of major general; a drill officer, a judge-advocate and four aides-de-camp, with the rank of colonels; a guard of twelve aides-de camp; a herald and armor-bearer, with the rank of captain.

As major general of the Legion, Bennett's staff included an adjutant general; a surgeon-general; a cornet; a quartermaster general; a paymaster general; a commissary general; a chaplain; two assistant inspectors general; four aides-de-camp; a war secretary, with the rank of colonel; a quartermaster sergeant, sergeant major and chief musician, with the rank of major; and four musicians and herald and armor-bearer, with the rank of captain.

Since practically every Mormon man in and about Nauvoo was a soldier, the problem of uniforms was never adequately solved — mostly because of the sheer numbers involved. Before the Nauvoo era came to its tragic close, some of the regiments had been adequately and colorfully clothed, but many a company did their wheels and turns in their every-day gospel clothes.

As always in the world of the military, the commissioned officers fared best. In the history of the Nauvoo Legion, the real unsung hero was John Bills, the Nauvoo tailor, who so tirelessly labored to clothe the gentlemen of the Legion. His newspaper advertisement, in the summer of 1841, states that he was prepared to "turn off work with despatch and in the best and most fashionable manner . . . all kinds of military coats made according to latest pattern."[9] Bills, a master of broadcloth, gold braid, fur and ostrich feathers, was probably the busiest man in Nauvoo.

General Daniel H. Wells once made the petulant complaint that John Bills had failed to "turn off the work" with "despatch" — the general having to wait an entire year for Bills to complete a promised military coat. The fact is that the poor tailor was probably paralyzed with the magnitude of his responsibilities. And besides, Bills, under the universal conscription, was himself a brigade major in the Legion. Not only was there cutting and sewing for the unprecedented panel of commanding officers, but the poor little tailor also had the task of preparing the army's muster rolls and official papers for dispatch to Springfield.

John Bills, the tailor, went through other problems as well. Bennett, and some of the other high brethren, once told him to submit their personal indebtedness to the State of Illinois for payment. The attorney-general, in turn, disallowed the claims, with the cryptic reminder that Illinois had already granted the Legion enough privileges, without assuming its personal tailor bills. In the end, Bills, the busy tailor, left Nauvoo a pauper.

IV

THE NAUVOO LEGION, whatever its stance and function, was a colorful and inseparable part of Mormondom's dynamic city, and remained so for the six years that the sect dominated Hancock County on the Mississippi. It added dazzle and splendor to many a civic and religious affair during the period it functioned in Illinois. Probably it was the most unique military body ever to serve as a segment of that state's militia.

Every community of any size followed the American tradition of providing a company or two of state's troops for the common defense. Many of these units, officered and recruited locally, were as efficient as they were colorful. Civic pride, and competitive community spirit, kept the towns vying with one another in the military spectrum of the day. But in the American west of the middle 1800s, there was nothing quite comparable to the Nauvoo Legion.

The Legion's first real day of glory was its participation in the ceremonies of laying the cornerstone of the great Nauvoo temple. It presence and function that day turned an ordinarily dull religious experience into a festive holiday throbbing to the sounds of bands, marching feet and the clup and rattle of cavalry. To the Prophet, and the Saints, there seemed to be nothing incongruous about dedicating a projected sacred building with all the pomposity of military might.

Shortly after sunrise, the troops were notified to assemble by the firing of cannon. At eight o'clock, Major-General Bennett began the formation of the Legion, and an hour and a half later, Lieutenant-General Smith was informed that it was organized and ready for review. Accompanied by his staff, four aides and twelve guards, in splendid uniforms, he approached the parade ground, and was met by the band, "beautifully equipped," which received him with the usual flourish of trumpets, and then swinging into line, preceded the party to the reviewing stand.

As the lieutenant-general passed along the line, he was appropriately saluted amid the firing of artillery. The sight was described as glorious, and it is beyond question, that in view of the number of troops paraded, and their proficiency in the drill, the sight was an unusual one to the people of the west.

GENERAL JOSEPH SMITH REVIEWING THE NAUVOO LEGION

— From Beadle's *Life In Utah.*

A graceful incident of the morning was the presentation of a silk banner to the Legion by a number of ladies of Nauvoo, who escorted by Major-General Bennett, drove up to General Smith and in appropriate language presented the patriotic emblem to the general, who had politely dismounted from his horse. The flag was turned over to the care of Cornet Robinson, and the Legion was reviewed by the commanding general. After the ceremony was over, the procession was formed under the direction of General Bennett, and the march to the Temple begun, in the following order:

Lieutenant-General Smith,
Aides-de-camp, and Conspicuous Strangers,
General Staff,
Band,
Second Cohort, (Foot Troops),
Ladies, eight abreast,
Gentlemen, eight abreast,
First Cohort, Horse Troops.

On arrival at the temple, the generals with their staffs and distinguished strangers took position inside the foundation, while around that historic spot were grouped citizens, strangers and the military. At the conclusion of the ceremonies here, Generals Bennett and Smith addressed the Legion in expression of their entire satisfaction with its conduct and appearance.[10]

It was only natural that a militia corps of such flash and dazzle would provoke envy and jealousy among other communities adjacent to Nauvoo. Many Gentiles, forsaking their own local militia companies, hastened to enlist in the Prophet's smoother functioning army. Complaints over the matter went all the way to Springfield, up to final review by the state's supreme court. Judge Stephen A. Douglas, frequent visitor to Nauvoo, and now politically friendly to Joseph Smith, handed down an opinion in the matter, in his capacity as Justice of that august body: "I have examined so much of the Nauvoo City charter, and the legislative acts, as relate to the 'Nauvoo Legion,' and am clearly of opinion that 'any citizen of Hancock county who may attach himself to the Nauvoo Legion has all the privileges which appertain to that independent military body, and is exempt from all other military duty, as provided in the twenty fifth section of the city charter; and cannot, therefore, be fined by any military or civil court, for neglecting or refusing to parade with any other military body . . .' "[11]

That the Nauvoo Legion was growing strong by cannibalizing other Hancock County militia units was one cause for the criticism; more of it sprung from jealousy and envy. A sense of alarm was spreading throughout Illinois over Nauvoo's accent on martial display, and the fact that, after all, the Legion was made up of soldiers with guns. And again, over Mormon heads, was rising the same problem that had plagued them in the past. Population growth meant political strength. Every aspirant to political office in the state, and every incumbent already in office, outdid one another in currying favor with Joseph Smith, John C. Bennett, and the Saints.

In September of 1841, General Joseph Smith, General Hyrum Smith, and General John C. Bennett were invited as guests of honor to a military parade held at Montrose, Iowa, directly across the river from Nauvoo. The officers in command, General Swazey and Colonel Fuller, who had invited the dignitaries from the Legion to review with them the Montrose militia units, were happy and proud to have the Mormons present. All went well until one of the militia members by the name of Kilbourn spoiled the affair by mounting the stand in front of the official staff. Publicly, and unafraid, he read his own proclamation:

CITIZENS OF IOWA

The laws of Iowa do not require of us
to muster under or be *Reviewed* by
Joe Smith or
General Bennett,
And should they have the impudence to
attempt it, it is hoped that every person
having a proper respect for himself will
at once LEAVE THE RANKS[12]

The parade went on in spite of the mutinous public demon-
stration, but the incident was promptly seized upon by such anti-
Mormon newspapers as Tom Sharp's *Warsaw Signal* as an example of the Mormon attempt to gain military power not only
in Illinois, but in other states as well. With Nauvoo as a city,
and the Legion as an army, growing with an immigration rate
that was frightening, the abrasive edges of public disapproval
and alarm began showing itself in the same pattern once familiar
to New York, Ohio, and Missouri.

V

THE CURIOUS welding of church and state, a concept always un-
popular in America, continuously irked the Illinois citizenry as
they watched the Mormon population grow to such proportion
as to become a political plum eagerly to be sought by every
office seeker. At the Legion's grand parade of May 7, 1842,
Judge Stephen A. Douglas adjourned the circuit court, then in
session at nearby Carthage, so he and all the prominent barristers
might witness Nauvoo's dazzling military display — which included a full-scale sham battle. General Smith, pleased at having
the prominent Gentiles as visitors, extended the invitation to
them to attend the lavish *repast militaire* held at his Mansion
House at the day's end. Douglas and his entourage were not the

only Springfield notables sharing the Prophet's hospitality during the years of Nauvoo's phenomenal growth.

The autonomy of both Nauvoo and the Legion, and the amazing powers granted to both by the Nauvoo charter, were the accomplishment of John C. Bennett. The plan and buildup of the Legion in its every complex facet came through the extraordinary skill of this man. The Prophet had rewarded Bennett handsomely, including the mayorship of Nauvoo, and the number two post in the church. It was inevitable that sooner or later the two glory-seekers must clash head-on.

For many months Joseph Smith had watched the insatiable ambitions of Bennett feed upon itself, until he had become silently convinced that this dashing entrepreneur harbored thoughts of eventual desposition of the Prophet and a takeover of his church. It was at this very May 1842 military display that the Prophet claimed to have thwarted a plot on his life. General Bennett, at this affair, twice solicited General Smith to take positions in the sham battle away from, and out of reach of his personal guard and staff. Sensing an attempt to assassinate him, in the thick of the melée, away from help and witnesses, and with no one the wiser, General Smith refused to accommodate General Bennett in any of his devious plans.

The worry of the Prophet for his personal safety was nothing new. Missouri had commenced a campaign for his extradiction, continuously thwarted by *habeas corpus* proceedings in Nauvoo's autonomous courts. More than one attempt had been made to kidnap him and haul him bodily across the river. And he had reason enough to fear for his life from certain elements within Nauvoo itself. He now kept himself continuously surrounded by an elite guard of ex-Danites, including John D. Lee, Orrin Porter Rockwell, Bill Hickman, Jonathan Holmes, and Hosea Stout. The guard consisted of a total of twelve men, tried and trusted friends all, bound by solemn oath to their duty. The

Prophet dressed these men distinctly in white. On muster day, and ceremonials, his guardian angels worse sashes of bright red. The Prophet, in turn, was reluctant to enter even a sham battle in his own Legion without the presence of the white guard. And these men were not the type of angels to be trifled with.

But the perfidy of Bennett was fast becoming the Prophet's major problem. As mayor, Bennett tightly ran the city. Outwardly it was free of public brothels, and if one wanted liquor, the purchase must be made from the city-church-owned dispensaries. Visitors were appalled by the fact that one could be arrested and jailed for loitering, and draw up to six months in jail, and five hundred dollars fine for such minor crimes as profanity. What astonished the Illinois citizenry was that under this facade of stern righteousness, Nauvoo had become the hiding place of river pirates, counterfeiters, and known criminals. The city, in spite of its pretensions to Godliness, possessed an underworld in the day when such things were scarcely known among the commonwealths. And there was little doubt but that Mayor Bennett, and certain other silent Saints, were hands deep in the chicanery.

But it was Mormondom's secret doctrine of "celestial marriage" and the "plurality of wives" which, if not one of the factors which brought John C. Bennett so eagerly to Nauvoo, was certainly one of the prime reasons for his later dramatic exit from the City of the Saints. Never morally scrupulous, with a physician's matter-of-fact outlook on the sexual mysteries, he refused to bother too much about wrapping a casual seduction in the elaborate spiritual ceremony which the Prophet had confidentially revealed and prescribed to the intimate circle of the hierarchy. Even though General Bennett was assistant president of the church, he still was a libertine at heart. And Nauvoo inwardly was seething with a secret as black and as dramatic as it was explosive.

It was back in Kirtland that Joseph Smith had started to pattern his new social organization in many ways that were strange to the accepted order of occidental society. His thinking, and even his writings, more closely followed Old Testament concepts than the prosaic, knuckle-edged thinking of Nineteenth Century America. That polygamy was acceptable to God and ancient Israel was reason enough to make it acceptable to the new prophet and the new order. The first stirrings of the philosophy were whispered to those close to the Prophet during the Missouri days. It began flowering simultaneously with the establishment of Nauvoo.

Apostle Parley P. Pratt, who early in 1840 had met Joseph Smith in New York City, during the Prophet's presidential and congressional mission of redress for the Saints, has written that "during these interviews he [the Prophet] taught me many great and glorious principles concerning God and the heavenly order of eternity. It was at this time that I received from him the first idea of eternal family organization, and the eternal union of the sexes in those inexpressibly endearing relationships which none but the highly intellectual, the refined and pure in heart, know how to prize, and which are at the very foundation of everything worthy to be called happiness."[13] Apostle George A. Smith also declared that the Prophet had revealed plural marriage to him as early as 1839.

By the time John C. Bennett had struck Nauvoo like a meteor, and had glowed for a year and a half in its midst, polygamy as a doctrine of the church had been fully established by the Prophet. Not only was it being secretly practiced by him, but by those of the hierarchy whom the Prophet deemed ready and ripe for the great charge. There can be no question that Bennett, at the very top of the church, willingly accepted its precepts. In plural wivery, it was in the manner of the taking, that finally brought the wrath of God down upon the head of General John C. Bennett.

Some of the Nauvoo women, shocked by the strange courtship of the already married Prophet and his apostles, had commenced to tattle. Some, like Martha Brotherton, had preserved their virginity by fleeing Nauvoo, and publishing accounts of the hot-lighted advances of those high in the church.[14] There were rumors aplenty flying around Illinois.

Joseph Smith had long suspected that Bennett was his most dangerous rival. Bennett was a brilliant, dazzling, unscrupulous rake. There was no doubt that his ambitions looked farther than city mayor, Legion generalship, or even second man in the church. Nothing but supremacy could ever satisfy such burning ego. And Joseph Smith had begun squirming with the thought that Bennett had plans to depose him and take over all.

However, it was not the battle for personal power, but rather the classic pattern and inevitability of these two men pursuing the same woman, which ultimately brought on the explosion. Nancy Rigdon, pretty nineteen-year-old daughter of Sidney Rigdon, became the flaming apex of the strange triangle involving these two hot and eager churchmen. It was a most embarrassing moment for Nauvoo and Mormondom when Smith and Bennett became eager rivals for the affection and favor of Nancy.

Bennett was a married man, though long previous to his arrival in Nauvoo his family had been deserted in the east by this smiling and adventurous hedonist. Joseph Smith, on the other hand, maintained a family — wife Emma Hale Smith and four sons — proudly and openly in Nauvoo. The number of his clandestine wives under "the new and everlasting covenant" were already a matter of constant rumor and conjecture. But the secret courtship of Nancy Rigdon by these two married men was the gravest sort of mistake for both.

If Nancy actually had any preference in the matter, it was probably for Bennett. For it was Bennett who forewarned her that the Prophet planned to "spiritually" proposition her at the home of Apostle Orson Hyde. When it did happen, Nancy not only resisted the Prophet's promise of celestial glory, but turned on him in howling fury. The next day the Prophet made the mistake of putting his courting hungers in a letter to Nancy. "Happiness is the object and design of our existence; and will be the end thereof, if we pursue the path that leads to it . . . Whatever God requires is right, no matter what it is, although we may not see the reason thereof till long after the events transpire . . ."[15]

Nancy in turn told all to her father, and showed him the Prophet's letter. Sidney Rigdon, the closest of all associates to Joseph Smith from Mormondom's beginnings, was shocked, and he was furious. He sent for the Prophet, and the scene between the two men was a dramatic one. Though neither Joseph Smith nor John C. Bennett ever succeeded in making a spiritual or plural wife out of Nancy Rigdon, this was the beginning of the end for the tough and dynamic Sidney Rigdon so far as Mormonism was concerned.

Nancy carelessly handed the letter over to a friend, who in turn gave it to Bennett, whose fury matched that of Sidney's. Later Bennett, in his published exposé of Mormonism, turned it with deadly effect upon the Prophet, and the inner affairs of Nauvoo.

Before the major trouble with John C. Bennett, Joseph Smith had taken on at least nine or ten spiritual wives, a number of them already married to Nauvoo brethren.[16] John C. Bennett had probably far outpaced the Prophet in the nuptial race, and in a considerably smaller space in time. The grave problem with Bennett, however, was that he seldom bothered to observe the spiritual formalities in the taking of a maid. He was a libertine by nature, and an accomplished abortionist by medical training. His debauchery had so far outpaced his military and political accomplishments in Nauvoo as to become a public scandal, and a cause of open indignation to the more virtuous Saints. Even without the quarrel, Joseph Smith would have been forced to publicly handle such a profligate, or witness the distintegration of his entire church and city.

In the full knowledge that Bennett would be an enemy more dangerous than any turncoat, apostate, or ex-communicant of the past, Joseph Smith, in May of 1842, drew up a bull of excommunication, backed by numerous affidavits from women Bennett had seduced or lived with in open adultery. Bennett claimed that the Prophet forced him to sign, at pistol point, a document exonerating Joseph Smith of any complicity or encouragement of such robust love life. There were weeks of indecision before the drastic documents were acted upon by the apostles and high council — including public confession of guilt, followed by public forgiveness by the Prophet. But the Bennett stench was too much for Joseph's associates, and he was finally forced to the public act. A month later, June 23, 1842, Dr. John C. Bennett was excommunicated from the church, shorn of his political power, and the ex-mayor of Nauvoo, and general of its Legion, became a public pariah so far as the Saints and their city were concerned.

VI

As COULD BE expected, Bennett's retaliation was deadly. He began a series of newspaper articles, opening in the *Sangamo Journal*, Springfield, July 8, 1842, that were copied and reprinted throughout the United States, to ultimately appear in a most devastating book against the Prophet and his Saints. His first installment was prefaced: "I write you now from the Mormon Zion, the city of the Saints, where I am threatened with death by Holy Joe, and his Danite band of murderers." In the foulest accusations possible the series, which ran until September, labeled Joseph Smith guilty of everything from immorality to murder.

The Nauvoo Legion, Bennett claimed, had for its sole purpose the subjugation of the American west, and the setting up of Joseph Smith as king and emperor. The Danite oath was the core and motivation of the army, with twelve of the most ruthless Sons of Dan "set apart" as Destroying Angels. Garbed in white, with sashes of red, the task of the Destroying Angels was to assassinate any man who dared challenge or speak ill of the Prophet.

The stories, and later the book, plunged sedition's knife into the center of Nauvoo. The city was never again the same, and the hate and suspicion toward it would never disperse until the ultimate tragedy. The fact that Bennett's attack was palpably vituperative, and his accusations so patently overstated as to reveal Bennett himself as a liar and opportunist, became the most handy and telling device the Prophet could use against him.

Joseph Smith answered Bennett with a barrage of affidavits by the very parties named as polygamists and adulterers. Church records, however, indicate that the women named as plural wives of the Prophet had truly been sealed to him, and for expediency's sake were forced to perjure themselves. The practice of polygamy in Nauvoo was categorically denied, notwithstanding the long list of notables who were even then secretly practicing it. For years this elaborate circumlocution of a most obvious fact would go on in the church. Not until 1852, and the church safely in Utah, would it officially admit something its practicing elders had for years publicly denied.

But the influence of John C. Bennett on Nauvoo lived long after his expulsion. The hurt was there years after his campaign of exposure and hate. Yet he had given the city the most liberal charter ever known. His military genius had created and forged a most remarkable army in the Nauvoo Legion. In spite of his claim to Danite influence, the Legion must remain a monument to the flash and dazzle of John C. Bennett. It was a well trained and efficient fighting corps, because Bennett had worked tirelessly at building it. And no city ever had a more handsome or a more debonair mayor.

VII

BENNETT'S FALL, and subsequent campaign of vituperation and slander against Joseph Smith, Nauvoo, and Mormondom in general, left scars that have not healed to this day. His was the voice that, more than anything else, started the hue and cry against the Prophet and the Saints — a campaign which would never cease until the Prophet was dead, and his followers expelled from an American state for the fourth time. But the Nauvoo Legion lived healthily on, long after Bennett's departure from Nauvoo.

His place was taken, first by Hugh McFall, as adjutant general, and later by Jonathan Dunham as acting major general. With Bennett in Missouri, stirring up old hates, and with an ominous arousal of anti-Mormon sentiment throughout Illinois, the Legion went through its periodic musters and parades with the new and solemn thought of possible defense. Such public display of martial strength, however, did nothing to placate the anxiety engendered in the west by its former commander's published statements to the effect that the Legion's intent and purpose was to conquer Illinois, Missouri and the western territories for the purpose of setting up a Mormon kingdom under the headship of Joseph Smith.

Out of the miasma of bitter hate and rumor came the story that the Prophet had predicted that Governor Carlin, of Illinois, would die in a ditch, and that Governor Boggs of Missouri would meet violent death within a year. There is nothing written in the annals to substantiate these prophecies, or that the Prophet ever actually uttered them. Also, of course, neither of them quite worked out. Carlin went out of office safely, and Thomas Ford was elected without publicly asking for the Mormon vote. What happened to Boggs is another matter.

Ex-Saint John C. Bennett, however, had done his best to keep alive the legend that the Prophet had propensity for bringing about fulfillment of prophecy, especially if they were concerned with those who had challenged or misused him. Bennett claimed that he had actually heard Joseph Smith offer five hundred dollars to any Destroying Angel who would lethally settle the score with the man who had issued Missouri's infamous extermination order against the Saints.

When Lilburn Boggs received a near-fatal blast of gunfire through the window, he was no longer governor of Missouri, but was running for the state senate. However, it was the man, not the office, the Mormons detested.

By coincidence, Orrin Porter Rockwell, one of the most feared of the Prophet's Destroying Angels, had returned from Missouri shortly after this attempt on Boggs' life. And all through Nauvoo had gone the happy news that Boggs was dead; that at last the Lord had visited retribution upon this monster out of the past. But, unfortunately, Boggs tenaciously clung to life. His assassin — Mormon or otherwise — had bungled the job.

When Boggs had recovered sufficiently to listen and act, John C. Bennett visited him. On the strength of Bennett's revealment and persuasion, Boggs preferred charges against Joseph Smith and Porter Rockwell for attempted murder, and succeeded in inducing Governor Reynolds to issue extradition papers on the pair as fugitives from justice. Governor Carlin of Illinois complied with a writ and warrant, which were duly served in Nauvoo. Both Smith and Rockwell submitted peaceably enough to arrest, but were immediately released under a writ of *habeas corpus* issued by the Nauvoo city court. To make doubly certain of the prisoners' freedom, the Nauvoo city council rushed through an ordinance granting power to the Nauvoo court to pass on the validity of every writ or process served on a Nauvoo citizen.

Thwarted by an ordinance which blatantly infringed on the jurisdiction of the state's courts, the sheriffs from Missouri hurried back to Springfield for conference with the governor. Assured by the state that Nauvoo's actions had no legality, the sheriffs returned again to take the men into custody. By that time the Prophet was safe in hiding, and his protective angel had taken flight to Philadelphia.

For half a year Joseph Smith hid out, while the Missouri sheriffs wore themselves into frustration hunting for him. From various concealments up and down the river, known only to his personal guard and church intimates, he conducted the business of his vast and growing ecclesiastical world. Finally wearying of this cat-and-mouse subterfuge, and at the urging of newly elected Governor Thomas Ford, who himself was anxious to test the validity of the Missouri extradition demands, Joseph gathered a protective coterie of Legion officers and militiamen, journeyed to Springfield and surrendered to the governor.

As Ford had predicted, the court and legislative findings were wholly in the Prophet's favor, the writ was held invalid, Missouri was rebuffed, and Joseph returned to Nauvoo a free man. But during his weeks of sojourn in Springfield, the blond and handsome Mormon leader won so many hearts with his charm and personality that he became the center of attraction in the Illinois capital. New Year's Day of 1843 occurred during the Prophet's Springfield sojourn. To honor him, the House of Representatives was thrown open to the Mormons present, and Apostle Orson Hyde delivered a sermon on Mormonism from the legislative dais.

The Prophet's easy victory, his ability to gain friends among the elite, and his immersion in high politics, whetted his own desire to shine brighter in that new and exciting world. In his mind, as he returned to Nauvoo, were some plans of his own. It was not enough to be revered as a Prophet, or to command an army of five thousand men. In the next national election, he would be a candidate for the Presidency of the United States.

But any thoughts that it was all over with the determined Gentiles from Missouri were soon dispelled. If they couldn't extradite Joseph Smith with the legal cooperation of Illinois, they would get him by stealth and force. There was enough reward money on the heads of Smith and Rockwell to make his kidnapping and deliverance on Missouri soil a profitable game for any man or set of men hardy and tough enough to attempt it. And there were plenty attempts.

On June 23, 1843, one such plan very nearly succeeded. Joseph Smith, visiting the Saints in the little town of Dixon, in Lee County, for a conference and sermon, was grabbed, after the meeting, by Constable Wilson, of Hancock County, and delivered over to a Missouri agent by the name of Reynolds. Enough men were in the Reynolds posse to get the Prophet downriver and across into Missouri, but Reynolds had not sufficiently calculated the alarm measures the Mormons had set up to insure the safety of their Prophet.

Quickly as Nauvoo learned that Joseph Smith had been abducted, the fastest riders from the Legion's mounted cohort were thundering down the roads toward Carthage and Warsaw. Generals Law and Rich, ignoring the legal steps necessary to muster out militia, personally led two hundred cavalrymen in the wild and desperate move to save the Prophet. The Mormon riverboat, *Maid of Iowa*, was commandeered, loaded with Legion men and gunpowder, and headed down the Mississippi.

After they had rescued Joseph Smith from their old-time enemies, and he once again was safe in Nauvoo, the Prophet immediately sued in the Nauvoo municipal court for a writ of *habeas corpus* to forestall not only the Missouri body-snatchers, but to dampen the ardor of the cooperating law officers in the non-Mormon communities of Illinois. The Prophet, in the autonomous courts of his unique city was, of course, immediately discharged as guiltless and free.

VIII

As THE YEAR 1843 progressed, the Prophet and his city were relentlessly swept ever nearer to the tragic drama which fate was storing up for the future. Springfield might have taken personal liking to the handsome giant of a man who ruled Mormondom, but the legislators and the citizenry at large were casting second hard looks at the power and autocracy they had blithely granted to the Prophet and his sect. No longer was there a John C. Bennett to smooth-talk and lobby for the Saints. Every politician had grown wary and fearful of the way Joseph controlled and manipulated his Mormon vote. Nauvoo was outstripping Chicago in population, with no end in sight. The frightening thing was that eventually Mormons would politically control the state.

Joseph Smith had now publicly declared himself as a candidate for the Presidency of the United States, and was turning his apostles and hundreds of missionaries into stump speakers who, by fall, would be declaring this candidacy throughout America with the same fervor and success with which they swelled the rolls of Mormonism with zealous converts. Neither Gentiles nor Saints had any doubt as to the power and persuasion of the Prophet.

The Nauvoo Legion had grown into the largest, best equipped and best drilled military unit in the state. While ostensibly it was a militia corps, patterned after the dozens of other units wheeling and turning in other Illinois towns and cities, it was there the similarity ended. Nauvoo Legion was an army, dangerously large, superbly trained, fanatically committed to the Prophet first, and state and national government second. John Bennett had publicly proclaimed that Joseph Smith planned to use it as an army of conquest and, while generally publicly discredited, Bennett's pronouncements were enough to bring shivers of apprehension up and down the collective spine of the west. After all, Bennett had promoted and commanded the Legion. Who could know better of its aims and its purposes?

Bennett's canny skill in wringing the Nauvoo and Legion charters out of an unsuspecting Illinois legislature had unleashed a monster that could possibly devour the state itself. Without a dissenting vote they had granted Nauvoo and its army such power as should be reserved only to the state. No other city — not even Springfield — possessed such a charter. The repeal of this fantastic blunder seemed not only necessary, but imperative.

Bennett's revelations had pictured Nauvoo as a Sodom of moral decay and depravity. In spite of Mormon claims that Nauvoo was the fairest of all examples of morality and virtue, enough seeds of suspicion had been sown to harvest perpetually in mistrust. The less favored and less fortunate towns in Hancock County were loud in their accusations against Nauvoo. The press of Illinois was turning sour and bitter against the Mormons. A storm was brewing. No man doubted it.

THE NAUVOO TEMPLE

Oddity was that while the Prophet was rising in affluence, not only among his people, but worldwide, an inchoate rebellion was brewing very close to home. With eyes on the Presidency, Joseph Smith had become a creature of consummate charm and ease. But at his heels, in spite of the Nauvoo Legion and his bodyguard in white, were men from Illinois just as anxious to "get the Prophet" as were those who persistently dogged at him from Missouri. His life had become a constant mixture of joy and jeopardy.

For Joseph, intoxicated with the heady dream of becoming President of the United States, there would no longer be truckling with local politicians — even though on several occasions it had been the local Whigs and Democrats who had saved him from the body-snatchers and process servers out of Missouri. He, as no other man, was conscious of the powers granted to Nauvoo through its unique charter, and was implacably against every attempt or mention of its repeal. Speaking before the city council, on February 25, 1843, he made a summation of its strength and its advantages. "We stand in the same relation to the state as the state to the union . . . Shall we be such fools as to be governed by its laws [Illinois laws], which are unconstitutional!"[17] To his thinking, Nauvoo stood equal with the state, and, in many ways, more sacrosanct.

The Nauvoo council, with seemingly crass contempt for constitutional law, became the tool of the Prophet in grinding out ordinances that were as peculiar as they were pernicious. One such law was passed providing arrest and, if found guilty, life imprisonment in the city jail, for any officer coming into Nauvoo with a writ for the arrest of Joseph Smith for the ancient Missouri difficulties. And, if found guilty, pardon could come only from the governor of Illinois — with the consent of Nauvoo's mayor. The mayor of Nauvoo, of course, was now Joseph Smith.

It had become a criminal offense for any officer to issue a warrant in Nauvoo without the approval and signature of its mayor. Dozens of other equally strange and autocratic decrees, including those aimed at preventing harassment of the Prophet for his debts, were enough to convince even the most skeptical that Joseph was putting personal aggrandizement and power above even the tradition of law.

But that was only one part of the high ride the Prophet was making as the dramatic year of 1843 came to its close. In December he drew up a petition to Congress asking that Nauvoo be designated a completely independent federal territory, with acceptance of the Nauvoo Legion into the United States regular Army as a separate corps. The petition went so far as to ask that the right be included for a granting to the mayor of Nauvoo the authority to personally call out federal troops when necessary. This strange petition asked so much, and went so far, that it alienated the last of the Prophet's friends in Springfield.

"I prophesied by virtue of the holy priesthood vested in me, and in the name of the Lord Jesus Christ, that, if Congress will not hear our petition and grant us protection, they shall be broken up as a government..."[18] Congress did not hear or heed it.

For the Legion, he set up an arsenal in Nauvoo, and began construction of a gunpowder factory. He surrounded himself with a proven and trusted inner organization, called the Council of the Fifty — as recondite and as oath-bound as the Danites. Within this mysterious inner circle the Prophet was actually crowned as Joseph — King of the Kingdom of God.

Nauvoo, many were certain, had become America's capital of intrigue and mystery.

IX

JOSEPH SMITH, though carried away by insatiable ambition and grandiloquent dreams, was not blind to the wave of hatred and criticism that had begun washing over the Saints in Illinois. Probably convinced that removal from the state would eventually be inevitable, he had begun casting eyes westward for space and territory to fit his expansionist and empirical hopes. In that fabulous decade, with Oregon, Texas and far-away California national topics of interest, he was not the only man intrigued with the challenge. But, in the Prophet, and the force he had unleashed upon the world, "manifest destiny" had a meaning considerably different than that of the Benton-Fremont congressional clique.

By summer of 1843, Joseph had begun talking westward migration. He sent Jonathan Dunham on a mission of exploration of routes to the Missouri River. At first break of spring in 1844 he began recruitment of a party of twenty-five men to seek out a location in California or Oregon "where we can remove to after the temple is completed, and where we can build a city in a day, and have a government of our own, get up into the mountains, where the devil cannot dig us out . . ."[19]

To the national agitation for expansion westward, a new fever had been added — the possible annexation of Texas — augmented and kept alive by the bloody border clashes of 1842-1843 between Texas and Mexico. Joseph and his Council of Fifty were as intrigued as other Americans by the possibilities offered in the sparse and open leagues of the great southwest. Agitators for this particular dream were Lyman Wight and George Miller. Lucian Woodworth, given the title of "minister to Texas" was dispatched by Joseph and his Fifty. Woodworth was to offer Texans the armed power of Mormondom in their battle against

Mexico in exchange for a colonization area that would have bitten an enormous chunk out of what is now Texas, New Mexico, Colorado, and southern Wyoming.

As if this were not enough, Joseph petitioned Congress, in March of 1844, for appointment as an officer of the United States Army, and as grantee of power and authority to raise an army of one hundred thousand men "to extend the arm of deliverance to Texas; to protect the inhabitants of Oregon from foreign aggressions . . . to open the vast regions of the unpeopled west and south . . . to supersede the necessity of a standing army on our western and southern frontiers . . . to break down tyranny and oppression and exalt the standard of universal peace."[20]

President Tyler's recommendation to Congress for the establishment of military posts along the Oregon Trail had, more than anything, prompted the Prophet to add filibustering on a grand scale to his already long list of personal ambitions. The effrontery and amazing scope of Joseph's petition stopped it short in the House of Representatives on May 25. The wildness of Mormon ferment, and the fact that its leader was bucking for not only the conqueror's role, but for the Presidency of the United States, had come under journalistic scrutiny throughout the nation. There were grave and disquieting fears over the tempest that was brewing in Illinois.

Although Joseph Smith had small chance of winning the highest office in the land, he showed himself as astute a politician as he was a Prophet and militarist, by shrewdly playing upon the stirring issues of the day. "I go emphatically, virtuously, and humanely, for a Theodemocracy, where God and the people hold the power to conduct the affairs of men in righteousness,"[21] he declared. He would reduce Congress by two-thirds, overhaul the penal system, and bring Texas into the Union. In a complete reversal of his Missouri stand, he advocated the abolition of slavery. This was the ticket his hundreds of missionaries were preaching throughout America in the spring of 1844.

Some of the newspapers laughed at the pretensions of the Mormon prophet, some jeered, others took thoughtful cognizance of this strange and infective force out of the west. Some of the closer Illinois newspapers, especially those of the rival town of Warsaw, were carpingly critical of the polygamist who wanted to be president. The *Warsaw Signal* started 1844 by labeling Joseph Smith as "that hoary monster who rules at Nauvoo; whose black heart would exult in carnage and bloodshed, rather than yield one iota of what power he has obtained by his hellish knavery."

On January 17 the *Warsaw Message* confessed: "We see no use in attempting to disguise the fact that many in our midst contemplate total extermination of that people; that the thousands of defenceless women and children, aged and infirm, who are congregated at Nauvoo, must be driven out — aye, *Driven* — *Scattered* — like the leaves before the Autumn blast! But what good citizen, let us ask, what lover of his country and his race, but contemplates such an event with horror?"

Thomas Gregg, who authored these and many other editorial blasts coming out of neighboring Warsaw took accurate measure of the temper of the times. He peppered the February 7 issue of his *Warsaw Message* with: "We claim not to be a prophet nor the son of a prophet, yet we tell you that your career of infamy cannot continue but a little longer! Your days are numbered!" Gregg's appraisal of Joseph Smith was defamatory and harsh but Gregg's qualifications as a prophet proved accurate enough.

The year 1844 was a climactic one for Joseph. He was riding the crest of fame and popularity. He was head of a dynamic and fast-growing religious movement, mayor of the largest city in Illinois, candidate for the Presidency in that year's national election, champion of western expansion, and lieutenant general of the feared and respected Nauvoo Legion. He was revered by his people as the greatest prophet of the ages, but he had not clawed his way to the pinnacle without scarring others and without gaining for himself a host of enemies.

Countless were the Gentiles who wished him ill — either because of his menacing and growing personal power, his peculiar religious precepts, morals, or the natural envy of any "comer" in politics or commerce. Nor could he longer be free of danger within the circles of his city. No man who had induced forty women to be "sealed" to him as plural wives — many of them already married to other brethren — could escape the fundamental and biological hates so intimately triggered to sex and mating. No longer now would Joseph Smith brook criticism, or tolerate personal guidance or counsel. His ambition and ego were like a bottomless well. The humble and contrite mien he so endlessly had preached for his followers, no longer were a part of his own life. Ruthlessly, and without mercy, he struck down any brother who thwarted his will or stood in his way.

Tens of thousands of Latter-day Saints revered him — and that was his immeasurable strength. The Nauvoo Legion, to a man, would have battled hell itself, in his name. The Quorum of the Twelve loved him enough to spread his name spiritually and politically throughout America and the world. The Council of the Fifty, and his guardian angels in white, were pledged to the death in his behalf. But that was not enough. The forces he had unleashed had brought the danger to his own threshold. Not even in Nauvoo was he safe.

William Law, an intelligent and wealthy Canadian convert, had come to Nauvoo, along with his brother Wilson Law. The ability and devotion of William had brought him fast advancement in the church, and the Prophet not only had made him his second counselor, but, after John C. Bennett's expulsion, had, because of Sidney Rigdon's illness and erratic behavior, leaned heavily on the able shoulders of this courageous and kindly man out of Canada.

As usual with most brethren of ecclesiastical standing in Nauvoo, William Law was honored with a commission in the Legion. William, however, was a deeply devout man, and his talents were more in keeping with civil administration, and the promotion and conservation of church and city. Militarily, a captaincy in the Mormon army was sufficient and satisfactory so far as he was concerned. No so Wilson Law, his brother. Wilson was a horseman and military strategist of high caliber, with similar administrative abilities. His career in the Nauvoo Legion was meteoric. By 1843 he was commanding its elite horse corps, the First Cohort, with a rank of brigadier general.

With the Prophet preoccupied in masterminding a church, building a temple, managing a city, commanding an army, visioning an empire, and running for the Presidency, William Law had assumed the difficult and exacting task of erecting the hundreds of dwellings and business structures necessary to the fastest-growing community in the American west. The Lord, by revelation, had commanded the Saints to erect the Nauvoo House — an imposing hostelry and public house, with perpetual and lavish quarters earmarked for the Prophet and his family descendants. It was William Law's obligation to see that all these things, including the Nauvoo House, were built.

As a practical business man, Law paid a decent wage to his workmen, and with phenomenal results. The Prophet, on the other hand, insisted that the temple and church edifices be constructed by the Saints, without pay, and by tithing their time and skills to the Lord. The Saints, however, considered eating-money more important than ethereal blessings and heavenly commandment, and the skilled workmen and artisans were ever so much more willing to work for William Law in preference to the Prophet. It was inevitable that conflict should arise between these two dynamic and strong-willed men.

To William Law the most maddening problem was that Joseph Smith literally controlled the purse-strings of both church and state. By heavenly commandment, money was subscribed by the Saints to the building of the Nauvoo House, in exchange for stock in the enterprise. But William, unable to use the money for the purpose it was subscribed, early began to suspicion that the Prophet was turning it to his own devices — purchase of Nauvoo lots, for the purpose of selling them at inflated prices to the eager Saints migrating to Illinois. The impossibility of any man carrying out his charges and obligations under so unworkable a financial structure, and to reap along with it, the complaints and criticism of the leader, finally became unbearable.

More than that, was the knowledge that polygamy permeated every strata of Nauvoo, and that the Prophet and his associates seemed obsessed with the idea of surrounding themselves with secret harems. William Law, instead of freely entering the marrying circles of his associates, was deeply shocked by what he saw. Devout Mormon though he was, he was too moralistic to hunt added spiritual wives for his "increase." The rift finally came when the Prophet approached Law's pretty wife, Jane, with the "new and everlasting commandment."[22]

Furiously Law lashed out at the Prophet. He demanded, on the pain of complete public revealment, an immediate end to the Sodom-like wickedness he claimed existed in Nauvoo. He demanded not only reformation within the church, but that Joseph Smith go before the High Council, humble himself, and make confession. Nothing less than this would suffice. If the Prophet refused, Law swore he would expose every bit of Mormon "corruption" to the world.

To humble himself, and beg forgiveness, was, of course, the last thing Joseph would do. Thwarted, William Law withdrew from active fellowship, and he and his brother Wilson joined such similarly disillusioned Saints as Dr. Robert D. Foster, William Marks, Francis Higbee and Hiram Kimball. The first hope of this group was that a reformation within the church might be possible — that it still might be cleansed, and restored to the purity and simplicity of the New York and Ohio days. But the Prophet was in no mood for guidance and counsel. He fought this apostasy, in the familiar pattern, by public denouncement of the disaffected ones — demanding that they, instead of himself, subject themselves to public confession and discipline.

But William Law believed fundamentally in the church, and was a stubborn man. His thesis was that Joseph Smith was not a false prophet, but a fallen one. That Joseph had been misled by pride, insatiable ambition, and corrupt men like John C. Bennett. William Law, like many another Saint, remained certain that Mormonism was the true gospel of Christ, and would return again to its pristine promise, when its accretion of false teaching and secret "sins" were pared away. When the Prophet, instead, began fighting this mutiny within the ranks, the Laws and their friends set up a church structure within the church. Excommunication and public denouncement came brutally quick.

But William Law was no man to be intimidated or terrorized. Nor was he an unprincipled knave like Bennett. He had the quaint idea one could operate in Nauvoo like a Luther or a Calvin, to bring sanity and morality back into the one true gospel. Nor was he exactly a poor man. At least he had salvaged enough of his wealth to purchase a printing press, type and paper, to carry home his message of reform. The first issue of the *Nauvoo Expositor*, with William Law and Sylvester Emmons on the masthead, appeared June 7, 1844. With sensational material so ripe for the plucking, it came out a remarkably restrained example of journalism. There was nothing lurid in what William chose to say, nor in the manner he said it. The tone of the whole sheet was disciplined, and as deeply spiritual as the church which William still professed to believe in. But the quiet voice, as usual, was the effective voice.

He confronted the Prophet and Nauvoo with intimate and unassailable facts. His exposure of polygamy, the whole spiritual wife business, and his criticism of Joseph Smith's arrogance and tyranny, hit deep and hard. There was only one issue of the *Expositor*. Joseph Smith called the city council into extraordinary session. He ordered a trial — not of the apostates — but of the *Expositor* itself. Without jury, without lawyers, without presence of the defendants, the verdict was passed. The mayor had declared the *Expositor* a civic nuisance. As commanding officer, he ordered the Nauvoo Legion to destroy it — which they did, with speed and dispatch. The Law brothers, and the "apostates" were forced to flee for their lives.

X

DESTRUCTION of the *Nauvoo Expositor* was Joseph Smith's fatal blunder. From Carthage, William Law and Robert Foster secured warrants for Smith's arrest on the charge of riot. These, like others in the past, were dexterously disposed of by the all-powerful Nauvoo courts on writs of *habeas corpus*. But this time there was no easy disposition of the tumultuous roar of indignation that swept the state.

The *Warsaw Signal* published Robert Foster's public statement, describing the high-handed and unwarranted destruction of the press. It listed innumerable crimes alleged to have been perpetrated by the Prophet and his zealots, including the alleged attempts on the life of Lilburn Boggs by Joseph's hired assassin, Porter Rockwell. It told of the wholesale seduction of women in Nauvoo by the lecherous Prophet and his apostles. "History affords no parallel to the iniquities and enormities of this tyrant, who dressed in a little brief authority, perpetrates deeds at which Heaven weeps and human nature falls back ashamed of her own depravity," Foster indignantly declared.

The theme was editorialized by Thomas Sharp, in the June 12 issue of the same newspaper: "War and extermination is inevitable! *Citizens arise, one and all!!!* Can you *stand* by and suffer such *infernal devils!* to *rob* men of their property and Rights, without avenging them? We have no time for comments; every man will make his own. *Let* it be made with *powder and ball!!!*" Indignation meetings were held in Warsaw and Carthage, and resolutions pledged to Mormon extermination were unanimously adopted. Armed Mormon-haters began crossing the river from Missouri and congregating in the excitement-filled towns south of Nauvoo. The mood was dangerous and ugly.

The Prophet, sensing the peril to himself and his city, wrote a long explanatory letter to Governor Ford, defending his stand against the perpetrators of the Nauvoo mutiny, the city's action in the destruction of their press, and begging the governor to come to Nauvoo. He dispatched urgent messages to the twelve apostles, and every Mormon dignitary out in the mission field stumping America for the Presidential candidacy of Joseph Smith. Not only did he urge their immediate return to Nauvoo, but for them to come back prepared to fight for their city and their homes.

Mormons from outlying areas began pouring into Nauvoo with tales of mob harassment and burnings. There was no mistaking now the tumult of war, and the necessity for defense. Every contingent of the Legion was mobilized, and never was its strength more impressive than on that June day when General Joseph Smith, resplendent in his blue and buff uniform, gilded buttons and epaulets, mounted the reviewing stand, to address the men who loved him, and would willingly die for him. Rank after rank of soldiery stood before his gaze. Women, children, men too young or too old to bear arms, were out there in a worried sea of humanity. These were his Later-day Saints. In their eyes, no matter how voiced the Gentile persecutors, he was their Joseph, a Prophet of the Living God, a man without sin or blemish. They revered him. They loved him. They would defend him to the last drop of their blood.

He read to his army and his people some of the inflammatory editorials daily pouring from the Illinois press, so they would be under no illusion as to the gravity of the situation. He recounted and defended the various steps of reprisal aimed at silencing the apostates, and leading to the climactic destruction of the *Expositor*. He felt encouraged and strengthened by their murmurs and shouts of approval.

It is thought by some that our enemies would be satisfied by my destruction, but I tell you as soon as they have shed my blood, they will thirst for the blood of every man in whose heart dwells a single spark of the spirit of the fulness of the gospel. The opposition of these men is moved by the spirit of the adversary of all righteousness. It is not only to destroy me, but every man and woman who dares believe the doctrines that God hath inspired me to teach to this generation.

We have forwarded a particular account of all our doings to the governor. We are ready to obey his commands, and we expect that protection at his hands which we know to be our just due.

We are American citizens. We live upon a soil for the liberties of which our fathers periled their lives and spilt their blood upon the battlefield. Those rights so dearly purchased shall not be disgracefully trodden under foot by lawless marauders without at least a noble effort on our part to sustain our liberties. Will you stand by me to death, and sustain at the peril of our lives, the laws of our country, and the liberties which our fathers have transmitted to us, sealed with their sacred blood?

A tumultous shout of "aye" by thousands of voices was his sustaining answer. "It is well," he said to them, with a shake of his handsome head. "If you had not done it, I would have gone out there." He pointed dramatically to the west. "And I would have raised up a mightier people." Many a man present knew of his interest and hopes for escape into the west.

"I call upon all men from Maine to the Rocky Mountains, and from Mexico to British America, whose hearts thrill with horror to behold the rights of free men trampled under foot, to come to the deliverance of this people from the cruel hand of oppression, cruelty, anarchy and misrule to which they have long been made subject..."

The Prophet drew his sword, pointed it heavenward. A wild cheer broke at this dramatic stance. "I call upon God and angels to witness that I have unsheathed my sword with a firm and unaltered determination that this people shall have their legal rights and shall be protected from mob violence, or my blood shall be spilt upon the ground like water, and my body consigned to the silent tomb. While I live, I will never tamely submit to the dominion of cursed mobocracy."[23]

XI

MARTIAL LAW was declared in Nauvoo, and in midst of preparation for defense of the city against the hysterical mobs and militia units assembling at Carthage and the surrounding towns, a message was received by the Prophet, from Governor Ford. The governor was at Carthage, and alarmed by the warlike preparation of western Illinois, and the fact that every community, including Nauvoo, had called up state militia without his authorization. He stated he was anxious to do all in his power to avert hostilities. He had established headquarters at Carthage

LAST ADDRESS OF JOSEPH SMITH TO NAUVOO LEGION

— *Contemporary.*

and, in the interest of peace, "he asked that well informed, discreet persons be sent to him at Carthage ... This request of the governor's was promptly complied with on the part of the people of Nauvoo; and John Taylor and Dr. J. M. Bernhisel were appointed to represent the situation at Nauvoo, and for that purpose were furnished with a copy of the proceedings of the city council, and the affidavits of a number of citizens bearing on the subjects that would likely be discussed."[24]

At Carthage, the two Nauvoo emissaries found the governor surrounded by the Laws, Higbee, Foster, and the most vociferous of the malcontents and Mormon-haters. The governor sided with the accusers in denouncing the *Expositor* affair, the unwarranted use of the Legion and state's arms in its destruction, the unauthorized calling up of the army in its show of force, and the refusal of the Prophet to stand trial before any other tribunal than his own city's biased municipal courts.

Ford ordered Joseph Smith to immediately submit to arrest under the original warrants, face trial at Carthage, and cease all warlike stance in Nauvoo. In vain did Taylor and Bernhisel argue that for the Prophet to appear in Carthage would be to face certain death at the hands of mobs pledged to his destruction. The governor was adamant. "Messrs. Taylor and Bernhisel called the governor's attention to the state of excitement in Carthage, and informed him that there were men bent on killing the Prophet, and that to insure his safety it would be necessary for him to be accompanied by an armed force which would doubtless provoke a collision. In answer to this the governor advised them to bring no arms, and pledged his faith as governor, and that of the state, to protect those who would go to Carthage for trial."[25]

The message out of Carthage brought panic to the Prophet, and gloom to Nauvoo. In his heart Joseph knew that the day he set foot in Carthage, he was a dead man. Hasty meetings were called by the church and city heads. At first it was decided that the Prophet would go at once to Washington, and lay the whole explosive situation before President Tyler. And, in a letter on the 22nd of June, Governor Ford was so informed.

The plan, however, was abandoned on the very day of its inception. Before the assembled council, and trusted brethren, Joseph Smith revealed that the spirit was whispering another wiser, solution: "The way is open. It is clear to my mind what to do. All they want is Hyrum and myself; then tell everybody to go about their business, and not to collect in groups, but scatter about. There is no danger; they will come here and search for us. Let them search; they will not harm you in person or in property ... We will cross the river tonight, and go away to the west."[26]

Within hours, plans for the hasty flight to the far security of "the Great Basin in the Rocky Mountains," was underway. W. W. Phelps was instructed to take the families of Joseph and Hyrum Smith to Cincinnati. Orrin Porter Rockwell, on that same night of June 22, rowed the Prophet Joseph Smith, his brother Hyrum Smith the Patriarch, and the trusted apostle Dr. Willard Richards, across the Mississippi to the Iowa shore. Rockwell left them safely in Montrose, and, with orders to procure horses and make all necessary preparation for the western flight, returned in the night to Nauvoo.

Next morning, at ten o'clock, the governor's posse arrived in Nauvoo to arrest the Prophet. Leaving a man by the name of Yates to watch Nauvoo for the return of the vanished leader, the posse returned to Carthage empty-handed. Yates warned the citizenry of Governor Ford's intention that, if Joseph and Hyrum Smith were not given up by the Saints to face the due process of law, the state would send troops into the city, and hold it until the day of the Prophet's appearance.

In the crisis, not all Saints were happy about the Prophet's decision to abandon everything and flee to the Rocky Mountains. Notes were sent to him, in his Iowa hideout, entreating him to return. "Some of Joseph Smith's friends instead of rendering him all possible assistance to escape from his enemies, complained of his conduct as cowardly and entreated him to return to Nauvoo and not leave them as a false shepherd leaves his flock when the wolves attack them."[27] These, with the pitiful plea of his wife Emma to give himself up, and trust to Governor Ford for a fair and honest trial, finally tipped the scales in favor of a return.

The retreat of Joseph Smith to Nauvoo was a cyclical moment in Mormon history.

Joseph, still burdened with a foreboding conviction that surrender and Carthage would cost him his life, sadly acquiesced to the entreaties. "If my life is of no value to my friends, it is of none to myself," he said. Under the protection of another nightfall, Rockwell rowed the three Mormons back across the Mississippi to Nauvoo.

Ford insisted the surrendering Mormons come to Carthage without armed escort. None of the Legion's trained and faithful soldiery rode at the Prophet's side on those long sad miles. None of his straight-shooting guardians in white were riding that day in his defense. It was early morning, June 24, 1844, when Joseph Smith, his brother Hyrum, and the little group of fellow Mormons listed in the warrants, took reluctant leave of their city.

Joseph, obsessed with the idea that he was going to die, looked out at beautiful but troubled Nauvoo. His eyes gazed fondly at the great white temple on the hill, now almost finished. He shook his head sadly, as he urged his huge black stallion into line with the other riders. Few of the Saints were up at the early hour, to wave him farewell. Little was said among the brethren, as they swung out of town toward the Carthage road. The Prophet knew he had only to speak a command, and he could march to Carthage with five thousand men. Instead, at the governor's insistence, he was surrendering, without aide or escort.

By ten o'clock the Mormon party had reached a point within ten miles of Carthage. There they were met by a company of mounted militiamen, dispatched by Governor Ford, and commanded by a Captain Dunn. They were a well disciplined group, from McDonough County. Their supposed purpose, at first, was thought to be the apprehension of the Prophet and his party. Their mission, instead, was to disarm the Nauvoo Legion. They were on the way to Nauvoo, with orders from the governor, to remove from the Legion and its arsenal, all state's arms in its possession.

To disarm the Legion meant quick and ignominious end to the military glory of the Mormon people. The Legion had been the Prophet's special pride. As its commander, he could have spoken a word, and the army would have overwhelmed Carthage, Warsaw, and driven every apostate and Mormon-hater into Missouri. Ford's crowning insult was this disarming of the Saints; to render them helpless before the howling mobs gathering downriver.

Captain Dunn was nervous about his assignment, and understandably so. The Legionnaires would have chopped Dunn and his sixty men into crow bait before surrendering their weapons to Gentiles out of Carthage, even though they entered Nauvoo as militiamen. But the Prophet was remembering Missouri, and how public resistance invariably bred public reprisal. He had already come to the conclusion that the only thing the people of Illinois wanted was surrender of the Prophet, for good or ill. Once the leader was taken, his Saints could live out their lives in Nauvoo, in peace and unmolested. When Dunn, in nervous fear, begged the Prophet to countersign the governor's order for the Legion's arms, Joseph did so without hesitation. His brother Hyrum, and the other brethren, were appalled at the Prophet's strange acquiescence.

"Do you realize what you're doing?" Hyrum asked.

"I do," the Prophet answered sadly. "If the Saints resist, they will die with me. If they stay calm, and cooperative, they will live."

"You keep talking as though you're facing death," said Apostle Willard Richards.

"I know what I am facing," the Prophet replied sadly. "I am going like a lamb to the slaughter; but I am as calm as a summer's morning; I have a conscience void of offense towards God, and towards all men. I shall die innocent, and it shall yet be said of me — he was murdered in cold blood."[28]

Captain Dunn was perfectly willing to interrupt the morbid certitude of the Prophet's stance, if he would take the time to turn about and ride back with him to Nauvoo. He knew, and the Prophet knew, that disarming the Legion, while its commanding officer was in jeopardy, would be no simple task. "If you'll go back with us, General Smith, and help us do our job, I'll pledge myself and my men to escort you safely into Carthage, and we'll protect you with our lives while you are there," Captain Dunn promised.

When the Prophet showed himself agreeable, the militiamen cheered. A message was sent to the governor, informing him of the change in plans, and the Mormon party joined Dunn's men in the return to Nauvoo.

There was no problem — with the Prophet on hand — to strip the arsenal of its weapons. But when Dunn and his men made demands on the individual soldiery for surrender of rifles and sidearms, they met confusion and reluctance. The men were remembering the great parade of a week ago. There they had seen a fighting Prophet, with upraised sword, defying the world. Now they were seeing a man, crushed, and hopelessly obsessed with the thought that he would die as the sacrifice and the martyr.

The result was that it was midnight before the Prophet and Dunn's men finally rode into Carthage. They were met by the Carthage Greys, the local militia company, long and impatiently awaiting arrival of the wanted men from Nauvoo. "Where's the damn Prophet?" they howled as Dunn and his men escorted the Mormons into town.

"Stand away, you McDonough boys! And let us shoot the damn Mormons!" And Joseph Smith now realized his premonition was by no means inaccurate. "God damn you, old Joe! We've got you now! Clear the way — and let's have a view of Joe Smith, the Prophet of God! He's seen the last of Nauvoo!"

And indeed Joseph Smith *had* seen the last of Nauvoo. He, his brother Hyrum, and Apostles Willard Richards and John Taylor, were placed in the "debtor's apartment" of Carthage jail. The jail, a two story affair, had been cleared of its other tenants, and the Mormons were given full run of the stout and solid structure. With the noise and agitation outside its windows, even the Prophet could see the logic of placing them safely out of reach of the mob.

Next day Governor Ford visited Joseph Smith in jail, and for hours the two men talked and argued over the rights and wrongs of the crisis that had come upon Mormondom. When Ford indicated that he intended going to Nauvoo, Joseph Smith pleaded to go with him — knowing that the moment the governor stepped out of Carthage, anything and everything might happen.

Two days were spent parading the Mormon notables to the militia companies stationed at Carthage, and arraigning them before the courts of law on charge of treason — stemming from the unwarranted use of the Nauvoo Legion in destruction of the

Expositor. Everywhere he went, Joseph Smith was howled at and vilified. For him it was Far West and the Missouri days in dramatic repetition — except for one thing. Thomas Ford was no Lilburn Boggs. Ford may have considered Joseph Smith a charlatan, and certainly a nuisance. But, whatever reprisals were due the state and its citizenry, it would be against the Prophet and his immediate associates. Even Joseph Smith was certain that, under Governor Ford, there would be no extermination order.

But at the same time the Prophet had no illusions as to his personal peril every hour he remained in Carthage. He knew, for certain, that without Ford and his authority on hand, his life would quickly be the forfeit. The fear was more than justified when, on the morning of the 27th, Ford took off on his promised trip to Nauvoo. With him went several companies of militia, including the friendly and trustworthy "McDonough boys." Left to guard the prisoners were the rabid and mutinous Carthage Greys.

When word was brought to the jail that Ford had taken leave of Carthage, and with him the only troops who could be trusted, the Prophet knew for certainty that he was trapped. Dan Jones, one of the Mormon party, brought word that a lynching party was being planned by the town's incendiaries. In desperation, Joseph Smith scribbled an order to Jonatham Dunham, ordering the Nauvoo Legion to ride for Carthage in all haste — to break the jail — to save their Prophet-Commander at all costs. In a matter of minutes the rider was galloping toward Nauvoo.

In Nauvoo, for some reason, Dunham, after reading the order, pocketed it. And the Mormon army neither knew, nor were able to save, the Prophet from his death.

It was late in the afternoon, on June 27, 1844, when the assault on the jail was made. Howling like the frenzied hosts of hell, the mob stormed the building. When it was over, Joseph Smith, the Mormon Prophet, and his brother Hyrum, lay dead under a riddling volley of shots. John Taylor was greviously wounded, but lived to eventually head the church. Only Willard Richards came out of the scene of fury and carnage unscathed.

In the little town of Carthage, the enraged citizenry of Illinois had provided the Mormon Church with its martyrs.

*　　*　　*　　*　　*

The Nauvoo Legion had failed to save its beloved commander. After the lynching, it neither marched as a conquering army, nor managed even to save Nauvoo. In the drama and tug-of-war of the next two years, during which time Illinois — like her sister state of Missouri — expelled the Mormon people from her borders, the Legion never did act in concert to save the Saints.

On the day the Prophet rode into Carthage the Legion had died in Illinois — and it had died with scarcely a sigh. Whatever fighting its men did was never in the phalanx formation envisioned by Bennett and Smith, but rather in the ridings of men to save their burning homes.

In a way, however, it did succeed in conquering the west — but with no remote semblance to the fearsome predictions that had been purveyed to the American public. Its men continued to live, and so did its spirit. Fate even decreed that the Nauvoo Legion should eventually be revived. But it would be in another time, and in another place.

NOTES — THE NAUVOO LEGION

1. *History of the Church*, IV, p. 40.

2. R. W. Young, *The Contributor*, IX, No. 2, p. 2.

3. *Charter*, Section 11.

4. *Ibid.*, Section 25.

5. Springfield letter, Dec. 16, 1840. Quoted in *History of the Church*, IV, p. 248.

6. *Doctrine and Covenants*, Section 124, v. 17.

7. See also *Contributor*, IX, No. 2, pp. 43-44.

8. *Ibid.*, p. 47.

9. *Ibid.*, p. 48.

10. R. W. Young, *The Contributor*, IX, No. 2, pp. 48-49.

11. *Ibid.*, letter, Douglas to John C. Bennett, p. 49.

12. *Contributor*, IX, No. 3, pp. 81-82.

13. Pratt, Parley P., *Life and Travels of Parley P. Pratt*, p. 297. 1938 ed.

14. *St. Louis Bulletin*, July 15, 1842.

15. See John C. Bennett, *The History of the Saints; or an Exposé of Joe Smith and Mormonism*, pp. 243-45. Published also as an essay on "Happiness" in *History of the Church*, V, pp. 134-36.

16. For detailed and intimate study of the Prophet, see Fawn M. Brodie, *No Man Knows My History*. Mrs. Brodie in her study of the Prophet gives biographical account of the forty-eight women who were known to have been "sealed" in marriage to the Prophet.

17. *History of the Church*, V, p. 289.

18. *History of the Church*, VI, p. 116. Another printing of the bombastic prophecy, in *Millennial Star*, XXII, p. 455, finishes it out in complete text with the Prophet's declaration "and God shall damn them, and there shall be nothing left of them — not even a grease spot!"

19. *History of the Church*, VI, p. 222.

20. *Ibid.*, VI, pp. 276-277.

21. *Nauvoo Neighbor*, April 17, 1844.

22. See Thomas Ford, *History of Illinois*, p. 322; John D. Lee, *Mormonism Unveiled*, p. 147. Fawn M. Brodie, in *No Man Knows My History*, pp. 368-370, gives a most excellent account of the Smith-Law controversy.

23. For a more detailed reporting of Joseph Smith's last speech see *History of the Church*, Period I, volume VI, pp. 497-498. Also *Comprehensive History of the Church*, II, pp. 241-242.

24. *Comprehensive History of the Church*, II, p. 243.

25. *Ibid.*, p. 245.

26. *History of the Church*, Period I, volume VI, p. 545.

27. *Ibid.*, p. 247.

28. See *Times and Seasons*, July 15, 1844. Quoted also in the martyrdom letter of Taylor and Richards, *Millennial Star*, volume XXIV, p. 775.

The Mormon Battalion

I

THE ONLY OTHER historical marches comparable to that of the
Mormon Battalion, are Xenophan's classic "Retreat of Ten
Thousand," and Doniphan's expedition into Mexico during the
Mexican War of 1846-1848 — the same war which produced the
Battalion. The incredible march of Xenophan's Greeks was
fifteen hundred miles. Alexander Doniphan's journey from
Santa Fe to Matamoras was a tremendous overland trek, but
still fell short of the two thousand miles foot-marched by the
Mormon Battalion in its long, dry journey into California. It
remains the longest infantry march in recorded history.

The winter of 1845-1846 was a cruel one for the Latter-day
Saints. Driven from their proud city of Nauvoo, their church
and leadership in chaos following the death of the Prophet, their
first wagons had crossed the Mississippi on the ice of winter,
to gather in the temporary Iowa camps of Mount Pisgah, Garden
Grove, and Council Bluffs. Death made frequent visit to the
tents of the weak and the ill. Babies were born while the wintry
winds shrieked over the thin canvas separating the bundled
mothers in travail from a sure and elemental death on the
prairie. Here among his homeless and dispossessed people,

Brigham Young was heroically at work attempting to restore order, harmony and courage to the thousands upon thousands of destitute victims of the Illinois purge.

Before his death, flushed with the glory and strength of military power, Joseph Smith had petitioned Congress for permission to raise and lead an immense army into the unclaimed west. In wake of the climactic anti-Mormon hysteria, which ultimately had led to his lynching, Congress had summarily turned down the petition. Joseph's projected private army would have capitalized on the patriotic fervor and expansionistic themes of the early 1840s by open declaration of its aim "to extend the arm of deliverance to Texas; to protect the inhabitants of Oregon from foreign aggressions and domestic broils . . . to open the vast regions of the unpeopled west and south . . . to supersede the necessity of a standing army on our western and southern frontiers . . . to break down tyranny and oppression and exalt the standard of universal peace."[1] The Carthage tragedy, of course, had buried the Prophet's grandiose plan, along with his presidential aspirations, his "new order," and the city of Nauvoo.

But the outbreak of hostilities with Mexico in 1845 quickly enough changed the thinking in Washington. Had the Prophet lived, it is not at all impossible that Congress would have favorably considered his "great delusion" along with some of the other desperate moves that were made at the time. Facing a war both west and south, and the fact that the Mormons had thousands of militarily trained men, homeless, on the prairies, and already headed into the west, the mood in Washington had suddenly become more than receptive.

In January of 1846, about the same time the first Mormon wagons were leaving Illinois, a shipload of Mormons, under the direction of Elder Samuel Brannan, had already sailed from New York City, headed around the Horn, and were destined for the Mexican province of California. The ship *Brooklyn* had loaded at New York with eager Saints seeking a new world free of persecution and oppression, its hold stuffed with agrarian and industrial necessities, and with enough guns and ammunition to secure and defend their projected colony on the Bay of San Francisco. The fact that they were seeking a foothold in what was now enemy country, was not only a little audacious, but seemed timed to manifest destiny.

Too, Elder Jesse K. Little, in his appointment as president of the Mormon Eastern States Mission, carried with him as instructions: "If our government shall offer any facilities for emigrating to the western coast, embrace those facilities, if possible. As a wise and faithful man, take every honorable advantage of the times you can."[2] Elder Little, fully cognizant of the desperate plight of his people, had moved with conviction, speed and dispatch.

Through a fortuitous meeting with Judge John K. Kane, former attorney-general of the state of Pennsylvania, while conducting a Mormon conference in Philadelphia, the road to Washington was made light and fortuitous for Elder Little. The Kanes were an old and honorable family in Pennsylvania. At the time of Elder Little's introduction to him, Justice Kane was serving as United States judge for the district of Pennsylvania, and was president of the American Philosophical Society. From this latter interest had sprung Kane's urge to study the peculiar and magnetic attraction which the Mormon doctrine seemed to hold upon the peoples of the world.

Judge Kane was also father to two rather remarkable sons, who likewise warmly responded to Elder Little's visit to the Kane home. One of these sons was Dr. Elisha Kent Kane, the famous arctic explorer. The other son, Colonel Thomas L. Kane, who would later serve with distinction as colonel and brigadier general in the Civil War, now suddenly stepped into the role

which would so profoundly affect the military course and history
of the Mormon people in America.

When Elder Little made known the desperate plight of the
Mormons, homeless, and encamped on the Iowa prairies,
Colonel Kane immediately drafted a letter of introduction to
the Honorable George M. Dallas, Vice-President of the United
States. "He [Little] visits Washington, with no other object than
the laudable one of desiring aid of the government for his
people," Kane's letter explained. Included with the Kane letter,
in Elder Little's portfolio, were other documents which had
come out of Little's previous visit to New York with Samuel
Brannan, and A. G. Benson. From Benson was a letter of introduction to Amos Kendall, former United States postmaster-
general.

So Mr. Little went to Washington — well sponsored. He found
Mr. Kendall ill, and his first visit there went unavailing. But, in
spite of this, the Kane letter worked fast and well for him. On
the very day of his arrival, the 21st of May, he was granted an
appointment with President James K. Polk. Present at the conference held that evening was a Mr. Dame of Massachusetts,
Mr. King, congressman from the same state, and Sam Houston,
whose presence had been preceded by the worrisome news of
Mexican attack on American dragoons on the Texas border.

Polk listened attentively and sympathetically to Elder Little.
But, preoccupied by the war problems confronting him, he was
non-commital at the time. Impatient with Washington inaction,
Little again searched out Amos Kendall, now recovered from
his illness, and receptive and ebullient to the idea of Mormon
participation in the coming hostilities with Mexico. Kendall
promised his own intercession with President Polk.

On the 27th, Little again met Mr. Kendall, who explained
that Polk and his cabinet had not yet decided on the matter.
But, as Little himself explained, "the plan offered was for me

to go directly to the [Mormon] camp, and have one thousand men fitted out and plunge into California, officered by our own men, the commanding officer to be appointed by President Polk; and to send one thousand more by way of Cape Horn, who will take cannon and everything needed in preparing defense; those by land to receive pay from the time I should see them, and those going by water from September 1st."[3]

Then followed more days of inaction, while Elder Little chafed over the Presidential indecision. Finally he personally wrote to Polk a long and desperate appeal in behalf of the homeless Mormon people. In its conclusion, he mentioned:

Our brethren in the west are compelled to go, and we in the eastern country are determined to go and live, and, if necessary, to suffer and die with them. Our determinations are fixed and cannot be changed. From twelve to fifteen thousand have already left Nauvoo for California, and many others are making ready to go. Some have gone around Cape Horn [Samuel Brannan's contingent on the *Brooklyn*], and I trust before this time have landed at the Bay of San Francisco.

We have about forty thousand [members] in the British Isles and hundreds upon the Sandwich Islands, all determined to gather to this place [California], and thousands will sail this fall. There are yet many thousands scattered through the states, besides the great number in and around Nauvoo, who are determined to go as soon as possible, but many of them are poor, but noble men and women, who are destitute of means to pay their passage either by sea or land.

They, as well as myself, are true-hearted Americans, true to our country, true to its laws, true to its glorious institutions — and we have a desire to go under the outstretched wings of the American eagle; we would disdain to receive assistance from a foreign power, although it should be proffered, unless our government shall turn us off in this great crisis and will not help us, but compel us to be foreigners.

... But Mr. President, were you to act alone in this matter, I full well know your course. I am not ignorant of your good feelings towards us, receiving my information from my friend Mr.

S. Brannan, who has gone to California, and also the Hon. Amos
Kendall and others;[4] believe me, when I say that I have the
fullest confidence in you, and we are truly your friends, *and if
you assist us at this crisis, I hereby pledge my honor, my life,
my property and all I possess, as the representative of this
people, to stand ready at your call,* and that the whole body will
act as one man in the land to which we are going, and should
our territory be invaded we hold ourselves ready to enter the
field of battle, and then like our patriot fathers, with our guns
and swords, make the battlefield our grave or gain our liberty.
We have not been fighting men, but when we are called into
the battlefield in defense of our country, and when the sword
and sabre shall have been unsheathed, we declare before heaven
and earth, that they shall not return to their scabbards, until the
enemy of our country, or we, sleep with the pale sheeted nations
of the dead, or until we obtain deliverance . . .

> [Signed] J. C. LITTLE,
>
> Agent of the Church of Jesus Christ of
> L.D.S. in the Eastern States.
> Washington, June 1st.[5]

Elder Little's florid and persuasive letter, either by reminding
Polk of some unwritten commitments, or by touching his sense
of justice and compassion, apparently started things moving in
Washington. For the next five days there were conferences with
the President and members of his cabinet. Moving in and out
of these gatherings, constantly attentive, guiding and advising,
was the ubiquitous presence of Amos Kendall. For Kendall
already had set himself up a rich stake in getting the Saints to
California. In his pocket was a contract signed by Samuel Brannan, A. G. Benson, and himself, specifically pledging the Saints
to deed over to these Washington speculators, every second lot
or parcel of land the Mormons might acquire. A copy of the
contract had been sent on to Brigham Young for ratification.
Had Kendall known at this time that Brigham would subse-

quently reject the whole specious proposition, he likely would not have been so attentive in gaining favors for Elder Little.

Apparently there were those high in government who were not so anxious as Kendall to set off a mass movement of Mormons to the great prize of California, which everyone in Washington seemed so eager and sure of pinching off from Mexico. Remembering Missouri and Illinois, they hesitated at any scheme, profitable or not, that would so patently grant a voting majority to Mormons, even in a new world yet to be conquered. Instead of a vast Mormon migration at government expense, as glowingly advocated by Kendall in his land scheme, Polk seemed to have been counseled by those of more conservative politics. One thousand Mormons in the American military would be enough — five hundred by land; five hundred by sea.

On June 5, Elder Little could record considerable progress: "I visited President Polk; he informed me that we should be protected in California, and that five hundred or one thousand of our people should be taken into service, officered by our own men; [he] said that I should have letters from him, and from the secretary of the navy to the squadron. I waived the president's proposal until evening, *when I wrote a letter of acceptance.*"[6]

It is possible that the influence of the Kanes, father and son, had a more persuasive though quieter effect on President Polk than the blatantly avaricious promotion of Kendall and his gang. For, only two days later, Colonel Kane was in Washington, guiding Elder Little through the political maze one must travel in search of governmental favor. There were visits by Kane to Kendall, and to Secretary of State James Buchanan. Armed with a letter of introduction from Kane, Little had conference with George Bancroft, Secretary of the Navy. Kane accompanied Elder Little to another meeting with the President and the Secretary of War. Finally it was decided that Kane should accompany the Mormon emissary west, to lend official assistance in recruiting the army.

Elder Little left Washington in company with Colonel Kane, and his father, Judge Kane. Judge Kane took leave of the party at Harrisburg, promising, according to Little, "to render any assistance in his power to influence the executive in our behalf." At St. Louis, the two men separated, Elder Little to make his way to the camps of Israel, by way of Nauvoo and the Iowa trail; Colonel Kane to hasten to Fort Leavenworth with the official dispatches.

The portfolio Kane carried to Leavenworth included governmental instructions to Colonel Stephen W. Kearny to enlist from the Mormon camps up to one-third of his projected "Army of the West." While this order preserved the politically essential preponderance of Gentiles over Mormons on the expected discharge of these troops in California, it did assure that a minimum of five hundred Mormon men would bear arms in the coming California campaign. The Mormon Battalion was to be enlisted for a period of one year, as regular soldiers, at regular military pay. Jesse Little, heading for the Mormon camps in Iowa, would inform Brigham Young of the plans for the Battalion's recruitment.

Acting under this order, Kearny immediately issued instructions to Captain James Allen, of the First Regular Dragoons, to proceed to the Mormon camps, to recruit from four to five companies for the Army of the West being gathered at Fort Leavenworth. Kearny's orders to Allen were clear and explicit:

Each company to consist of any number between 73 and 109; the officers of each company will be a captain, first lieutenant and second lieutenant, who will be elected by the privates, subject to your approval; and the captains then to appoint the noncommissioned officers, also subject to your approval. The companies, upon being thus organized, will be mustered by you into the service of the United States, and from that day will commence to receive the pay, rations and other allowances given to the other infantry volunteers, each according to his rank. You will, upon mustering into service the fourth company, be considered as having the rank, pay and emoluments of a lieutenant-colonel of infantry, and are authorized to appoint an adjutant, sergeant-major, and quartermaster-sergeant for the battalion.

The companies, after being organized, will be marched to this post [Leavenworth] where they will be armed and prepared for the field, after which they will, under your command, follow on my trail in the direction of Santa Fe, and where you will receive further orders from me.

You will, upon organizing the companies, require provisions, wagons, horses, mules, etc. You must purchase everything that is necessary and give the necessary drafts upon the quartermaster and commissary departments at this post, which drafts will be paid upon presentation.

You will have the Mormons distinctly to understand that I wish them for volunteers for twelve months; that they will be marched to California, receiving pay and allowances during the above time, and at its expiration they will be discharged, and allowed to retain, as their private property, the guns and accoutrements furnished to them at this post.

Each company will be allowed four women as laundresses, who will travel with the company, receiving rations and other allowances given to the laundresses of our army.

With the foregoing conditions, which are hereby pledged to the Mormons, and which will be faithfully kept by me and other officers in behalf of the government of the United States, I cannot doubt but that you will in a few days be able to raise five hundred young and efficient men for this expedition.[7]

Captain Allen arrived at the Mormon camp of Mount Pisgah, in Iowa territory, on the 26th of June, considerably ahead of Jesse Little, who was to have alerted the Saints on the plans and details of raising the Mormon Battalion. With no news having yet arrived out of Washington, it is understandable that the leaders of the Pisgah camp were a little surprised and uncertain when Allen made known his intention. Nor did they cooperate with alacrity in his distribution of the "Circular to the Mormons," which explained the plan, and the terms of enlistment.

II

THE MORMONS, fresh from the tragedy of the Illinois expulsion, and in the absence of knowledge of Elder Little's Washington conferences, at first reacted with surprise and suspicion. To them it seemed a little odd that the government of the United States, which had turned eyes and ears away in their time of greatest need, should now have the temerity to urge them to soldier for a cause which seemed far remote from their own desperate problem. The presiding brethren at Pisgah, having neither inclination nor authorization to aid Allen in the recruitment, gave him a letter of introduction to Brigham Young, and sent him and his three dragoon aides-de-camp on their way to Council Bluffs, to take the matter up personally with Brigham and the Mormon presidency.

Allen arrived at Council Bluffs June 30, and on the following day, at a meeting with Brigham Young and the council, presented the whole question of raising a Battalion from the Mormon camps. Again lacking knowledge of Little's Washington overtures, there were questions as to the honest intent of the government in their behalf, and the crippling effect certain to come to the Mormon migration by bleeding it of its manpower in a time of most acute need.

Already the problem of wintering the thousands upon thousands of homeless Saints, and finding forage for their stock, were questions uppermost in the mind of Brigham Young. Mormon eyes and hopes had been turned on Grand Island, in the Platte River, one hundred and fifty miles to the west. The island was fifty-two miles long, well timbered, with adjacent river-bottom land lush with grass and rushes, which could be cut and dried for hay to feed the Mormon stock for the coming wintering. Brigham realized this area, as well as the Iowa camps, were within the domain of the Louisiana Purchase, and would necessitate governmental approval before they could be occupied. Cannily, now, Brigham sought this approval, as one of the conditions for Battalion enlistment.

Allen, sensitive and sympathetic to the dire Mormon problem, unhesitatingly assumed responsiblity for this grant, and further promised that he would write President Polk, seeking permission for Mormon encampment at any point necessary during the prosecution of the war. Appreciative of this friendliness and cooperation on the part of Captain Allen, Brigham called a public meeting for that afternoon, and Allen was introduced to the assembled Saints. Vocally, and without restraint, he was allowed to present Kearny's proposal for enlistment of a battalion. The Mormon leader himself followed Allen, as speaker. His remarks, while couched with the worries and problems that plagued the Saints, were still affirmative to the idea.

I addressed the assembly; wished them to make a distinction between this action of the general government and our former oppressions in Missouri and Illinois. I said, the question might be asked, "Is it prudent for us to enlist to defend our country?" If we answer in the affirmative, all are ready to go.

Suppose we were admitted into the Union as a state and the government did not call on us, we would feel ourselves neglected. Let the "Mormons" be the first to set their feet on the soil of California. Captain Allen has assumed the responsibility of saying that we may locate on Grand Island, until we can prosecute our journey. This is the first offer we have ever had from the government to benefit us.

I propose that the five hundred volunteers be mustered and I would do my best to see all their families brought forward, as

far as my influence extended, and feed them when I had anything to eat myself.[8]

Leaving Apostles John Taylor, Parley P. Pratt and George
Albert Smith at Council Bluffs to aid Allen in the recruitment,
Brigham Young, accompanied by his first counselor Heber C.
Kimball, set out for Mount Pisgah to persuade the brethren
there as to the wisdom and merit of the government's offer.
When within eleven miles of Pisgah, Brigham was met by Elder
Jesse Little, who not only brought the Mormon leader up to
date regarding the Washington conversations, but added logic
and urgency to the cause with the showing of the official letters
and dispatches from President Polk and the highest officers of
the nation.

And even as Brigham Young sat in council with Elder Little
at Mount Pisgah, Colonel Thomas L. Kane rode into Council
Bluffs. There Kane added his own voice and persuasion to
Captain Allen and the apostles in selling the idea of the battalion
to the still reluctant Mormon refugees.

After his talk with Elder Little, and the implication and advantages became increasingly apparent, Brigham Young now
threw weight into the thing with his own authority and enthusiasm. The change in attitude among the brethren was magical.
By lectures at Pisgah, and by letters by special messenger to
other camps, Brigham laid hard on the call of duty. To the
brethren encamped at Garden Grove, he penned:

... Elder Little, president of the New England churches is
here [at Mount Pisgah] ... direct from Washington, who has
been to see the president on the subject of emigrating the saints
to the western coast, and confirms all that Captain Allen has
stated to us. *The United States wants our friendship, the president wants to do us good and secure our confidence.* The outfit
of this five hundred men costs us nothing and their pay will be
sufficient to take their families over the mountains. This is war
between Mexico and the United States, to whom California

must fall a prey, and if we are the first settlers, the old citizens cannot have a Hancock or Missouri pretext to mob the saints. *The thing is from above, for our good,* has long been understood between us and the United States government, but the first blow was struck sooner than we anticipated. *The church could not help the twelve over the mountains, when they wanted to go, and now we will help the churches.*[9]

With the return of Brigham Young to Council Bluffs, the enrollment went on in earnest. A huge rally was called by President Young on July 13. An American flag, rescued out of Nauvoo, was hoisted to a tree mast, and under it the recruitment took place. There were repeated speeches by Brigham Young, the apostles, and Captain Allen.

"We have lived near so many old settlers, who would always say, 'get out' that I am thankful to enjoy the privilege of going to settle a new country," said Brigham enthusiastically. "You are going to march to California; suppose that country ultimately comes under the government of the United States, which it ought to, we would be the old settlers; and if any man comes and says 'get out' *we* will say 'get out.' . . . *The president of the United States has now stretched out his hand to help us, and I thank God and him too.* It is for us to go, and I know you will go."[10]

In three days the Battalion muster rolls were filled, and Captain Allen officially took the Mormon army under his command. After a final meeting, for sermons and blessings by the Council of the Twelve, the Battalion's newly elected captains marched them in double file from "Redemption Hill" across the Missouri River bottoms, seven miles to their bivouac site at the ferry.

Leavetaking was climaxed by a "ball" at the Council Bluffs camp, held in the afternoon, on the hard-packed earth, beneath the camp's "bowery." Colonel Kane, who was there, made his own observations:

... A more merry dancing rout I have never seen, though the company went without refreshments and their ball room was of the most primitive kind ... To the canto of debonnair violins, the cheer of horns, the jingle of sleigh bells, and the jovial snoring of the tambourine, they did dance! None of your minuets or other mortuary processions of gentles in etiquette, tight shoes, and pinching gloves, but the spirited and scientific displays of our venerated and merry grandparents, who were not above following the fiddle to the Foxchase Inn, or Gardens of Gray's Ferry. French fours, Copenhagen jigs, Virginia reels, and the like forgotten figures executed with the spirit of people too happy to be slow, or bashful, or constrained. Light hearts, lithe figures, and light feet, had their own way from an early hour till after the sun had dipped behind the sharp sky line of the Omaha hills.[11]

On July 20 the Mormon Battalion started its long march to Fort Leavenworth. There was bound to be some consternation as Allen, without apology, marched his Mormons through Missouri. In the Missouri settlements there were cat calls, and bitter remembrances, but the journey was completed without serious incident or mishap. On August 1 the Battalion swung wearily into Fort Leavenworth.

III

THERE HAVE been those who have written the Battalion into history as an "unfriendly" act on the part of the American government against the Mormon people, especially when construed as a requisition on their manpower at the lowest ebb of their fortunes. It is true that their leaders had only recently been murdered, their public arms for defense taken from them, and they had been expelled from the body politic of the nation. But this censure loses validity when measured against the almost frantic efforts of Jesse Little and Samuel Brannan in seeking military preference for Mormons as an aid to accomplishing their great move into the west.

Had Elder Little not been in Washington at the opening of the Mexican hostilities, had Brannan not convinced Kendall and Benson that Mormon colonization in California would be to American advantage, had not Thomas L. Kane unselfishly given of time and talent to a people in deep stress and trouble, there would certainly never have been a Mormon Battalion. It was born of sudden events, and of fate unexpected.

Still, even though Mormon solicitation was parent to its birth, and its recruitment eventually was hailed as a monetary and material advantage to the Saints, it nevertheless brought to the volunteers, their families, and the movement generally, unbounded sacrifice. The recruitment program, paced as it was through a matter of days, caught the camps at a time when the young men were spread about the northwest settlements working anywhere they could for the wages necessary to finance the great removal. Consequently the military complement of the Battalion was enlisted heavily by married men with families and dependents. When the Battalion marched away, five hundred Mormon wagons were left without able teamsters, and hundreds of families faced the long trek westward conscious of an almost excruciating need for their men.

To face an infantry march of two thousand miles, and the prospect of war and death, when one's loved ones were left to the mercy of their own devices and the aid of friends, was a sobering prospect, no matter how roseate were played up the promises or the advantages. Bitter resentment for the callous and murderous experiences at the hands of politicians and the American citizenry, remembrance of the deaf ear turned by federal and state governments to unprecedented suffering and abuse, had built in the Saints a skepticism and disbelief that anything government did could ever be to their advantage.

There was reason for hesitancy, when Allen unfolded the plan. It took all the persuasiveness of Brigham Young to make the far and distant war acceptable or palatable. The march out of Council Bluffs was not without reluctance, sadness and misgivings.

IV

AT FORT LEAVENWORTH the Mormon brethren were more thoroughly indoctrinated into the stern and harsh pattern of life as an infantryman. One hundred tents were issued to the Battalion — one tent for every six privates. For arms, the best Fort Leavenworth could yield were flintlock muskets of rather ancient vintage, with a few caplock Jaegers issued to each company for sharpshooting and hunting.

Each man drew forty-two dollars as clothing allowance for one year — a sizable portion of which was turned over to Apostles Parley P. Pratt, Orson Hyde, and John Taylor, who had accompanied the Battalion from Council Bluffs. Elder Jesse Little was also on hand. The men, in addition, generously donated toward the travel costs of these dignitaries in the missionary efforts of the church — Pratt, Hyde and Taylor to pursue a European mission; Elder Little to resume his presidency in New England. The bulk of the money, however, entrusted to Apostle Pratt, was for the purpose of aiding the families of the Battalion members to make their own journey westward, and for the general help of the church in the crisis that was upon it. What was left bought a rather skimpy wardrobe for each soldier. Most of the men made do with the clothes they had worn out of Council Bluffs, or their faded blues from the Nauvoo Legion. The Battalion, in its march to California, was not one of the more smartly dressed units in Kearny's corps.

What surprised the paymaster at Leavenworth was that every member of the Battalion was able to sign his own name. Illiteracy among the Missouri and Illinois volunteers pouring into the Fort ran so high that not one out of three of the men could write his name on the payroll. Colonel Allen was just as agreeably surprised with the willing, almost eager attitude with which his Mormon soldiers buckled into the marching and drilling process so necessary in turning a recruit into an efficient and dependable infantryman. This, coupled with the marked absence of drinking, brawling and gambling, in contrast to those tough nuts filling the Gentile contingents, pleased the commander mightily. He was satisfied with the little army he had brought out of Council Bluffs. He was certain, once he had whipped it militarily into shape, that it would score well in the California campaign.

And the men were just as pleased with their commander, and just as confident in his abilities as a leader. In the last week of their intensive round of training, however, Colonel Allen became suddenly ill, and was forced to direct Battalion operations from his hospital bed. On the 12th of August, he ordered the Battalion to start its long march toward Santa Fe, to follow the route already being traversed by Kearny and his dragoons, and Doniphan with his Missourians. Allen promised that, after a few additional days of recuperation, he would join his men.

Colonel James Allen and the Mormon Battalion never met again. On the 23rd of August he was dead. The Mormon soldiers were already nearing the Kaw River when the news reached them. Loss of their beloved commander was a shock and a sorrow. The Battalion paused in its march to hold a prairie funeral for their leader. Eulogistic sermons were preached by Adjutant George P. Dykes and Senior Captain Jefferson Hunt. Unstinted were the words of praise the brethren lifted to Allen's memory.

But now the Battalion was leaderless; without a commander. So, acting on the supposed authority of its articles of enlistment, the Battalion's council of officers unanimously elected Captain Jefferson Hunt to fill the vacancy left by the untimely death of Colonel Allen. Hunt not only was a former major in the Nauvoo Legion, but was senior captain in Company A, and a sober, able soldier, well liked by the brethren. Hunt marched the Battalion as far as Council Grove. There an express messenger caught up with the troops. The orders out of Leavenworth made it abundantly clear that the Mormons had not properly reckoned with the ways and protocol of military professionals.

Major Horton, in command at Fort Leavenworth, had other ideas as to the succession of leadership in the Battalion; that the command, by military necessity, must go to a commissioned officer from the regular army, rather than an officer of volunteers. A day or so later, the official party from Leavenworth arrived — a Major Walker, Lieutenant A. J. Smith, and a military physician, by the name of Dr. George B. Sanderson. The Battalion tarried restlessly at Council Grove while the military tangle was straightened out.

Lieutenant Smith presented himself as the Battalion's appointed commander, with a letter from Major Horton not only confirming the appointment, but explaining that the property of the Battalion, because of Allen's sudden death, had not been properly receipted for. This, it was explained could only be accomplished by a signatory from the regular army. By the appointment of Smith, from the regulars, this and other matters could be quickly and properly attended to.

Captain Jefferson Hunt, the unanimous choice of the Battalion, elected commander according to articles of enlistment, boldly and forthrightly defended his right to leadership. He claimed not only the capability and experience for the command, but that he entertained no fears as to the responsibility it entailed. In spite of Hunt's defense, and the wishes of the Battalion itself, the command, pending Kearny's decision upon reaching Santa Fe, went to Smith. When Major Walker returned to Leavenworth with the equipment properly receipted for, a pall of gloom, equal in sadness to Colonel Allen's death, settled over the camp of the Battalion.

That a fuzzy-faced young lieutenant should be tendered command of the proud little army, without putting the decision to a regular soldier's vote, as promised, seemed unbelievable. Misgivings were lessened none when Smith, with complete lack of warmth and understanding, put the Battalion through parade, and made known the whip-cracking discipline which could be expected for the remainder of the march. The Battalion's new physician, Dr. Sanderson, was introduced. It was bad enough to have Smith. But within a week Sanderson was anathema.

True, there was sickness in the camp. The men, physically depleted by the rigors of Iowa, and exhausted by the heat and the long and fast march, had fallen prey to malaria. As an army surgeon, Sanderson doctored his men in the army way. With resumption of the march westward from Council Grove, every ill and wilted soldier, at the begining of each day, was forced to "jim along joe" to the surgeon's tent, for liberal dosage of calomel and arsenic, out of the communal "old iron spoon." In vain did the men protest — and to protest brought them under the wrath and retribution of martinet Smith. The Latter-day Saint method of healing was by herbs, prayer, and "laying on of hands" by those "in authority." Sanderson scoffed at faith healing, considered that he was authority, and the men got their calomel and arsenic in spite of God, the Prophet, and the creed.

From Council Grove, still chafing under the toil and hurt of the new and harsh command, the Battalion followed the Arkansas River to a little beyond Fort Mann. There, in order to avail themselves of a better known route, they crossed the Arkansas River, and followed it in the direction of the Cimarron. After crossing the Cimarron, they traveled its south fork, known as Cimarron Creek, until again reaching the Arkansas. This last crossing of that wide and familiar stream was accomplished on the 16th of September.

Smith seemed obsessed with the necessity for driving the army forward, perhaps in hopes of closing the vast distance between it and the commands of Kearny and Doniphan. But the men, in spite of Sanderson, arsenic and calomel, were failing under the rigors of the march. The corps, too, was hampered by a distinctly unmilitary rear guard consisting of wives and families of a number of the soldiers. Their wagons, ox and mule drawn, plodded along behind the marching troops in their own cloud of dust. Before a final leave of the Arkansas, Smith ordered that this rear guard, save for wives and servants of the command, and the more stout and robust laundresses, be immediately detached from the Battalion.

This "division" brought additional groans of protest. Those who put it more vociferous to the commander, were militarily dressed down. The "division" not only proceeded as ordered, but the rejected ones were sent to the settlement of Pueblo, on the east base of the Rocky Mountains to the north, under a guard of ten men. The sick and emaciated soldiers included in this "detachment," were turned over to Captain Nelson Higgins.

The Battalion, of course, considered this another violation of the Council Bluffs agreement, but their protests went unavailing so far as Smith was concerned. Still, in the interests of the corps as a whole, this weeding out, and sending the unfit up the Arkansas to Pueblo, was unquestionably to the best interest of the Battalion. Certainly, neither the families nor the sick ones could have survived the rigors of what lay ahead.

IV

UNDER SMITH's relentless drivings, the main and less hampered body of the Battalion now continued its march southwestward to San Miguel. Rounding the lower point of the mountain range, it swung northwestward. The first detachment — made up of the healthiest and most mobile — clumped wearily into Santa Fe on October 9. Three days later, October 12, the second detachment, a conglomerate of those sickly and exhausted men who had failed to keep up the pace, arrived in this ancient Mexican town.

Here they found Colonel Alexander Doniphan, their legal friend of the Missouri days, and his army. In the captured city, Doniphan was allowing his men pause and rest preparatory to his own historic march upon Chihuahua. To the weary and discouraged Mormon soldiers there was a thrill and an uplift when Doniphan ordered his troops to greet the marching Saints with a salute of one hundred guns.

Other than utterly wearing down the men, Smith's forced march had availed little. The Battalion had failed to catch up with Kearny and his California-bound dragoons. But Kearny, before his own departure westward from Santa Fe, had solved the pernicious problem of Battalion command. He, too, had passed over the articles of Battalion recruitment, which had promised the men a voice in their choice of officers. The new commander, awaiting the Battalion's arrival, was Colonel Philip St. George Cooke.

Like Smith, Cooke was a West Point graduate, and an officer of the regular army, but considerably older, wiser, and more experienced than the young lieutenant who had led the men west from Council Grove. Again the Mormons requested their beloved Jefferson Hunt to lead them. Again they were disappointed. And once· more there were murmurs of discontent.

To Cooke, Kearny had tendered a double obligation — to march the Battalion westward in support of the opening of California hostilities, and to haul the wagons and vehicles, which Kearny had abandoned in Santa Fe, all the way to the coast. This latter obligation meant changing a foot-trail into a road, and with the failing mule-power represented in the worn-out beasts the weary Mormons had brought with them, Cooke faced a formidable task.

Nor was Cooke especially encouraged by first inspection of his new command. "Everything conspired to discourage the extraordinary undertaking of marching this Battalion eleven hundred miles, for the much greater part through an unknown wilderness, without road or trail, and with a wagon train," was Cooke's own comment.

"It was enlisted too much by families; some were too old and feeble, and some too young; it was embarrassed by many women; it was undisciplined; it was much worn by traveling on foot, and marching from Nauvoo, Illinois; their clothing was very scant; there was no money to pay them, or clothing to issue; their mules were utterly broken down; the quartermaster department was without funds, and its credit bad; and animals were scarce. Those procured were very inferior, and were deteriorating every hour for lack of forage or grazing...

"With every effort, the quartermaster could only undertake to furnish rations for sixty days; and, in fact, full rations of only flour, sugar, coffee and salt; salt pork only for thirty days, and soap for twenty. To venture without packsaddles would be grossly imprudent, and so that burden was added."[12]

Faced with dwindling food supplies, and a condition of want in Santa Fe growing daily more acute, Cooke had no other alternative than to push the Battalion westward with all possible haste. To do it meant stripping the corps of its impedimenta of those unable to stand up to the stress, fatigue and exposure of a forced march. With the thoroughness of an experienced campaigner, Colonel Cooke invalided eighty-six of the men physically unfit for the journey. These, with all the remaining wives and family members still attached to the Battalion, and every one of the laundresses, were sent on to Pueblo, to join those previously ordered there by Lieutenant Smith.

Captain James Brown, and Lieutenant Elam Luddington were ordered to escort this strange company of the ill, infirm, and unfit from Santa Fe to Pueblo — a distance of two hundred miles. Under short rations, and almost inconceivable hardship, they arrived at the Pueblo encampment, previously set up by Captain Nelson Higgins, on November 17. The only women now left in the Battalion rear guard were wives of five of the officers, whom the stern and uncompromising Colonel Cooke allowed to accompany the corps only if they provided their own transportation, and faced their own risks.

In Santa Fe, besides overhauling the Battalion, Cooke shook up its command. Lieutenant A. J. Smith, who, in spite of Mormon complaints, had ably led the Battalion to Santa Fe, became its acting commissary of subsistence. Later, in the Civil War, Smith would rise to the distinguished office of major general. Another West Point graduate, who would likewise rise high in American military stature, was Lieutenant George Stoneman. He became the Battalion's acting quartermaster, to take the place of Lieutenant Samuel E. Gully. Gully, a Mormon officer, had resigned his command in anger over the despotic attitude of the army's regular officers, and the contemptuous disregard for the recruiting promises. He returned to Council Bluffs, joined the Mormon migration to Salt Lake Valley the next year, and died en route. In Battalion memory, Gully is still revered for his courageous but futile stand.

That everlasting scourge, Dr. Sanderson, was retained by Cooke as the Battalion's physician-surgeon. But as guides for the almost trackless country ahead, the hard-headed colonel hired three of the greatest mountain men in America's history — Pauline Weaver, Baptiste "Pomp" Charbonneau, and Antoine Leroux. Stephen C. Foster, known in all Battalion narratives as "Dr. Foster," was employed as "interpreter." Foster, a young Yale graduate, would later become the first American mayor of Los Angeles.

V

STILL WEAK, but infinitely improved by Cooke's drastic pruning, the Battalion marched out of Santa Fe on October 19. Its course generally was southward, down the valley of the Rio Grande. By November 10, fifty-five more men had been knocked out by the strenuous push. They too were invalided, and, under the command of Lieutenant W. W. Willis, sent on to Pueblo to join the other sick ones.

Breakdown of the men came from the obsessive drive of Colonel Cooke to fullfill his obligation to General Kearny — to get the wagons through. It was one thing to march the endless miles, with full pack, half rations, and dry canteen, without having to tug and pull at the cumbersome and heavy vehicles through the desert sand. "Our course now lay down the Rio del Norte [Rio Grande]," says Sergeant Daniel Tyler. "We found the roads extremely sandy in many places, and the men while carrying blankets, knapsacks, cartridge boxes (each containing thirty-six rounds of ammunition, and muskets on their backs, and living on short rations, had to pull at long ropes to aid the teams. The deep sand alone, without any load, was enough to wear out both man and beast."

"On the 30th, we had to leave the river for a time," the faithful Tyler observed, "and have twenty men to each wagon, with long ropes to help the teams pull the wagons over the sand hills. The commander perched himself on one of the side hills, like a hawk on a fence post, sending down his orders with the sharpness of — well, to the Battalion, it is enough to say — Colonel Cooke."[13]

For two hundred and twenty-eight miles the army doggedly pushed its way southward, following the general course of the Rio Grande, to the point where Kearny had found it necessary to abandon his own wagons. The men and the beasts of the Battalion had likewise reached the same measure of exigency — the guides themselves declaring the impossibility of following, with the vehicles, Kearny's Gila route from this point. But Cooke was adamant about getting the wagons through, irrespective of the obstacles, or the toll on men and mules. After a council with the guides, it was decided to circuit south through Sonora, on a well defined roadway skirting Janos and Fronteras.

By now everyone — from the walking Mormons to Cooke himself — were worn to discouragement by the continued southing into Mexico, rather than the westward travel so necessary to get them into California. Cooke's apprehension had a justification not readily apparent to the weary men. The Battalion was a part of Kearny's Army of the West. Every mile deeper into Mexico brought him closer to General Wool's command area. And, once within hailing distance, the Battalion faced the possibility of being drawn into Wool's "Army of the Center." In that case, none of them would ever see California in this war.

As the Battalion marched ever deeper into Mexico, and the Janos road bore them southeastward instead of westward, a sense of gloom fastened itself upon the little army. At night there were prayers in the tents, in the hopes God might persuade the stubborn commander to the fact that California could only be reached by a change of course. "All of our hopes, conversations and songs," says Tyler, "were centered on California. Somewhere on that broad domain we expected to join our families and friends."[14]

On the morning of November 21, either the Lord's influence, or an old soldier's intuition, finally prevailed on the crusty colonel. Rising in his saddle, he ordered a halt. "This is not my course," he growled. "I was ordered to California...and I'll go there, or die in the attempt!" With a rare sample of barrack room profanity, he ordered the bugler to "Blow the right!"[15] It was at a point about thirty miles north of present-day El Paso, that the Battalion heeled to the west.

"At this juncture, Father Pettegrew involuntarily exclaimed, 'God bless the Colonel!' The Colonel's head turned and his keen, penetrating eyes glanced around to discern whence the voice came, and then his grave, stern face for once softened and showed signs of satisfaction."[16]

For nearly a month the little army battled sand, desert and thirst as slowly it moved westward. The only enemy encountered in the great and empty desolation were an occasional Apache — more curious than warlike — until they reached the valley of Rancho San Bernardino. The rancho, once a populated Mexican hacienda, with many cattle and horses, had been reduced to desert solitude by Apache depredations. Vacant and neglected, San Bernardino's horses and cattle had reverted to nature's wildness. The few horses that could be caught were ferocious under the saddle, and demolished any semblance of harness put upon them. But it remained for the wild bulls of San Bernardino to give the marching Battalion its most fantastic encounter.

The entry of the Battalion into the valley was met with repeated charges by the enraged animals. Wagons were upset, mules gored, and the men had to shoulder guns in defense of their lives — not against Mexicans, but against a natural enemy far more ferocious and dangerous than any buffalo herd in the west. Hair-raising experiences were recorded by Battalion members in their "battle of the bulls." The greater gain was that, for once, the men had fresh meat along the march. And many a fractious Mexican bull went into the dried jerky which the thrifty Colonel Cooke ordered his men to manufacture for the commissary.

VI

ON DECEMBER 17 the plodding army finally reached the presideo of Tucson, to face their first encounter with the Mexican army. Commandant Comaduran made a first warning that any entry of Tucson by American troops would be resisted by the Mexicans garrisoned there. When Cooke ordered the men to advance on the town, with muskets loaded and primed, the Mexicans changed their mind. In their flight, they took with them half the town's population.

In Tucson, after a conciliatory speech, in which he expressed regret for the necessity of militarily taking the presideo, that the Battalion was not there to make war on Sonora, and that the citizenry might return to their town without fear of molestation, Colonel Cooke marched the Battalion out of the walled settlement, and encamped it in the saguaros beyond. In his remarks he let it be known that the Battalion had an additional duty, besides defense of its country — the opening of a road to the Pacific Coast, and that such road would be of immense benefit to the Sonorans.

With such amicable end to hostility, the Mexicans, with wide smiles and friendly faces, began filtering back to Tucson. Soon there was lively trading in quinces, semi-tropical fruit, beans and corn. When the men marched away, a day later, their

THE MORMON BATTALION REACHES A STREAM
ON ITS MARCH ACROSS THE ARIZONA DESERT

knapsacks were stuffed with the mementoes of Tucson that would, for a short time at least, relieve the monotonous and skimpy diet of army fare, and arrest the scurvy that now walked endemic among them.

The Battalion spent Christmas eve encamped alongside a cornstalk-and-straw village of the Maricopa Indians. The Maricopas, and the neighboring Pimas encountered along the trail, the Mormons found especially docile and friendly. Months previously, Kearny had left in Maricopan care a number of trail-spent mules and some baled supplies — with instructions that they were to be picked up by Cooke and the Battalion. The natives, true to their promise, had carefully preserved the animals and army property, and readily delivered them over to their new visitors.

It was here that a few of the hungry Mormons of Company E filched some of the mules' ration of corn to boil for Christmas porridge. Apprised of the theft, Colonel Cooke ordered the ration of beef due Company E to be fed to the mules. Since the animals were not accustomed to eating meat, the humbled miscreants of that company were forced to watch, sad eyed, while the mules trampled the precious beef underfoot.

Christmas day was spent marching eighteen miles uphill through sand, to a waterless camp far west of the villages. Next day, after a dry and strenuous twenty-three miles, the Battalion had reached the Gila River, and the troops — hitched to the wagons with the failing mules — followed its rough, circuitous and sandy course generally westward toward its confluence with the Colorado. By now the last of the San Bernardino beef had been eaten, and its lush plenitude only a tantalizing memory. As the Battalion's own famished sheep, oxen and mules dropped in the trail, they were butchered on the spot, and their carcasses minutely doled out to the equally famished men. Hides and entrails were rationed, to be broiled over the campfires for whatever food value they might contain. And by now the men were not at all fussy.

The Colorado River was reached on January 9, and the next day, using the water-tight boxes of the "damnable" wagons, the Battalion's supplies were safely ferried across the wide stream. Men and animals had to make it on their own. Worse, after the Colorado was crossed, the struggling little army faced two hundred miles of desert hell.

The diaries and journals that have come out of this epic march, all concur that this final segment of the journey was the supreme test of human endurance. Like drunken men, they staggered at their ropes, dragging the rickety wagons, now hub-deep in sand. Maddened with thirst, the men earned precious water only by digging wells into the earth, and ladling out the seepage a quart at a time. But it was these desert wells, dug at such frenzy and cost, that made possible the crossing of this hostile terrain by later travelers.

By now many of the men were barefoot, their shoes long since disintegrated by the endless miles. Every scrap of raw-hide, not eaten in hunger, was meticulously saved to be in-geniously fashioned into crude boots to protect bleeding feet from the rocks, sand, and thorny plants of this dry and lethal desert. "Some used, instead of shoes, rawhide wrapped around the feet, while others improvised a novel style of boots by stripping the skin from the leg of an ox," says Sergeant Daniel Tyler. "To do this, a ring was cut around the hide above and below the gambrel joint, and then the skin taken off without cutting it lengthwise. After this, the lower end was sewed up with sinews, when it was ready for the wearer, the natural crook of the hide adapting it somewhat to the shape of the foot. Others wrapped cast-off clothing around their feet, to shield them from the burning sand during the day and the cold at night."[17]

It took the Battalion five days of indescribable hardship to cross this last great desert. Only a body of men steeped in brotherhood, with a faith transcending reason, could ever, in like condition, have made it. Cooke never ceased to marvel at the patience and endurance of the men over which he had been given command. And Cooke himself was fashioned of the stern flesh of great leadership. He respected his men, and they respected him. Historically, it made a great team.

At the end of this five days of torture was Carrizo Creek, the first running water the glazed eyes of the Mormons had seen since leaving the Colorado crossing. No semblance of march now, as they staggered to it.

But Carrizo was only temporary surcease. The men were facing starvation. Cooke, in an urgent plea for help, had dispatched two of the guides, Charbonneau and Leroux, for the California city of San Diego, in full knowledge that they were entering enemy country, and that fighting between Kearny's forces and the Californians was still reported in progress near Los Angeles to the north.

All but five of the government wagons had by now disintegrated, or had been abandoned to the desert. The mules, on scant forage, were almost useless in drawing the loads, and, as usual, the men themselves staggered at the ropes. Remaining yet was still one more high and formidable mountain range between the chopped-up desert and California's lush coastal plain.

The Battalion's final assault on the stubborn terrain was through the Carrizo corridor, only to end in a narrow canyon, up a dry wash, with walls of solid rock too narrow for wagon passage. Fresh mules had arrived from San Diego, and a small drove of sheep. The sheep were promptly butchered for food. But not even good mules could draw the wagons through a box canyon too narrow for their passage.

Any less stubborn commander would have abandoned the useless vehicles at this point — but not Cooke. General Kearny had ordered him to bring wagons through to California. The Mormon Battalion would do what Kearny had found impossible — if they had to tear down the mountains, and use up every last Mormon on the march. In his obsession, Cooke very nearly did both.

With scant tools, and Mormon brawn, the rock walls of the box canyon were widened enough to clear the wagon hubs. With last frenzied labor, the narrow passage was negotiated. The few wagons that got into California stood as a sorry, battered lot. But no one could deny that Colonel Cooke and his courageous Mormons had accomplished the miracle.

VII

ON THE 21st of January, 1847 the Mormon Battalion encamped at Warner's Rancho, circled by the mountains they had won. Weather was like May, grass high and green, the streams of water full, clear and abundant. Here the brethren saw their first white man's house since leaving Tucson. Here, at last food was plentiful, and generously issued. Warner sold beef from his endless herds to the Battalion's depleted commissary for three dollars and fifty cents apiece — Warner to keep the hides, as the only thing of value about the animals. The beef was roasted over open fire, or by the California style of burial in hot coals. But the famished men were allowed to eat to surfeit — which they did. Some of the fortunate ones augmented the good fat beef with corn cakes purchased from the Cahuilla Indians, who shared the wondrous and peaceful valley with them.

No Battalion member ever forgot "Mr. Warner," his valley, or his ranch. Jonathan Trumbull Warner, a native of Massachusetts, had settled in this land of promise many years previously. To the Mexicans he was known as Juan José. Hopeful, if not convinced, of American success in the war for California, he generously welcomed any troops coming to the support of Kearny, Fremont, and the sailors from the American warships at Monterey and San Pedro. The news of Kearny's bruising at San Pascual, and the fighting around Los Angeles, had not been too encouraging, but the Battalion had arrived to lend aid, and that brought new hope. Still, in light of the news, the Mormons knew that Warner's paradise of high grass and fat beef, could not, of necessity, be theirs to enjoy for long.

On January 23 Cooke had become convinced of the necessity of immediately getting the Battalion northward to support Kearny in his campaign for the reduction of Los Angeles. The bivouac at Warner's, at the same time, had suddenly changed from an earthly paradise to a quagmire of wet and mud with a sudden rainstorm which, in the California winter months, can be hammered from the sky in a veritable deluge. The men who had been parched, dehydrated; who had prayed for water through many a desert thirst; now, in a space of twenty-four hours, were seeing enough moisture to float them to the sea.

It was a sodden, cold and wet Battalion that marched out of Warner's. On the 25th they were in the Temecula Valley, when Cooke received dispatches from Kearny, ordering the Battalion back to San Diego. The uprising of the Californios had been successfully put down. On January 27 the weary army reached the now-deserted Mission San Luis Rey, and a mile farther the Mormons were looking upon the Pacific Ocean for the first time. Gazing out on its endless leagues of water, they realized at last how truly they were in California. Many a Mormon soldier that day penned into his sweat-stained notebook the homesickness and nostalgia he felt for his loved ones somewhere on the trackless prairies of America.

"The joy, the cheer that filled our souls, none but worn-out pilgrims nearing a haven of rest can imagine," Sergeant Tyler describes it. "Prior to leaving Nauvoo, we had talked about and sung of 'the great Pacific sea,' and we were now upon its very borders, and its beauty far exceeded our most sanguine expectations. Our joy, however, was not unmixed with sorrow. The next thought was, where, oh where were our fathers, mothers, brothers, sisters, wives and children whom we had left in the howling wilderness, among savages, or at Nauvoo, subject to the cruelties of the mobs . . .? We trusted in God that they were in the land of the living somewhere, and hoped we might find them on our return in or near the valley of the Great Salt Lake, within the limits of California, then a Mexican State, but this was only hope . . ."[18]

On the 29th the Battalion came in sight of the town of San Diego, and encamped a mile below its old and venerable mission. With the successful termination of its epic march, even the austere and grumpy Colonel Cooke thawed enough to make public mention of the accomplishments of the strange soldiers he had led westward.

"The Lieutenant-Colonel commanding congratulates the Battalion on their safe arrival on the shore of the Pacific Ocean and the conclusion of their march of over two thousand miles.

"History may be searched in vain for an equal march of infantry. Half of it has been through a wilderness where nothing but savages and wild beasts are found, or deserts where for want of water, there is no living creature. There, with almost hopeless labor we have dug deep wells, which the future traveler will enjoy. Without a guide who had traversed them, we have ventured into trackless table-lands where water was not found for several marches. With crowbar and pick and axe in hand, we have worked our way over mountains, which seemed to defy aught save the wild goat, and hewed a passage through a chasm of living rock more narrow than our wagons ... Thus, marching half naked and half fed, and living upon wild animals, we have discovered and made a road of great value to our country ..."[19]

Though the commendation was not read to the assembled Battalion until February 4 — six days after it was written — it was gratefully and happily received by the ragged and weary troops. "One of those simple acts of justice so rarely done to 'Mormons,' " was Tyler's wry appraisal.

VIII

BEFORE the Battalion could even sample the civilized and community life of San Diego, they were marched back to Mission San Luis Rey, with orders to turn the deserted but thick-walled religious structure into a garrisoned and fortified military post. Men were detailed to cleaning up the place, and Cooke was just as adamant in demanding that, at the same time, the men clean up themselves.

Beards and hair were ordered clipped to military specifications, "no beard be allowed to grow below the tip of the ear; hair must be clipped even with the tip of the ear." Clothing had to be washed clean. Daily military drill, and Sunday parade, were now obligatory.

At the first parade, even Colonel Cooke must have been shocked at the sight. The men were utterly destitute of clothes and shoes. Pants had been improvised out of discarded wagon covers. Shoes in many instances were entirely absent, or were the trail-fashioned bootees fashioned of rawhide or ox fetlocks and gambrels. What clothing was available from the army sutlers was now priced so high as to be completely out of the realm of the impoverished Mormons. But, though naked as Indians, or in their rags, Cooke made his strange little army do their wheels and turns with precision.

Other than California's endemic fleas and vermin with which the great crumbling mission was liberally infested, San Luis Rey was welcome rest to the Battalion, and a happy improvement over the long and arduous march. "The public square of the mission, with a large adobe Catholic Church and a row of minor buildings forming the outside wall, contained about four acres of ground, with orange and tropical trees in the center," observed Sergeant Tyler. "The olive, pepper, orange, fig and many other varieties of semi-tropical fruit and ornamental trees grew in the garden. There was also a large reservoir, used for bathing, washing clothes and watering the garden. Two large vineyards were also connected with the mission."[20]

Then, just about the time the Battalion had made of San Luis Rey a home away from home, Kearny decided he had use for the Mormons elsewhere. The conquest of California had ended with a few dying skirmishes, and the Battalion had marched in too late to share even the terminal phases of the struggle. Other American troops were now arriving, both overland and by sea. But even with this increasing show of strength, there still remained pro-Mexican bitterness for the abrupt and highhanded way the Americans had taken military advantage of this vast and weakly guarded Mexican province. As a preventive measure against uprisings, Kearny decided to garrison the cities. The Mormon Battalion was ideal for this.

So, on February 15, Company B of the Mormon Battalion was ordered to the port of San Diego. On the 19th, leaving only a token force of thirty-two men under command of Lieutenant Oman and Sergeant Brown to guard San Luis Rey, the remaining companies of A, C, D and E were ordered to march to the Pueblo of Los Angeles. Eventually the guard, left at San Luis

Rey, joined the Battalion at Los Angeles, but Company B remained at San Diego.

Among the American forces it was generally conceded that the Californios were "whipped but not conquered," and there was constant apprehension that uprisings among the natives were not only possible but probable. At San Diego, the Battalion's Company B set itself to the immediate erection of a fort commanding the town. But the natives in that far southern community, instead of resenting the *gringo* Mormons, took them to their heart and friendship — so much so that there was genuine sorrow at the time of their leaving.

The main corps at Los Angeles found things less tranquil. The Pueblo was one of the wildest, most lawless spots in California. Gambling, drunkenness and debauchery were there in sufficient measure to shock and surprise the sober Mormons. Here, as in the outlying ranchos, there was resentment over loss of the province to the Americans. More than once Cooke called his Battalion to battle posts, in expectation of general insurrection.

To counter this threat, and give the Battalion something to do, Cooke set his Mormons to work building a substantial fort atop a hill immediately west of the city. Fort Moore, it was called, named after Captain Benjamin D. Moore, who had died in the Battle of San Pascual. The fort's seven cannons were so mounted that Los Angeles could be raked with shot any time its Californios might decide to reopen the war. In May, a detachment of the Battalion was sent to Cajon Pass to put an end to the Indian incursions upon the southern California ranchos.

For years the Californios had been plagued by the skilled and daring raids of Ute Indians under leadership of the renowned war chief Walkara. The thieving bands of Walkara, joined at times by white mountain men and adventurers, had stolen thousands upon thousands of California horses, with the rancheros virtually helpless against their skilled and merciless raids. The Battalion soldiers fought one battle with the renegades, killing six of them. Walkara's Utes, of course, were too well entrenched in their nefarious traffic to give up with one skirmish. But meeting American soldiers, instead of Mexican ranchers, marked the beginning of the end for this greatest of all horse thieves.[21]

As spring moved into summer, and the date grew nearer for their discharge from military service, the members of the Mormon Battalion grew ever more anxious to join their families, wherever they might be on the American plains. Meetings were held, plans discussed, horses and supplies were purchased, awaiting that day in July when they would be free from military servitude.

Word had come from San Francisco Bay that Samuel Brannan's colony, brought in on the *Brooklyn,* had practically taken over Yerba Buena and the Bay area. And, with the first months of summer, had come news that Brannan himself was crossing the mountains eastward, to search out, and guide Brigham Young and the Saints into California. As the day for discharge grew nearer, hope and excitement filled the Mormons stationed at Fort Moore, in Los Angeles, or with Company C, at San Diego.[22]

"On the 15th [July 15, 1847], Company B arrived from San Diego, preparatory to being discharged, and the next day at three o'clock, p.m., the five companies of the Battalion were formed according to the letter of the company, with A in front and E in the rear, leaving a few feet of space between. The notorious Lieutenant, A. J. Smith, then marched down between the lines in one direction and back between the next lines, then in a low tone of voice said: 'You are discharged.' This was all there was of the ceremony of mustering out of service the veteran corps of living martyrs to the cause of their country and religion. None of the men regretted the Lieutenant's brevity; in fact, it rather pleased them."[23]

IX

EXCEPT for a small number who had been talked into reënlisting for an additional six months, the Mormon veterans gathered up their horses and supplies, and headed out for the long and desperate search for their loved ones. For travel, they maintained a semblance of military order, organizing as companies "after the ancient and modern Israelitish customs, with captains of hundreds, fifties, and tens," as Tyler explains. On August 26, after a forced but uneventful journey through California's great Valley of the San Joaquin, the ex-soldiers arrived at Sutter's Fort, and went into camp two miles up the American River.

Here they paused long enough to get their horses shod, lay in supplies, and generally prepare for the arduous journey over the mountains, and eastward, in search of Brigham Young and the Saints. In their haste to make the Sierran passage before summer ran out, they deliberately had bypassed San Francisco Bay, where they would have found the colony of Saints brought in by Samuel Brannan and the *Brooklyn,* the previous summer.

At Sutter's the news that Elder Brannan was already on his own journey in search of Brigham Young and the Mormon vanguard was verified. News too had already trickled in, via emigrant train, that Salt Lake Valley had been chosen for Mormondom's new promised land, rather than the lush and beautiful California that the Battalion itself had anticipated as the gathering place.

Jobs were offered to any or all of the brethren, at good wages, and a number of the men who were anxious to improve their stakes before entering the new Zion, or those who were still convinced Brigham Young would eventually choose California, elected to stay. After prayers and affectionate leave-taking over those who remained, the main body of the Battalion headed eastward for the high mountains.

On August 28 they were at Johnson's mill and ranch, on Bear Creek. By September 3 they had reached the spot in the Pass where the Donner party had perished the winter previous. The command of General Kearny, riding back to Washington to report on the California conquest, and taking Colonel Fremont along to be court-martialed for insubordination, had passed this spot a month previous. They had buried most of the Donner dead, but enough grisly reminders remained in the outlying camps to give shudders to the Mormon men and an urge to clear the Sierran snow traps while weather would still permit.

On the morning of the 6th, in a valley near Lake Tahoe, they met Elder Samuel Brannan, returning to California after his historic quarrel with Brigham Young in Salt Lake Valley. Brannan, fully expecting to lead Brigham and the Saints into the beautiful world of San Francisco Bay, and the endless green acres he had set aside for Mormondom, at New Hope on the Stanislaus, had been appalled at Brigham's choice of the barren valley of the Great Salt Lake.[24]

"We learned from him [Brannan] that the Pioneers had reached Salt Lake Valley in safety, but his description of the valley and its facilities was anything but encouraging. Among other things, Brother Brannan said the Saints could not possibly subsist in the Great Salt Lake Valley, as, according to the testimony of mountaineers, it froze there every month in the year, and the ground was too dry to sprout seeds without irrigation, and if irrigated with the cold mountain streams, the seeds planted would be chilled and prevented from growing, or, if they did grow, they would be sickly and fail to mature. He considered it no place for an agricultural people, and expressed his confidence that the Saints would emigrate to California the next spring."

Surprised and worried by this dire news, the Battalion boys pressed for clarification of Brigham's stand in the face of such calamitous factors. Brannan revealed that there had been hot words between himself and the leader. Unsure and unsettled now, the men begged his advice as to what they should do. "He thought all except those whose families were known to be at Salt Lake had better turn back and labor until spring, when in all probability the Church would come to them; or, if not, they could take means to their families."[25]

They camped overnight with the man who had audaciously sailed his colony of Mormons from New York, around the Horn, to San Francisco Bay, and who, like themselves, saw in California a most promising opportunity for the homeless Saints. But apparently Brigham Young was seeing differently. Brannan, however, did bring the happier news that the Pueblo contingent of the Battalion, those who had been invalided from the march by Smith and Cooke, were now in Salt Lake Valley, and already plowing and planting. Their Captain James Brown, Brannan explained, was only a day behind him on the trail. Brown was on his way to California for official verification of the Pueblo detachment's discharge from service, and to collect their pay.

Next day, after Brannan had taken leave of the Battalion camp, Captain Brown rode in. With him was a trail guard of Mormon brethren from Salt Lake Valley. Brown had brought letters from the brethren's loved ones, and all the news of Pueblo and Salt Lake Valley, and the epic journey of the Mormon Pioneers from Iowa westward. He had also brought an "epistle" from Brigham Young and the Twelve Apostles "advising those who had not means of subsistence to remain in

California and labor, and bring their earnings with them in the spring." With this to confirm the advice already freely rendered by Samuel Brannan, more than half of the Battalion turned back to labor and winter at Sutter's Fort and San Francisco Bay.

X

THE Mormon Battalion made its own peculiar mark in American history by its unparalleled march to California. The men comprising this little army were good soldiers, and so attested by the commanders of the long march. They were brave, sober, and obedient. They exhibited a rare quality of patience and fortitude under a condition of thirst, destitution and hunger seldom asked of even the commonest soldier. They were visionary, prayerful, temperate, and morally clean — but, like their brethren everywhere in Mormondom, they were a tough breed of men.

With the group who elected to go on to Salt Lake Valley, as well as with the Pueblo detachment already there, went seeds and agricultural ideas picked up from the Mexican-Americans of the great southwest, including the knowledge of irrigation which transformed barren Utah into a garden land. With them went the horses, purchased cheaply in California, and of great material aid to the Saints in their new world. Their soldiers' pay had already made possible the migration of their families from Iowa. The Battalion, with all its suffering, had been a good thing for the Saints. It had been a good thing for their church.

Of even more momentous import, however, were the events forced by the discovery of gold in California. And the Battalion boys who had elected to remain yet another winter away from their families, and those who had turned back to Sutter's after listening either to the disgruntled report of Samuel Brannan or the more priestly advice of Brigham's "epistle," had a direct hand in the dramatic event which changed the history of America.

The men had found no difficulty in selling their seasoned brawn, or the exceptional skills that had helped build Nauvoo, and for comparatively good wages. Sutter offered day work to any and all of the Mormons who would remain at the Fort. One group of forty of the brethren entered into a contract with Sutter for the erection of a flour mill, six miles from the fort, and a saw mill on the American River, some forty-five miles into the hills. The frame of the flour mill, only a short distance from what is now the city of Sacramento, was raised by Christmas day of 1847, and the saw mill a few weeks later. The jobs were under the direction of Sutter's foreman and overseer, James Marshall.

The races for both mills were dug by the Battalion boys, but it was the crew at the American River saw mill who uncovered the gold. "On or about the 24th of January, 1848, the water was turned into the race above the saw-mill," says Sergeant Tyler. "The race was found good, but the water, in leaving the flume and reaching the head of the tail race, having considerable fall, washed a hole near the base of the building. Being turned off, Superintendent Marshall went below to ascertain what effect the wash was likely to have. While thus examining, his eyes caught sight of yellow shining metal, which he picked up, not knowing what it was, but believed it to be gold."[26]

It was gold all right. And history was made.

The sober and industrious Mormons finished their contract with Sutter, but when the news of the gold strike exploded upon the world, the mills were short lived. Some of the Mormons took to the streams after their work day, with anything that would serve as a pan — pie tins to skillets. Mormon Island, on the American River, became famous because of the rich diggings discovered and worked by these walking soldiers who were first upon the scene.

Unless one has clear comprehension of the hold of the Mormon faith on the souls of men, it is almost impossible to believe that, with the warming days of spring and summer of 1848, these Battalion ex-soldiers turned their collective backs on Sutter's Fort, Mormon Island, and the American River. They gathered up their gear, saddled their California horses, and with what nuggets and dust they had in their buckskin pouches, they set off for Salt Lake Valley.

Samuel Brannan had been proven wrong. Neither Brigham Young nor the church were coming to California. It was time to go home at last.

For men, at the call of duty, to turn away from the very spot which half the world was already frantically trying to reach, becomes an odd finale to the epic march of the Mormon Battalion. But to these strange and unheroic followers of the Prophet and his church, the gospel proved greater than gold. Salt Lake Valley was the gathering place — not California. All the riches of the world could not keep them from going home to Zion.

NOTES – THE MORMON BATTALION

1. *History of the Church,* VI, pp. 276-277.

2. Little's Report, *History of Brigham Young, Ms.,* 1846, bk. 2, p. 11, Salt Lake City. Quoted also in *Comprehensive History of the Church,* III, p. 67.

3. Little's Report, *History of Brigham Young, Ms.,* bk. 2, p. 16. Quoted also in *Comprehensive History of the Church,* III, p. 71.

4. There seems to be little doubt that the Benson-Kendall-Brannan agreement covering the Mormon *Brooklyn* expedition to California, was tied high and influentially in Washington. Here, Little seems to indicate that Polk himself not only is cognizant of the agreement, but may have been one of the several silent parties to it. See Paul Bailey, *Sam Brannan and the California Mormons.*

5. Little's Report, *History of Brigham Young, Ms.,* bk. 2, pp. 20-22. For *extenso* quotation and comment, see *Comprehensive History of the Church,* III, pp. 72-73.

6. *Ibid.,* p. 73.

7. See Daniel Tyler, *A Concise History of the Mormon Battalion in the Mexican War,* pp. 113-114.

8. *History of Brigham Young, Ms.,* bk. 2, p. 4. Quoted in *Comprehensive History of the Church,* III, p. 79.

9. *Ibid.,* bk. 2, 1846, pp. 26-30. *Comprehensive History of the Church,* III, p. 81. Letter is dated July 7, 1846.

10. *Ibid.,* bk. 2, p. 46.

11. Kane, Thomas L., *The Mormons,* pp. 30-31. Philadelphia: King and Baird, 1850.

12. Cooke, *Conquest of New Mexico and California;* New York: G. P. Putnam and Sons, 1878, pp. 91-92.

13. Tyler, *A Concise History of the Mormon Battalion in the Mexican War,* pp. 180-181.

14. *Ibid.,* p. 206.

15. *Ibid.,* p. 207.

16. *Ibid.,* p. 207.

17. *Ibid.,* p. 245.

18. *Ibid.,* p. 253.

19. Cooke, *Conquest,* p. 197. See also Tyler, pp. 254-255.

20. Tyler, p. 264.

21. See Paul Bailey, *Walkara, Hawk of the Mountains;* also Bailey, *The Claws of the Hawk.*

22. See Paul Bailey, *Sam Brannan and the California Mormons.*

23. Tyler, p. 298.

24. See Paul Bailey, *Sam Brannan and the California Mormons.*

25. Tyler, p. 315.

26. *Ibid.,* p. 333.

LIEUTENANT GENERAL BRIGHAM YOUNG

— From *Contributor, Vol. IX.*

The Utah War

I

"GIVE us ten years in this valley, unmolested, and we'll ask odds of no man," Brigham Young had prophesied upon Mormon entry into Utah. It took exactly ten years before the Mormons again flexed their military muscles before the Gentiles.

After the Illinois expulsion the Nauvoo Legion had vanished as a martial necessity to Mormon living. And after the incredible march of the Mormon Battalion, and the mustering out of its men, the ex-soldiers were only too glad to forget the misery and dangers of army life in favor of the challenge which went with maintaining family and a community pattern in the new Zion of the Rocky Mountains.

For those who had seen California, and compared it with the barren valleys which Brigham Young insisted as theirs to keep and hold, there was a certain restlessness. A few of the Battalion boys never accepted it. Some of the Saints re-loaded their wagons and went on to the coast; to follow the persistent lure and cry of the gold fields. They, like Samuel Brannan, apostatized, and were lost to the church. But by far the greater number remained loyal and obedient to the counsel of Brigham Young, turned deaf ears to the siren song of California and its gold, and buckled down to the task of making another secure and prosperous homeland, on the western slopes of the Rocky Mountains.

This was the fourth time the Saints had endeavored to build a commonwealth. In this final attempt went the desperate hope that their efforts would not be thwarted by any of the factors which, in the past, had brought down upon them the wrath of the Gentiles. Brigham Young shrewdly surmised that for the church now to set up colonization operations in California, would be open invitation to be over-run by the Gentiles who, by land and sea, were being drawn there by the magnet of the gold rush. He knew, and wisely, that the only way Mormons could ever know peace, was to build their commonwealth in a land coveted by no man or set of men. To him, California, and the Brannan-Benson-Kendall contract were dismissed and forgotten. So far, no one had cast covetous eyes on the Great Basin. No one had yet asked the Mormons to share it.

Colonizing a wilderness, especially one as contemptuously referred to as Brannan's appraisal, while free from the competition of other claimants, was not without its hazards — especially one as raw and as little known as the table lands of the Great Basin. In the north, resentful of Mormon intrusion, roamed the Blackfoot, and the Snakes, or Shoshone Indians. South of the Mormon colonies were the Piedes, Pahvants, and the powerful Utes who, under a confederation of war chief brothers, claimed that immense territory bordered by the Navajo country to the south, the nations of the Sioux to the east, and the Shoshones to the north. It took only a few Mormon brushes with the hot-blooded aborigines of the Great Basin to point up the necessity of military protection should there be failure in the more desirable evangelization of the tribes.

Since Salt Lake Valley for ages had served as an undisputed sanctuary, a council ground, a sort of Indian no-man's-land, its

first settlers were not challenged. But as the colonists pushed
out southward and northward, they were soon treading on the
toes of the redman, who could see no particular merit in this
new and unprovoked intrusion into his homeland. Instead of
Gentile "old settlers" resenting and disputing the ground with
the Saints, it was now the dark-skinned "Lamanites," to whom
the brethren were bringing the salvation promised in the *Book
of Mormon*. They were proving even less receptive to the gospel
message than Missourians. After a few pitched battles, particularly in Utah Valley, with violent death and constant harassment
a part of Mormon missionary efforts and colonization, the need
for military protection was dramatically brought home.[1]

The projected State of Deseret, as planned and envisioned for
the Mormon homeland, was no timid concept. It included all of
the present states of Utah and Nevada, most of the state of
Arizona, and sizable portions of New Mexico, Colorado, Wyoming, Idaho, Oregon and California. The seaport of San Diego,
known to the Battalion boys, was purposely included in a line
drawn due south from the state's western boundary of the Sierra
Nevada Mountains. This assured Deseret an outlet to the sea,
and a point for Mormon migration by way of the Isthmus of
Panama. As conceived, it truly was a vast empire.

One of the first acts of the legislature of the provisional government of the State of Deseret — the earliest governing body
of the territory — was provision for organization of a militia
corps. In remembrance of Illinois, and what had been lost to the
Saints, it was no accident that this military body should be
called by the old and familiar name of "Nauvoo Legion." Daniel
H. Wells, one of the military actives out of Nauvoo, was named
as its commanding officer, and given the rank of major general.
Steps were at once taken to organize the new Legion into
companies, battalions and regiments — the whole corps to be

at the disposal and use of the governor. The governor, of course, was Brigham Young.

Before it could be effectively organized, there was work for it to do. Its first action was against the militant Utes harassing Fort Provo in Utah Valley. Legion effectives at the time, fifty mounted volunteers under the command of Colonel Peter W. Conover, found the Saints at Provo under siege by a large band of Timpanogos Utes under leadership of Elk, an implacable foe to the colonists. With a fair-sized war on its hands, Conover sent an urgent appeal to General Wells for more troops. Wells, bringing additional men, drove the Utes into retreat, but the Mormon dead and wounded threw focus on the absolute necessity of a trained and mobile fighting force.

Other engagements with the Indians followed, and General Wells, in his organizational efforts with the newborn Legion, kept pace with the demands. Under his direction the Legion quickly answered the necessity for an effective peace-keeping force to the growing Mormon colonies on the American frontier. On March 27, 1852, additional territorial laws were enacted aimed at strengthening the reactivated Nauvoo Legion into a fully coordinated and mobile military structure capable of dealing with any situation threatening public security.

Brigham Young, besides filling the vacancy left by the murdered Joseph Smith as head of the Latter-day Saints, was once again "sustained" as governor of Utah Territory and the hoped-for State of Deseret. He also received federal appointment as territorial Indian agent. Under the new law, Daniel H. Wells was once more the choice to head the Legion as its lieutenant general — with Generals James Ferguson, Lewis Robison, Albert P. Rockwood, James W. Cummings, and Woodville M. Andrews, composing his staff. All of these men had either served the Legion in its Nauvoo days, or had made the historic march with the Mormon Battalion, or both. As commanders, they were tough, trained, and experienced men.

As in the days of Nauvoo, all male citizens from eighteen to forty-five years of age were required to be enrolled in the Legion. Again, as before, there was universal conscription. An elaborate system of fines and courts-martial was established, and rules laid down for periodical drills and musters. In addition, a battalion of "life guards," independent of any other organization, was formed in Salt Lake City. These elite troops were on constant and special call to Governor Brigham Young and the lieutenant general of the Legion.

At the close of 1852 the reactivated Nauvoo Legion numbered over two thousand men. By July 1855 Salt Lake County alone was mustering more than fifteen hundred, commanded by that fiery zealot, Jedediah M. Grant, with a rank of major general. Included in the fast expanding army was a regiment of cavalry, headed up by Colonel Ira Eldredge; three regiments of infantry under command of Brigadier General H. S. Eldredge, with Henry Harriman, William Burgess, and David J. Ross as colonels of the First, Second and Third regiments respectively. Other effectives included a company of artillery, and two companies of riflemen.

At a session of the territorial legislature held in the winter of 1852 and 1853, a substantial sum was appropriated for the construction of a suitable building to house the arms and property of the troops. Out of it came the arsenal, atop Arsenal Hill. One thousand dollars additional was appropriated to put into effective condition the ordnance and public arms; and a like amount to be expended "in the encouragement of a military school, wherein engineering, mathematics and other branches of science of importance to the military art might be taught."[2]

Within a year after activation of the Nauvoo Legion, it found itself embroiled in the "Walker War," a vicious uprising of the

Utes against the Mormons, headed by the famous war chief
Walkara [or "Walker" as it was anglicized]. This was the same
unconscionable adventurer whose skilled and savage bands had,
through the years, struck terror to the southern Californians. As
a horse thief, Walkara remains supreme. Untold thousands of
California's horses had been stolen in repeated and vicious
raids, and his reputation as a slaver had made Walkara's name
a thing of terror among the more peaceful "walking" tribes of
the Great Basin, upon whom he and his men constantly preyed
for the women and children he forcibly took for sale as menials
to the Mexicans of California and New Mexico.[3]

American victory in the war with Mexico had blunted and
endangered Walkara's lucrative pattern of horse thieving and
slaving, and when the Mormons began spreading across his
once untrammeled homeland, and were more reluctant than
the Mexicans about trafficking with him in horses and women
and children, he turned with ferocity upon them. With this
wily chief as antagonist, the Saints soon found themselves embroiled in a bitter struggle, fought in a pattern that was dis-
tinctively Walkara's.

For two hundred miles, up and down Utah, the Mormon
colonies were struck in the hit-and-run strategy which left the
towns counting their dead, their burned out homes, and minus
their precious horses and livestock. In the "Walker War," the
Legion had its hands full.

But Walkara quickly found that the Mormons were of a
different breed than the Mexicans, and in drawing steel with
them, he met his match. The Legion handled its campaign both
intelligently and effectively — in a manner that could have been
studied with great profit by the troops then being fielded across
America by the United States Government. Even while the
colonists were besieged, they "forted up." Within a matter of

months, the little towns of Utah were walled and garrisoned. A great wall even began rising around Salt Lake City.

The defensive factor was important, but the Legion, once aroused, was fighting no passive war. Mormons had cavalry equal to Walkara's own. Without hesitance they moved it into the Ute strongholds in the Wasatch and Sanpete. The war chief quickly found his family camps just as vulnerable to surprise attack as had been the Mormon towns. He learned too that the Mormon soldiers, while hard and tough in extracting victory, were just and compassionate to his people when that victory was won. To them, no Indian, not even a fractious Ute, was ever turned away hungry. The Mormons had a message of "salvation," and a book to prove it, for their "Lamanite" brethren. Their big chief, Brigham, wooed the recalcitrant Walkara in his stronghold, with notes of peace and love, and generous presents of tobacco.

A year later, Walkara was suing for peace, and his war against the Israel Tribe was over. In the spring of 1854, Governor Brigham Young lent great dignity to the contumacious war chief by personally going south for the formal council and a smoking of the peace between Mormons and the Utes.

The result was that Walkara quit his slaving, gave up his raids on California, and joined the church. Though he fretted constantly under his new halo, and was probably the most fractious Mormon elder ever to wear a loin cloth, Brigham managed Walkara up until the famous chief's death, by pneumonia, a year later. But now the Mormon towns had become forts, the Legion had become an all-inclusive army, alert and powerful. And never again would Mormondom be caught unprepared.

II

WITH Utah as part of the vast land prize awarded America through its victorious conclusion of the Mexican War, the Mormons once more began coming under the scrutiny and jurisdiction of the American commonwealth. The fact that out in Utah the Saints once more were building a vast and effective colonization structure, governed by their peculiar ecclesiastical hierarchy, complete with courts and army, could not fail to stir up the old suspicions and ferment.

Mormon petition for recognition of its own State of Deseret was repeatedly rejected by Congress. For Mormons now, and on into the uncertain future, territorial status only was granted. And the fact that even here the Saints continued to elect and sustain Brigham Young as governor of the still mythical State of Deseret, and to insist on his continued appointment as governor of Utah Territory, was rankling to the populace, and a bone of contention in Congress and the American press.

Along with this new awareness of Mormons and their antlike cohesiveness and industry came another flood of lurid stories concerning them — most of it sensational concoctions of the fictioneers of the day. Polygamy, secret murder, Danites, Avenging Angels, formed basis for the tales coming out of Utah — their dramatic and mysterious character heightened by distance and the insularity of the Mormon promised land. The pattern by now was repetitively familiar. As in Ohio, Missouri and Illinois there was emerging a determined and sustained effort to depose and tumble the militant and unanswerable Mormon leadership in favor of the more familiar and understandable American politicians and congressional appointees.

Brigham Young, of course was the focal target. This polygamous and defiant martinet, irrespective of the fact that he was the unanimous and elected choice of the Mormon people, must be shuffled out of office. All America was rapidly uniting to the urgent cause and necessity of desposing him, and striking down his deadly alliance of church and state.

Mormon bishop's courts, while eminently workable to the Saints, were completely unacceptable to the American system of jurisprudence — and Utah was suddenly heir to a flood of judicial appointees to remake all her courts more in keeping with the American image. That the judges and territorial officers sent out to Utah seemed invariably to be broken-down hacks chosen to repay political debts, without thought as to qualification, ability or understanding of a problem, became an endless source of irritation to the Mormons — who had hoped desperately for peace, and an end to harassment.

The Mormons — as cut away and isolated from their fellow Americans as a bat cave in Cibola — not only underestimated the threat of the rising storm, but seemed unaware of the pitch of hysteria already motivating the campaign against them. All they knew was that the battle for power out of the east, and the constant friction, was becoming increasingly tense. With impolitic bluntness Brigham Young and the Mormon leaders spoke out defiantly against the humiliation imposed upon them by the Gentile politicians sent out to regulate a world they could not and would not understand, and in which they had small sympathy. As with the Prophet, Brigham Young's tabernacle sermons to his people [the "old" tabernacle, used until 1866] were trumpeted back to Congress and the American press as the ranting of a dictator steeped in treason.

While the Nauvoo Legion was gaining experience and skill in its subjugation and pacification of the Indians of the Great Basin, its motives and necessity were completely distorted into an added menace in the Mormon picture. Any other state or territory could have its militia — but Mormon militia was pictured as an army of defiance and conquest — Mahomet with the sword. Not only was Brigham Young dominating his holy empire in defiance of American tradition, but he posed a lethal threat to the nation at large by this maintenance of troops pledged and operative to his slightest whim.

Brigham's inflammatory sermons, the flood of words by sensation-mongers, and the disgruntled reports of the political appointees bucking a tightly-knit ecclesiastical organization, could not fail, in a climate of hate and misunderstanding to have an adverse effect upon the Saints. What the Saints seemingly failed to realize was that these things were being interpreted by congressional hot-heads and American editors as treason on the part of Governor Young, and rebellion on the part of the Mormon people and their loyal and obedient Legion.

It took the American political campaign of 1856 to raise the "Mormon problem" to an inferno of hate. General John C. Fremont, now the popular hero of the Mexican War, after his victorious emergence from the critical censure of its real hero, General Stephen W. Kearny, was nominated as presidential candidate by the newly-formed Republican Party. The most stirring and heeded plank in his platform was the pledge to secure the "abolishment of slavery and polygamy; the twin relics of barbarism." Anti-Mormon venom so saturated this vicious campaign that any man with any obscure hope for office faced an imperative mandate to move with speed and dispatch to "put down the Mormon rebellion" and wipe polygamy and treason from the face of the earth.

Fremont, with all his aura as "pathfinder," and with all his promises, failed to gain election. The victor, James Buchanan, however, was fully as attentive to public clamor. One of his first orders of business, as President, was the "Mormon problem." Brigham Young, by governmental fiat, was unceremoniously, and without notification, dumped from his office as Utah territorial governor. Alfred Cumming, of Georgia, was appointed to take his place. Cumming had served, in another appointee role, as Superintendent of Indian Affairs on the Upper Missouri. But this time he was not going out to Utah to manage Indians.

Pressed by Congress and fevered public clamor, Buchanan was leaving the gubernatorial seating of Cumming to nothing resembling chance. Almost every movable unit of the United States Army was ordered out to Utah. Brevet Brigadier General W. S. Harney, commander at Fort Leavenworth, was original choice to lead the military expedition. When, however, it became indicative that Harney was himself over-anxious to "put down the Mormon rebellion," the command was shifted to Colonel Albert Sidney Johnston. By late spring and early summer the "Utah Expedition" was on its way westward. Its entourage included the politically safe Governor Alfred Cumming, and a coterie of appointees to territorial offices of lesser rank.

The first division, twenty-five hundred strong, cleared Fort Leavenworth July 18, 1857. Within another sixty days the entire corps was moving westward. The expeditionary force, including teamsters and civilians, totaled around five thousand men. This formidable army, the best the government could field on such short notice, had the dignity of official order. John B. Floyd, Secretary of War, on June 29, 1857, charged its commander: "The community and, in part, the civil government of Utah Territory are in a state of substantial rebellion against the laws and authority of the United States. A new civil governor is about to be designated, and to be charged with the establishment and maintenance of law and order. Your able and energetic aid, with that of the troops to be placed under your command, is relied upon to insure the success of this mission."[4]

By the enormity of the contractual and speculative forces set in motion, it would appear that this was intended to be only the beginning of military operations. Contracts were let for the expenditure of $6,000,000 for 4,500 wagons, 50,000 oxen, 4,000 mules, and the hiring of 5,000 teamsters, blacksmiths, herders and laborers. Contract for transporting 8,000 tons of supplies to Utah was awarded the firm of Russell, Majors and Waddell "without advertisement or subdivision." The quartermaster general calculated that the supply train that followed Johnston's Army to Utah would, if bunched mule nose to tailgate, make a line fifty miles long.

Before another year was out the American public, outraged by the gouging, graft and waste of the expedition, would be labeling it the "contractors' war," and "Buchanan's blunder." Far more money was being sunk in this punitive force against the Mormons than the Saints had up to this point invested in their reputedly rebellious promised land. Some of the supplies foisted on the expedition and dispatched to Utah by grafting and crooked contractors with their hands in the public till, were ludicrous and utterly useless in waging war. Before it was over, it would stand as America's comic opera of military stupidity and political corruption. But to the stern and uncompromising Colonel [later General] Johnston, and the citizens of Utah Territory, there was nothing comic about the army, or the government's reprisal.

III

FIRST NEWS to the Saints that an army was on its way fell dramatically upon them — July 24, 1857 — the tenth anniversary of their first arrival in Salt Lake Valley. In line with the commemorative importance of "Pioneer Day" this particular year, a public celebration, social and picnic was in progress, far up Big Cottonwood Canyon. Governor Young and every church and civic dignitary was in attendance. And it was no small affair.

"The main encampment of the celebrants was formed at Silver Lake, where three spacious 'lumber-floored boweries' had been provided...and a large number of the encampment passed the evening of the 23rd 'in the joyous dance.' ...There were 2,587 persons in the company; with 464 carriages and wagons, 1,028 horses and mules, and 332 oxen and cows...Captain Balloo's band, the Nauvoo brass band, the Springville brass band, the Ogden City brass band, and the Great Salt Lake City and Ogden Martial bands, were in attendance; also the 1st company of light artillery, under the command of Adjutant General James Ferguson, a detachment of four platoons of life guards and one platoon of the lancers, under the command of Colonel R. T. Burton, and one company of light infantry under the command of Captain John W. Young."[5]

"The stars and stripes," reported the *Deseret News*, "were unfurled on two of the highest peaks in sight of the camp, and on the tops of two of the tallest trees... The different bands played at intervals throughout the day, and greatly added to the zest of the varied sources of enjoyment."[6]

Into this scene of gayety and joy clattered a light wagon drawn by a double span of travel-lathered horses. Porter Rockwell, accompanied by Abraham O. Smoot, and Judson Stoddard, seeking Brigham Young, and not finding him in Salt Lake, had frantically driven the miles up Big Cottonwood Canyon. Rockwell, Stoddard and Smoot had been tending the far flung stations of the Mormon Y. X. Express Line to the east. At first news of the army's move westward, they had driven frantically across the plains to Utah, sparing neither animals nor themselves. This was the grim news they brought with them to the Mormon Pioneer Day celebration.

General Wells of the Nauvoo Legion passed the announcement on to the assembled Saints at sunset, called for united prayer, and told the celebrants to break camp on the morrow, and go quietly to their homes. There was no doubt in the general's mind as to what lay ahead.

IV

As NEWS of the advancing army permeated the thinking of the Utah communities there was, contrary to what might have been expected under the circumstances, little indication of excitement or hysteria. "The colonists of Utah were too inured to opposition — even to organized opposition — to be easily excited by its appearance, though it approached in a new form and seemed more formidable than hitherto. There was to be resistance to manifest injustice, of course, yet there would be no hysterical nervousness in that opposition. Confidence in the righteousness of their cause, and confidence in their leaders was too great to admit of undue excitement."[7]

Immediate steps were taken to alert all district commanders of the Legion that it was "tolerably well authenticated" that an army was on its way to "invade Utah territory." The official communication went out from Salt Lake City on August 1, and was signed by Daniel H. Wells, lieutenant general commanding. As could be expected, the alert was sharp and bristling.

It made pointed mention of the fact that the people of Utah had lived "in strict obedience to the laws of the parent and home governments, and are zealous for the supremacy of the Constitution and the rights guaranteed thereby;" but "in such times, when anarchy takes the place of orderly government, and mobocratic tyranny usurps the power of rulers," the citizenry "have left the inalienable right to defend themselves against all aggression upon their constitutional privileges."

It reminded that the Saints "for successive years" had stood witness to the desolation of their homes, the "barbarous wrath" of mob reprisals upon their unoffending brethren and sisters; their leaders murdered; and finally the Saints themselves forced to cull life from the inhospitable desert, amid the savages of the American west. It declared that Latter-day Saints were no longer willing to endure these unceasing outrages; that if this be an exterminating war proposed against them, and blood alone must cleanse this pollution from the nation's bulwarks, then *"to the God of our fathers let the appeal be made."*

The district commanders were ordered to hold their respective divisions of the militia in readiness for immediate march to any part of the territory; to make certain that the law was strictly enforced in regard to arms and ammunition; and "as far as practicable, that each ten be provided with a good wagon and four horses or mules as well as the necessary clothing, etc., for a winter campaign ... *Avoid all excitement, but be ready.*"[8]

Along with the preparation for war, urgent appeals went out of Salt Lake City by Mormondom's own pony express, for return to Zion of all Mormon leaders on missions to the east and Europe, and the abandonment of the thriving colonies of Genoa, in Nevada Territory, and San Bernardino, in California. All Saints in the San Francisco Bay area, and the gold camps, were ordered back to Salt Lake City — although plenty of these prospering brethren now turned deaf ear to Brigham Young's frantic call.

Samuel W. Richards, in a fast ride eastward, carried saddle-bags stuffed with letters reflecting the Mormon attitude toward the army's approach. When these were properly placed in the eastern mails, he was to continue on to England with urgent instructions for Apostles Orson Pratt and Ezra T. Benson to return to Utah at once. Richards was to detour through Washington, D. C. long enough to present Mormon memorials of grievance to President Buchanan, and to inform the national head that his army could not enter Utah until "satisfactory arrangements" had been made by commission and otherwise.

Among Elder Richards' dispatches were copies of the *Deseret News* of August 12, containing a caustic but carefully worded editorial stating the views of the presiding authorities of the church regarding the outrage of hurling an army against an inoffensive minority of the American commonwealth. These he delivered to Colonel Thomas L. Kane, the one stalwart and true friend the Mormon people possessed in this eastern mill of hate and misunderstanding. Kane promised to personally get them into the hands of the President and congressional leaders.

Before sailing for England, Elder Richards was interviewed by the *New York Times,* which fortunately aired the Mormon side of the grievance to a vast readership, and did much to temper the rising tide of prejudice and misconception so generally rife throughout the east. Elder Richards' mission, though a hasty one, was to prove both effective and fruitful.

V

THE FIRST movement of Utah forces in the field was a special "corps of observation" from the Nauvoo Legion, comprising seventy-five men under command of Colonel Robert T. Burton. Their orders upon leaving Salt Lake City, August 15, was to protect and aid the twelve hundred Mormon immigrants already on the plains, and headed for Utah. An even more important detail was for Burton's command to locate the invading army, assess its strength and equipment, and report its progress and movements by fast express to Salt Lake City. Burton was also ordered to make note of every strategic point along the route which might avail the Mormon troops in opposing the army before it could enter Utah. He was not, however, to interfere or seek battle with the westbound troops.

Another company was dispatched to the vicinity of Fort Hall. Its commander, Captain Andrew Cunningham, was to use his forty-three men in watching the northern approaches, should the "invading" army make the detour by way of Soda Springs. Later, with the coming of winter, and it became more and more certain that the Utah Expedition would utilize the more direct route by way of Fort Bridger and Echo Canyon, Cunningham and his men were recalled to Salt Lake City.

Burton and his men, however, reached Fort Bridger on August 21. Five days later, at Pacific Springs, he met the first of the Mormon immigrant companies headed westward. Next day they watched in astonishment as three huge government supply trains passed, their wagons loaded with army supplies, but completely unprotected by any military escort. Leaving a portion of his command on the Sweetwater to scout this strategic approach, Burton moved on to Devil's Gate, which he reached August 30, encountering many companies of Mormon immigrants en route.

On the 8th of September he sent a scouting party to the Platte. Four days later the men returned. They had seen the army — and it was no small one. From that time on, Burton had it under surveillance.

When Colonel E. B. Alexander's division of the Utah Expedition camped at Devil's Gate, on September 22, Burton and three of his men not only had it under scrutiny, but made their own observation camp only half a mile away. The fact that it comprised the 5th and 10th United States infantry regiments, with the batteries of Phelps and Reno, were duly made note of, and, as news, was carried by fast express to Salt Lake Valley. This advance contingent of the U.S. Army was never out of sight of Mormon soldiers until the day it went into bivouac at Ham's Fork.

In Utah, up to late August, it was generally supposed that General W. S. "Squaw Killer" Harney was in command of the Utah Expedition. Harney's utterances had been openly contemptuous of the Mormons, he had boasted of his own planned reprisals against them, and from Fort Laramie and other army posts it was no secret that he was determined to remove all Mormon express and emigrant stations along the westward route.

August 26 Governor Young stated: "I have sent word to General Harney that I wish for peace, and do not want to fight anybody; but he must not come here with a hostile army, and if he undertakes it, we shall prepare to defend ourselves."[9] As the late summer's crop of Mormon pioneers began arriving in Salt Lake City, however, they brought the news that Colonel Albert Sidney Johnston had replaced Harney in command of the Utah Expedition. They brought with them, too, the first shocking knowledge of the hate and hysteria prevailing in the east.

The Mormons, in light of the sudden and dramatic apparition of an army marching upon them, had no possible way of knowing that the War Department's orders to the Utah Expedition were actually temperate, sensible, and certainly not vindictive or destructive. True, any such sudden appearance of armed might, accompanied by the nihilistic tone of press, pulpit and politicians, could scarcely be construed as anything less than an invasion. But the army carried with it a complete complement of civil authorities, from territorial governor down, and with instructions were for it to serve more as a posse to back up new leadership rather than outright warfare on the Mormon people. But the Saints were anything but convinced of this. If it were a posse, it was "one hell of a big one."

The expedition was officered by men of high caliber. Practically every man in its command, from Johnston down, would, in a few years serve with distinction on one side or other of the great war between the states. Many would emerge as America's most revered heroes. But the Mormons, who had been under the gunsights of their enemies too long, were not impressed by military record or integrity of soldier or gentlemen. Utah was being invaded. The homeland they had spent ten sacrificial years in building would soon, like their other homelands of the past, be under siege. They would resist this outrage to the last man.

Seemingly, the War Department's only sensible act in this moving of an army to Utah in response to public hysteria, was to dispatch Captain (afterwards Major General) Van Vliet as advance courier to the expedition. Van Vliet, at the time, was assistant quartermaster, U.S.A., to General Harney's staff. He had been known to the Mormons during their sojourn in the Iowa camps. In Iowa, Van Vliet had employed hundreds of Mormon males out of their Winter Quarters colony, in government service, had treated them well, and the Saints, in turn, respected him.

Van Vliet arrived in Salt Lake City September 8. By that time, Alexander's forces were moving into bivouac at Ham's Fork. He was received kindly and courteously by Brigham Young and the leading brethren. Brigham went even further than mere courtesy. He introduced Captain Van Vliet to the Saints in the tabernacle. "From the day of his [Van Vliet's] visit to Winter Quarters," Brigham warmly and honestly told his worried audience, "many of this people have become personally acquainted with him, both through casual intercourse with, and working for him. He has invariably treated them kindly, as he would a Baptist, a Methodist, or any other person, for that is his character. He has always been found to be free and frank, and to be a man who wishes to do right; and no doubt he would deal out justice to all. Many of you have labored for him and found him to be a kind, good man; and I understand that he has much influence in the army through his kind treatment of the soldiers."[10]

Van Vliet, of a certainty, was the right man to establish liaison with the Saints. The only problem was that, in the government's haste and muddle to get the army west, it had failed to provide the captain with the kind of answers that would allay the worry, or put to silence the interminable questions with which the Saints now plied him. Underneath it all, he found a smoldering anger engendered by the hate and hysteria rocking the east, a deep hurt at the government's hasty action in mounting a military campaign against them, and an implacable determination to resist the army in any attempted entry. Neither friendship nor urbanity were enough to counter these impressions and influences.

The good captain had come to quiet the fears of the Saints before the army's arrival. He endeavored to convince them that there was no intent to conquer or destroy the Saints. But the Saints had been shot at enough times before, to be chary of any kind of promise. The Utah Expedition was an army. An army — any army — meant war, not peace. To the Saints it spelled out, at the very least, coercion, and the likelihood of subordination of civil authority to the military. Bringing with it new territorial officers could mean only a despotic wresting from the Utah citizens of their constitutional right to govern themselves. "The coming of that armed 'Expedition,' therefore, meant to the Latter-day Saints of Utah the subversion of their constitutional rights, the destruction of their liberties — their religious freedom; their right of community self-government; perhaps, even, their community existence."[11] Against these arguments, the captain had few answers.

Van Vliet had been charged with the necessity of seeking supplies for the army, once it arrived, and scouting out a favorable area for it to encamp within the valley. His negotiations with the polite but stubborn Mormons proved of no avail. "The governor [Brigham Young] informed me that there was abundance of everything I required for the troops, such as lumber, forage, etc., *but that none would be sold to us.*"[12] Once in Salt Lake Valley, the army faced bleak prospects.

With the finesse of a diplomat, the captain tried to persuade Brigham and the brethren that it would be the rashest sort of folly to resist the federal troops. "We do not want to fight the United States," Brigham replied, "but if they drive us to it, we shall come off conquerors, *for we trust in God.*"[13] The picture of Missouri and Illinois, the murder of the Prophet, and all the remembered hurts, were paraded before the captain. And to this he had no convincing answer.

On the 14th, Van Vliet made one last interview with Brigham before departure to join his command. The leader bitterly declared that, had the government sent its new territorial officers without an army, they would have been as well received in Utah as had been the captain himself. "We would still have received their governor and officers, had they sent them here without an army; but inasmuch as they are disposed to send an army here to hold us still while others run their hot iron into us and then kill us, we will now say that we will not have either their soldiers, armies, or officers any more here at all, and you may tell them so. We will fight from this day forth ... If the government of the United States persists in sending armies to destroy us — in the name of the Lord we shall conquer them!"

Brigham drew a picture of the havoc that would be wrought on Mormonism's colonial experiment when the thousands of teamsters, camp followers, army opportunists, whores and gamblers were discharged in Salt Lake at the end of the march. Mormon spies had made him bitterly aware of the human flotsam traveling with the troops.

He cited his record as Indian agent in holding the Utes, Blackfoot and Shoshoni in check. But, "if they [the United States] commence the war, I shall not hold the Indians still by the wrist any longer ... but I shall let them go ahead and do as they please ... And even should an army of 50,000 men get into this valley, when they get here they will find nothing but a barren waste. We will burn everything that is wood, and every acre of grass that will burn, and you may tell them that they must bring with them their forage for their animals, *for they will not find anything in this territory when they come.*" And, with Mormon restraint unloosed from the Indians, maintaining supply lines into the west would be precarious, if not impossible. "The Indians will kill all who attempt it."

Van Vliet again used every effort to persuade the angry Brigham that it was not the intention of the government or the army to make war on the Saints, but merely to put Utah's territorial house in order.

"Congress could send out an investigating committee to Kansas, or any other place but to Utah," Governor Young argued, "but upon the mere rumor of liars they send out 2,000 armed soldiers to Utah to destroy the people, without investigating the subject at all."

"They never did anything against Joseph [the Prophet] till they had ostensibly legalized a mob, and I shall treat every army and every armed company that attempts to come here, *as* a mob. You might as well tell me that you can make hell into a powder house, as to tell me that you could let an army in here and have peace.

"Liars have reported that this people have committed treason, and upon their lies the President has ordered out troops to aid in officering this territory, and if those officers are like many who have previously been sent here ... they are poor, miserable blacklegs, broken down political hacks, robbers and whoremongers ... men that are not fit for civilized society ... I feel that I won't bear such cursed treatment ...

"I do not lift my voice against the great and glorious government guaranteed to every citizen by our Constitution, but against those corrupt administrators who trample the Constitution and just laws under their feet."[14]

Van Vliet's meetings with the Saints, and his conferences with Brigham Young, had convinced him that hostilities were inevitable the moment the troops appeared upon the scene. He carried out of Salt Lake City a portfolio of bad news.

VI

VAN VLIET, on his return east, was accompanied by Dr. John M. Bernhisel, Utah Territory's delegate to Congress. On meeting the slowly advancing troops, just then emerging from South Pass, he advised the command not to attempt any entry into Salt Lake Valley that winter. He had been completely unsuccessful in arranging for either forage or supplies. Not only would they find the Mormons uncooperative and hostile, but, he was convinced, any attempted entry would be at the price of fighting their way through. The Mormons, he was certain, were not bluffing.

Some of the officers were inclined to take lightly the somber warnings of Van Vliet. Not only were they confident they could push their way into Salt Lake City, but so eager were they for the fight, they began doubling their usual progress of fifteen miles per day. Oddly enough, not even exuberance, determination, nor forced marches were to gain them Salt Lake Valley this winter.

Moreover, Van Vliet had not underestimated the Mormon will to resist. The day following his departure from Salt Lake City, September 15, 1857, the still undeposed Governor Young issued a proclamation to his people.

Citizens of Utah:

We are invaded by a hostile force who are evidently assailing us to accomplish our overthrow and destruction

For the last twenty-five years we have trusted officials of the government, from constables and justices to judges, governors and presidents, only to be scorned, held in derision, insulted and betrayed. Our houses have been plundered and then burned, our fields laid waste, our principal men butchered while under pledged faith of the government for their safety, and our families driven from their homes to find that shelter in the barren wilderness and that protection among hostile savages, which were denied them in the boasted abodes of Christianity and civilization.

The Constitution of our common country guarantees unto us all that we do now, or have ever claimed. If the constitutional rights which pertain unto us as American citizens were extended to Utah, according to the spirit and meaning thereof, and fairly and impartially administered, it is all that we could ask, all that we have ever asked.

Our opponents have availed themselves of prejudice existing against us because of our religious faith, to send out a formidable host to accomplish our destruction. We have had no privilege, no opportunity of defending ourselves from the false, foul, and unjust aspersions against us before the nation. The government has not condescended to cause an investigating committee or other persons to be sent to inquire into and ascertain the truth, as is customary in such cases.

We know those aspersions to be false, but that avails us nothing. We are condemned unheard and forced to an issue with an armed, mercenary mob, which has been sent against us at the instigation of anonymous letter writers ashamed to father the base, slanderous falsehoods which they have given to the public; of corrupt officials who have brought false accusations against us to screen themselves in their own infamy; and of hireling priests and howling editors who prostitute the truth for filthy lucre's sake.

The issue which has been thus forced upon us compels us to resort to the great first law of self-preservation and stand in our own defense, a right guaranteed unto us by the genius of the institutions of our country, and upon which the government is based.

Our duty to ourselves, to our families, requires us not to tamely submit to be driven and slain, without an attempt to preserve ourselves ...

Therefore, I, Brigham Young, governor, and superintendent of Indian affairs for the territory of Utah, in the name of the people of the United States in the territory of Utah,

1st — Forbid all armed forces, of every description, from coming into this territory under any pretense whatever.

2d — That all forces in said territory hold themselves in readiness to march, at a moments' notice, to repel any and all such invasion.

3d — Martial law is hereby declared to exist in this territory, from and after the publication of this proclamation; and no person shall be allowed to pass or repass into, or through, or from this territory, without a permit from the proper officer ...

[Signed] BRIGHAM YOUNG.[15]

With this proclamation, and declaration of martial law, Utah Territory — and the Legion with all its mustered strength — moved speedily to back their stance with warlike preparation. Companies of the Legion, aggregating twelve hundred and fifty men, were ordered into Echo Canyon, to hold it by force of arms. On Sunday, September 27, Daniel H. Wells, lieutenant general of the army, with members of his staff, and apostles John Taylor and George A. Smith, serving as "counselors," took leave of Salt Lake City to inspect and supervise the troops and the field of possible conflict. Before departing, each of these brethren, by the solemn imposition of hands, was blessed and "set apart" by the presidency of the church. To them, as to the lesser soldiers, it was accepted and acknowledged that they were serving, in the defense of Zion, a sacred mission for God and church. Should there be battle, heaven's hosts were on their side, and next to their skin, they wore, inviolate, protection's holy garment of the priesthood.

The western mouth of Echo Canyon, about forty miles from Salt Lake City, was the site selected by General Wells and his staff as the best possible defensive point. Here at the "narrows," Wells set the Legionnaires to work, under command of Colonels N. V. Jones and J. D. T. McAllister. Fortifications and breastworks would be constructed, not only on the canyon floor, but on the heights along the whole length of this rocky and denuded mountain gorge. No man could enter this pass without coming under the gunsights of the Mormon soldiers.

With a small escort, General Wells hurried on to Fort Bridger, where, on September 30 he met Colonel R. T. Burton and General Lewis Robison. They, of course, having shadowed the army westward, had news and information to impart of utmost value. The first division of the big army, under command of Colonel E. B. Alexander, were now bivouacked at Ham's Fork, about fifteen miles above its juncture with Black's Fork, a tributary of the Green River. Here at "Camp Winfield" — named in honor of General Winfield Scott, lieutenant general of the United States Army — they were awaiting impatiently the arrival of Johnston and the main command, with units of Alexander's division riding protective patrol for the endless wagons of supplies being brought westward by the civilian contractors and teamsters.

From the Mormon camp at Fort Bridger, General Wells forwarded to Colonel Alexander two copies of Governor Young's proclamation, and with it a letter Brigham had expressly addressed to *The officer commanding the forces now invading Utah territory.* To abbreviate this unique document would destroy its flavor:

Governor's Office, Utah Territory,
Great Salt Lake City, September 29, 1857.

Sir: — By reference to the act of congress passed September 9, 1850, organizing the territory of Utah, published in the laws of Utah, herewith forwarded, pp. 146-7, you will find the following:

Sec. 2. And be it further enacted, That the executive power and authority in and over said territory of Utah shall be vested in a governor, who shall hold his office for four years, *and until his successor shall be appointed and qualified,* unless sooner removed by the president of the United States. The governor shall reside within said territory, shall be commander-in-chief of the militia thereof, etc., etc.

I am still the governor and superintendent of Indian affairs for this territory, no successor having been appointed and qualified, as provided by law; nor have I been removed by the president of the United States.

By virtue of the authority thus vested in me, I have issued, and forwarded you a copy of my proclamation forbidding the entrance of armed forces into this territory. This you have disregarded. I now further direct that you retire forthwith from the territory, by the same route you entered. Should you deem this impracticable, and prefer to remain until spring in the vicinity of your present encampment, Black's Fork, or Green river, you can do so in peace and unmolested, on condition that you deposit your arms and ammunition with Lewis Robison, quartermaster-general of the territory, and leave in the spring, as soon as the condition of the roads will permit you to march; and should you fall short of provisions, they can be furnished you, upon making the proper applications therefor. General D. H. Wells will forward this, and receive any communication you may have to make.

Very respectfully,

[Signed] BRIGHAM YOUNG,
Governor and Superintendent of Indian Affairs, Utah Territory.[16]

Colonel Alexander politely acknowledged receipt of the proclamation and the letter, and gave General Lewis Robison and Major Lot Smith, the Mormon emissaries from Fort Bridger, the only answer possible. As senior officer in command of Camp Winfield, he would submit the communications to Colonel Johnston when he arrived. But in the meantime, he would remind the Mormons that the troops at Camp Winfield were there by orders of the President of the United States. Their future movements would be dependent upon "orders issued by competent authority." And that, of course, did not include Brigham Young.

With Alexander's curt answer, the issue was now joined. A council of war was held at Fort Bridger by the high officers of the Nauvoo Legion, on the afternoon of October 3. If the army was to be stopped before the gates of Zion, hostilities must immediately commence. The war would be fought Fabian style, by destroying the enemy's forage and supplies.

To Major McAllister who, with his men, were now on the Oregon Road watching for movement of the troops, Orrin Porter Rockwell was immediately dispatched with orders to burn the grass on every route leading into Salt Lake Valley via Soda Springs. Colonel Burton, whose command was then encamped at Fort Supply, was to take the field to harass and annoy the "Expedition" in every way possible, "without risking his men."

Since Fort Bridger and Fort Supply would of certainty fall into the hands of the advancing army, it was decided to destroy both bases, and render them useless as winter quarters to the enemy. After caching all the Mormon grain that had been raised in the vicinity, both posts were burned to the ground. Trapper Jim Bridger had, some years previously, fled the fort and post that had made him famous. On October 3 — the same day of the council of command — Lewis Robison applied torch to the renowned outpost. "It burned very rapidly, and made a great fire."

Two days later, Fort Supply went up in flames. The buildings, mills, houses and property destroyed in these two fires were estimated at better than $50,000. For miles around, the grass was burned by the energetic and determined Mormons. Not a "seed or a blade" would be allowed the Expedition. If they managed to get into Utah, they would find scorched earth for every mile they moved westward.

"Use every exertion to stampede their animals and set fire to their trains," General Wells ordered. "Burn the whole country before them, and on their flanks. Keep them from sleeping by night surprises; blockade the road by felling trees or destroying the river fords where you can. Watch for opportunities to set fire to the grass before them ... Keep your men concealed as much as possible, and guard against surprise ...

"If the troops have not passed, or have turned in this direction, follow in their rear, and continue to annoy them, burning any trains they may leave. *Take no life, but destroy their trains, and stampede or drive away their animals, at every opportunity.*"[17]

VII

THE MOST spectacular success under this "harass and burn" policy was achieved by Major Lot Smith and his intrepid little company of Legion cavalry. They were to intercept the army's supply trains then advancing from South Pass, and "either turn them back or burn them." Aiding Major Smith and his forty-four dedicated raiders were Captains Horton D. Haight, Thomas Abbott and John Vance.

Their first encounter was with the ox train in which a Captain Rankin was chief skinner. When Rankin was told by Smith to "turn around and head back for the states," he brusquely inquired: "By whose authority?"

Major Smith pointed to his men. "You're looking at the authority," he said. "And there are more men concealed in the brush."

With a thunderous oath, Rankin turned his cumbersome train around and headed it eastward. But being a hard and stubborn man, he switched it to westward again when the Mormons were gone. This was repeated several times, until finally he was overtaken by a contingent of United States mounted troops and their army supply wagons. While Lot Smith and his men watched, unwilling to fight a pitched battle with the U.S. regulars, Rankin's train was relieved of its lading, repacked in the army wagons, and the teams and empty vehicles left standing on the open plain.

The Mormons had harassed this particular train, with results that were considerably less than spectacular. The next encounter would necessitate a more drastic handling. Obviously turning the trains back was not enough.

Dividing his little command, Lot Smith ordered Captain Haight, with nineteen men, "to see if he could get the mules of the 10th regiment on any terms." Taking the remaining twenty-three men, Smith headed for Sandy Fork, to intercept anything approaching from South Pass. At the Big Sandy, a tributary of the Green River, Smith's scouts reported a train of twenty-six large freight wagons on the old Mormon trail, fourteen miles south and west. It meant back-tracking, but it was a prize worth trying for.

By the time the Mormon riders reached the train, it was encamped for the night. But by the sounds of music and hilarity, and the sight of its numerous campfires, its teamsters and guards were very much awake. Keeping his men in ambush, Smith sent scouts forward in the darkness to ascertain the number and position of the wagons. "Twenty-six wagons, in two lines, a short distance apart," came the report. When Smith and his men made their bold ride into the center of the camp, he quickly discovered how faultily he had read the report. Instead of twenty-six wagons in two lines a short distance apart, there were two lines a short distance apart, of twenty-six wagons each. The lines seemed to stretch out to infinity in the darkness.

Hopelessly in it now, there was only one thing to do, and that was to act quickly and decisively. "Where's your commander?" Major Smith demanded, as the Mormons swept into the fire-light.

"I'm the commander," came a bull-like voice. "Name's Dawson. Who the hell are you?"

"We're Utah militia," Smith shouted. "You've got time to take your personals from the wagons. But don't wait!" These wagons are going to make a big fire!"

"For God's sake," howled Dawson. "Don't burn the trains!"

"It's for His sake that I'm going to burn them!" Smith replied.

Without hesitance the men were disarmed, weapons stacked, and the men put under guard. While Dawson, guards and teamsters watched, convinced that hundreds of Mormons lurked in the shadows, the torch was put to fifty-one wagons.

While they burned, a government messenger rode in. He was from Colonel Alexander. At Mormon gunpoint he delivered over the message from the American commander. "Mormons are in the field," the message stated. "Captains and teamsters are not to sleep, but keep night guard on the trains. Four companies of cavalry and two pieces of artillery will come over in the morning to escort you into camp."[18]

The frightened soldier, as he delivered the message; the teamsters and the guards; were thinking strange thoughts as the flames from the burning wagons mounted eerily into the night.

Two nights later, Smith's raiders intercepted a third train at a point on the Big Sandy now known as "Simpson's Hollow." When the Mormons rode impudently into the train, and Major Smith demanded to see its train master, he was informed that the "captain" was out rounding up cattle. While the men kept the teamsters under guard, Smith rode out alone to get "Simpson." He met the captain, about half a mile from the train.

"I told him," as Smith himself describes it, "that I came on business. He inquired the nature of it, when I demanded his pistols. He replied: 'By God, sir, no man ever took them yet, and if you think you can, without killing me, try it.' We were all the time riding towards the train, with our noses about as close together as two Scotch terriers would have held theirs — his eyes flashing fire; I couldn't see mine — I told him that I admired a brave man, but that I did not like blood — you insist on my killing you, which will only take a minute, but I don't want to do it. We had by this time reached the train. He, seeing that his men were under guard, surrendered, saying: 'I see you have me at a disadvantage, my men being disarmed.' I replied that I didn't need the advantage and asked him what he would do if we should give them their arms. 'I'll fight you!' 'Then,' said I, 'We know something about that too — take up your arms!' His men exclaimed, 'Not by a d - - n sight! We came here to whack bulls, not to fight.' 'What do you say to that, Simpson?' I asked. 'Damnation,' he replied, grinding his teeth in the most violent manner, 'If I had been here before and they had refused to fight, I would have killed every man of them.' "

"Captain Simpson was the bravest man I met during the campaign," Lot Smith declared. "He was a son-in-law of Mr. Majors, a large contractor for government freighting."[19] Smith allowed Simpson and his men two wagons to haul out their own rations and personals. The remaining wagons of the train were soon burned to the iron.

Economic loss to the Utah Expedition by Lot Smith's guerrilla raids had reached disaster proportions. The seventy-four wagons burned on the Green River were loaded with foodstuffs and rations, without which no army could move. When wagons were not handy, the Mormons swept down on the horses and mules, with the result that a thousand animals were herded through the canyons, by the Mormons, into Salt Lake Valley. With forage destroyed by fire for hundreds of miles along the trail, additional thousands of animals perished from starvation.

Like wraiths in the night — swift, sure — trained to wilderness tactics — the Legionnaires struck and struck again. Not a man was lost by the Mormons; not a soldier was killed by their guns. But already they had put the long lines of the Utah Expedition into deep trouble. How deep, the approaching commander, Albert Sidney Johnston, was soon to find out.

VIII

COLONEL ALEXANDER, with his division encamped on Ham's Fork, faced a time of increasing perplexity. The ubiquitous Colonel Johnston, with the remainder of the army, had not yet arrived. Without official direction — whether to move forward, sit still, or retreat — Alexander sat paralyzed with his restless and disgruntled troops. Supply trains, loaded with vital food, had been put to the torch. Forage grass for his animals had been burned for hundreds of miles before him, and hundreds of miles behind him. He and his men were not yet in Salt Lake City, but thousands of the army animals were there — driven in joyously by Mormon raiders. Remainder of his animals, and possibly even his men, faced starvation, unless help soon arrived.

And now the mountain winter was upon them. The howling winds and snow squalls were harbingers of a time of suffering.

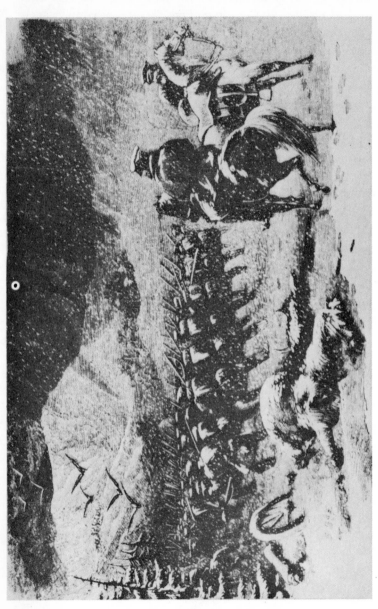

THE "UTAH EXPEDITION" (JOHNSTON'S ARMY) SNOWBOUND IN THE ROCKIES

— From *Harper's Weekly*, April 24, 1858.

So far, Alexander had been given no definite instructions from the War Department as to the actual intent and purpose of the Utah Expedition. With these secrets locked in Colonel Johnston's breast, and Johnston himself still far to the east, Alexander was as helpless in giving logical answers to his command as Van Vliet had been when standing before the Mormon questioners. One thing he did know — the Expedition had started west far too late in the season. If he were guilty of blundering in attempting to winter quarter at Ham's Fork, the smart heads at Leavenworth and Washington had blundered even more.

A council of officers was called in midst of these perplexities. With hope of peaceably getting Alexander's advance division into Salt Lake Valley now all but abandoned, three possible sites for winter quarters were put under discussion — the east side of the Wind River Mountains, to the northeast; on the Green River, at Henry's Fork, and Brown's Hole; adjacent to Fort Hall, at Beaver Head Mountain, one hundred and forty miles west of Fort Bridger. All these sites had been scouted, and reported on favorably. And all of them were an improvement over the frigid and exposed Ham's Fork.

The decision was made for the Fort Hall area. "After much deliberation...," Colonel Alexander wrote in his report, "I have determined to move the troops by the following route: Up Ham's Fork about 18 miles to a road called Sublette's cut-off; along that road to Bear river, and Soda Springs. On arriving at Soda Springs two routes will be open, one down Bear river valley towards Salt Lake, and one to the northeast towards the Wind river mountains, where good valleys for wintering the troops and stock can be found . . . If the force under my command is sufficient to overcome the resistance which I expect to meet at Soda Springs, I shall endeavor to force my way into the valley of Bear river and occupy some of the Mormon villages, because I am under the impression that the Mormons, after a defeat, will be willing to treat and bring provisions for sale ... and if I can get possession of a town in Bear river valley, I can easily fortify and hold it all winter."[20] Alexander's troops, cautiously spied on by the Mormons, began moving out on October 11.

Snow was already falling, and, because of the weakened condition of the draft animals, three miles a day marked the best in their capacity to do. The vanguard of the enfeebled train could be observed going into the camp ahead before the rear guard had left its camp of the previous day. A week of supreme effort brought the army but little nearer Fort Hall. The driving snow, while possible to broach in the plains country, utterly stalled them in the mountain passes.

Another council of officers was held — this one raucous, almost mutinous. The more reckless among them wanted to try for Salt Lake Valley, by forced marches, regardless of the cost. Final decision was to turn down Ham's Fork to the point of juncture with Black's Fork. The start had scarcely begun when word finally got through from Colonel Johnston. He and his troops had cleared South Pass. His orders were for Colonel Alexander to move his troops to Fontenelle Creek, another tributary of the Green River, thirty miles directly north of the point now reached by Alexander on Ham's Fork.

Another start was made, and another express arrived from Johnston. The new decision was for Alexander and his men to again turn about, and head down Ham's Fork, past the old camping ground, to *three miles below* the juncture with Black's Fork. There the commanding officer, and the remainder of the Expedition would join him.

The return for Alexander was more disastrous than had been his upriver journey. The cold was all but unbearable. Mountain blizzards cut and froze the flesh of the men. Draft animals by the hundreds dropped dead in the trail, and were abandoned along with their wagons. When Johnston finally caught up with Alexander, the historic meet was amidst a scene of military ruin.

With the Utah Expedition hopelessly stalled at Ham's Fork, and King Winter supremely allied to the Mormon cause, the Legion began drawing its men from guerrilla warfare, and back through the passes to Zion. Echo Canyon, and the Soda Springs and Bear River routes remained heavily guarded, but the Saints, wise and knowledgeable as to their country, knew that they were safe for at least one more winter. As a gesture of concern for the deprivation and suffering of the men and animals of the mighty army the Saints had humbled, Brigham Young sent a wagon load of salt out to the troops at Ham's Fork. The proud and angry Johnston turned it back with disdain.

But the Mormons, though safe inside their natural mountain fortress, were not without thoughts as to the future. Spring would bring a time of reckoning, and now, with the issues clearly drawn, stood the certainty of a shooting war. The arrival of Johnston, with fresh troops and supplies, had lifted the morale of the Utah Expedition; infused it with new strength. Johnston, as an officer, even though he had arrived late, was no blundering ass. The Nauvoo Legion, arming and training for the months ahead, were under no illusions as to the nature and capacity of their enemy.

Brigham Young, as territorial governor, still remained unnotified and unchallenged as to his office. But Alfred Cumming, with Johnston at Ham's Fork, carried the official portfolio. Civil judges were there to back him up. And Brigham and the leading Mormons were tried for treason, in absentia — by both civil and military authority. There were reasons for some soul-searching in Zion.

But likewise, with the Utah Expedition stalled far short of its objective, there was thinking, and comment back in Washington. "The more you send men to the 'Mormon War,'" thundered Gen-

OFFICERS OF LIEUT. GENERAL WELLS' STAFF

COMMANDING OFFICERS, NAUVOO LEGION

AS REORGANIZED IN UTAH, 1850S

eral Sam Houston of Texas, from the Senate floor, "the more you increase the difficulty. They have to be fed. For some sixteen hundred miles you have to transport provisions. The regiments sent there have found Fort Bridger and other places, as they approached them, heaps of ashes. They will find Salt Lake, if they ever reach it, a heap of ashes... Whoever goes there will meet the fate of Napoleon's army when it went to Moscow. Just as sure as we are now standing in the senate, these people, if they fight at all, will fight desperately. They are defending their homes. They are fighting to prevent the execution of threats that have been made, which touch their hearths and their families; and depend upon it they will fight until every man perishes before he surrenders...

"If war begins," Houston warned, "the very moment one single drop of blood is drawn, it will be the signal of extermination. Mr. President, in my opinion, whether we are to have a war with the Mormons or not, will depend on the fact whether our troops advance or not. If they [the troops] do not advance; if negotiations be opened; if we understand what the Mormons are really willing to do; that they are ready to acquiesce in the in the mandates of the government, and render obedience to the Constitution; if you will take time to ascertain that, and not repudiate all idea of peace, we may have peace. But so sure as the troops advance, so sure they will be annihilated. You may treble them, and you will only add to the catastrophe, not diminish human suffering. These people expect nothing but extermination... from your troops... and they will oppose them."[21]

The stalling of Johnston's Army at Ham's Fork not only had averted catastrophe, but was working abundantly to the benefit of the Mormons. The winter of inaction while the American troops shivered and groused an hundred miles short of their destination, gave the American Congress, press, pulpit and people a needed pause while they mulled the propriety and necessity for pitching an army without warning at Utah. Mormon declaration of resistance, their courageous guerrilla campaign and defense, had caught public sympathy. Brigham Young, in popular esteem, was emerging from an established role as treasonable lecher, into a sort of valorous Prince of Orange, willing to immolate ten years of Mormon industry rather than surrender to the army hammering at the gates of Zion.

IX

AND WHILE the Utah Expedition, at Ham's Fork, battled snow and deprivation instead of Mormons, the Saints, temporarily safe behind their mountain barrier, worked frantically to prepare for the uncertain months ahead. Legion drills on the public squares of Salt Lake City were arduous and grim. The city, already stuffed to bursting with Saints called home from every Mormon colony in the west, now resembled an armed camp. With martial law ruling Zion, there could be no question but what Mormons would die in defense of their principles.

The calls upon the people for donations, food, clothing, horses, guns and ammunition, were deep and sacrificial. Every serviceable musket, rifle and pistol in Utah had gone into the Legion arsenal for distribution to the Mormon troops — including all the arms and equipment allowed the Battalion boys according to the terms of their enlistment and discharge. From San Bernardino had come five hundred revolvers, the Carson Valley colonists had brought back with them twenty-seven hundred pounds of church ammunition and eight hundred dollars worth of arms purchased in San Francisco. The thousands of government mules and horses herded into Salt Lake Valley by Lot Smith's guerrillas were put to good use in this winter's frantic preparation.

And, while Zion buckled on its armor, the spies, even through the winter months, kept the Utah Expedition under constant surveillance. When Johnston decided to shift the great camp to the burned-out shell of Fort Bridger, the Mormons at first interpreted the move as the commander's decision to attempt Salt Lake Valley in spite of winter. It was quickly apparent, however, that when the American troops required fifteen days to make the thirty-five miles to Bridger, there was little to fear on that score. The cost in dead draft animals for even this slight move was appallingly high. Johnston's own report of this tedious and expensive operation is tragedy unembellished:

"The loss of battery horses, draught mules and oxen of the contractors has been very great... Our marches each were necessarily short on account of the extremes of coldness and inclemency of the weather... and the failing condition of the draught animals starving from cold and hunger... Shelter for our thousands of animals seemed indispensable for the preservation of life, yet a more rapid advance to attain it would, we believe, be attended with immense loss... The thermometer ranged from ten degrees above to sixteen degrees below zero ... The country between this and the South Pass, with the exception of narrow valleys of water courses, is a great desert, affording no shelter by its conformation or by its woods, or even bushes from the furious blasts in these high regions; and no fuel, except wild sage or willow bushes. There was no alternative but to press forward perseveringly, though slowly marking our route by the frozen horses, mules and oxen..."[22]

The new camp, gained at such incredible suffering and cost, was in the Green River country on Black's Fork, two miles above the ruins of Fort Bridger. Johnston named it Camp Scott, in honor of General Winfield Scott. It quickly took on an air of permanency, and, sheltered by the high bluffs above it, the new place was doubtless a vast improvement over Ham's Fork. While the military erected a small city of log huts and Sibley tents, the civil officers, headed by Governor Cumming, were set up in a little nook in the woods above the military camp. This little colony, housing the governmental and judicial appointees to head up Utah Territory — once they had gotten there — was named "Eckelsville," in tribute to the new chief justice of the territory.

"It was from Camp Scott that Governor Cumming issued his proclamation, 'To the People of Utah Territory,' on the 21st of November, announcing that on the 11th of July, 1857, the president of the United States had appointed him governor for the territory of Utah; that he arrived at the point from which he addressed them on the 19th of November; that he would probably be detained some time in his present location in consequence of the loss of animals during the recent snowstorm; that he would proceed at this point to make the preliminary arrangements for the temporary organization of the territorial government.

"He announced that many treasonable acts of violence had been committed by lawless individuals, supposed to be countenanced by the late Utah executive [ex-Governor Young] — such persons were in a state of rebellion; proceedings would be instituted against them in a court organized by Chief Justice Eckels, held in Green River county; this would supersede the necessity of appointing a military commission for the trial of such offenders . . . He came among the people with no prejudices or enmities, and hoped to command their confidence by a just and firm administration. Freedom of conscience and the use of their own peculiar mode of serving God, he recognized as sacred rights guaranteed by the Constitution, with which it is not within the province of the government to interfere, neither is it the disposition of its representatives to so interfere.

"By virtue of his authority as commander-in-chief of the militia, he ordered all bodies of individuals, by whomsoever organized, to disband and return to their respective homes; disobedience to the command would subject the offenders to the 'punishment due to traitors.' "[23]

It was considerably later before the proclamation of Governor Cumming could, by government express rider, get through the guarded and snowbound mountain passes, but once arrived in Salt Lake City, Brigham Young finally had his official notice of deposition. Still Camp Scott was not Salt Lake City. If Brigham was perturbed by this notice, there was no indication of the fact. Engrossed with the problem of the defense of Zion — treasonable or not — he went methodically ahead. To the Saints he was still president of the church; still governor of the territory.

Included with the proclamation was a personal letter from Cumming. In it he reiterated his own appointment to governorship; expressed the regret he felt for the many warlike acts of violence committed by the Mormons against the property and personnel of the United States Government; and reminded that these acts would indicate that the territory was in a state of rebellion. For these ex-Governor Young would be held responsible. Serving in evidence was the copy of the ex-governor's proclamation found in the possession of Joseph Taylor, a Mormon prisoner.

A month later came the report that a grand jury, composed of civilian teamsters at Camp Scott, and backed by the Utah's stranded panel of governmental jurists, had returned bills of indictment against Brigham Young and the sixty Mormon associates. The major crime was treason.

All this scarcely made a ripple in Salt Lake City. While military preparation went doggedly on, the Utah territorial legislature, headed by Ex-Governor Young, carried on its busy sessions. Memorials to president and congress, setting forth Mormon reasoning and grievances, were prepared, acted upon, and sped across the wintry plains to Washington. And through all these months the American people, abetted by an aroused and lively press, had plenty of time to review the comic opera situation of a nation's stranded army and territorial officers, as they attempted to both castigate and regulate a commonwealth from their snowbound hideout above Fort Bridger.

X

IT WAS in midst of this odd and unparalleled stalemate that Colonel Thomas L. Kane made his appearance in Utah — as unexpected and as dramatic as a page from a novel. This loyal and considerate friend of the Saints arrived in Salt Lake City on the 25th of February, 1858, after a most hectic and difficult journey from New York, *via* the Isthmus of Panama to Los Angeles. From thence he had ridden the southern overland route. Sick and exhausted, he drove into Salt Lake City in a heavy spring carriage gratefully provided by the Saints of southern Utah.

Carried on in a delicate state of health, Colonel Kane had made the long journey over the protests of his father, Judge John K. Kane, and other members of his family. Traveling under the cognomen of "Dr. Osborne," Philadelphia botanist, he had circled a continent accompanied only by a single companion, his servant. He maintained, even in Salt Lake, the elaborate subterfuge of "Dr. Osborne." But to his friends among the Saints there was no mystery.

Apostle Wilford Woodruff, who met with the little group of leaders officially greeting Kane on his day of arrival, made a record of this interview in his journal. After a formal introduction of "Dr. Osborne" to the brethren, by Joseph A. Young, the strange visitor announced himself as authorized to lay before these assembled church leaders "most fully and definitely the feelings and views of the citizens of our common country, and of the feelings of the executive towards them, relating to the present position of officers of this territory, and of the army of the United States now upon your borders."

"After giving you the most satisfactory evidence in relation to matters concerning you now pending," Kane continued, "I shall then call your attention, and wish to enlist your sympathies, in behalf of the poor soldiers who are now suffering in the cold and snows of the mountains, and request you to render them aid and comfort, and to assist them to come here and to bid them a hearty welcome into your hospitable valley."[24] He then requested a private conference with Governor Young, and begged excuse of the other brethren for this secrecy and formality.

When the two men returned, the meeting was finished out in pleasant and informal conversation. Whatever secrets were imparted as to the special mission of Colonal Kane, nothing more was mentioned regarding them.

Many interpretations have been made as to Kane's role in solving the impasse of the Utah War; some historians claiming that he officially represented President Buchanan in a governmental attempt to back out of an awkward situation, and to avert the imminent probability of bloodshed. The evidence, however, would indicate that Kane made the long journey at his own initiative, and at his own expense. He greatly respected the Mormon people, had vigorously defended them in the past, and had lent them genuine aid in the Battalion crisis. The lengthy and dangerous pilgrimage out to Utah seems to have basis only on the humanitarian impulse of a deeply sensitive and understanding man.

Certainly "Dr. Osborne" was not in Utah in any official capacity from the United States President, nor as "an ambassador from the chief executive of our nation," as Apostle Woodruff had phrased it. Definitely he was not an "agent of the administration," as Tullidge reports him, or "a private envoy of the government," as Whitney claims. He had, however, before leaving the east, conferred with a number of governmental heads, including President Buchanan. And in his possession was a letter from Buchanan commending Kane for his willingness to voluntarily serve "the Mormons, at his own expense, and without official position."

But there was caution, too, in the letter's acknowledgment. "I could not at the present moment, in view of the hostile attitude they [the Mormons] have assumed against the United States, send any agent to visit them on behalf of the United States."[25] Kane held another note from Buchanan, commending him to favorable regard by any officers of the United States whom he might meet in his travels, and suggesting that they render any aid and facilities in their power toward expediting the philanthropic and humanitarian journey of the colonel.

Actually, Brigham Young was not impressed by the package for peace which "Dr. Osborne" unloaded in Salt Lake City. The colonel, deeply concerned by the imminence of Mormon annihilation, was disturbed by the nonchalance of Brigham Young and the leaders in face of the almost certainty of military reprisals against them for their treasonable conduct, and actual armed resistance. The half hour secret conference with Brigham apparently failed to impress the deposed governor with the necessity of treating with the military and civil officers at Camp Scott, or to dissuade him from his intentions toward further resistance.

"When Colonel Kane came to visit us," Brigham later explained, "he tried to point out a policy for me to pursue. But I told him I should not turn to the right or left, or pursue any course, only as God dictated . . . When he found that *I would not be informed,* only as the Spirit of the Lord led me, he felt discouraged and said he would not go to the army. But finally, he said, *if I would dictate he would execute.* I told him that as he had been inspired to come here, he should go to the army and do as the Spirit of the Lord led him, and all would be right. He did so, and all was right. He thought it very strange that we were not afraid of the army. I told him we were not afraid of all the world; if they made war upon us the Lord would deliver us out of their hands, if we did right. God controls all these matters."[26]

Colonel Kane remained in Salt Lake City from February 25 to March 8, still maintaining his posture and disguise as "Dr. Osborne." He was treated well, and allowed to occupy the rostrum of the tabernacle. For the long, rough journey to Camp Scott, Brigham furnished him an escort of mounted Legionnaires, and a letter properly accrediting him, so far as Mormons were concerned, as an acceptable mediator in the difficulties. Kane's Mormon escort accompanied him to within twelve miles of Camp Scott, from which point he finished the journey alone — arriving there on the evening of March 12.

The visit started off badly, with an altercation with the sentry who challenged him. One historian [Tullidge] claims that the fiery little colonel broke a gunstock over the sentry's head, before he was allowed audience with Colonel Johnston. In view of the paucity of corroborative information to sustain the story, it is increasingly difficult to believe. It is true, however, that Kane made little headway with the haughty commander. From the first, Johnston resented Kane's intrusion into the military commitments against the Mormons. They were enemy; he was to march against them in a matter of months. A winter of inaction had whetted his determination and resolve to move this army into Utah, and any attempt to cloud or interfere with that decision, no matter how noble or altruistic, was anathema in his eyes.

Rebuffed, snubbed, and humiliated in his attempts to negotiate with Johnston, Kane retired to the quarters furnished him, and with equal haughtiness. When, unbowed and stubborn, Kane sought Governor Cumming and Judge Eckels for his campaign of peaceful settlement, he gained ears that were considerably more receptive. Johnston apparently resented this move.

Relations between Kane and Johnston were further strained when an orderly, dispatched from headquarters with an invitation for Colonel Kane to an officers' dinner, either inadvertently or maliciously got his orders mixed. Instead of tendering the invitation, the orderly pretended to have mistaken his instructions, and instead, placed Colonel Kane under arrest. If the gesture was intended to humiliate the colonel, it backfired. Kane considered the arrest no less than a studied insult, and promptly challenged Johnston to settle the matter on the field of honor.

The duel was averted by prompt action of Governor Cumming and Judge Eckels. The Judge ordered immediate arrest of every party to the affair, should it proceed one step further. Elaborate apologies were made, but there was little of friendship between the two officers.

Through it all, Kane was persistent and dedicated in his efforts toward averting bloodshed with the Mormons. At the end of a three week stay in Camp Scott, he persuaded Governor Alfred Cumming to make the journey into Salt Lake City. But the military escort provided by Camp Scott would, he explained, be wholly unacceptable to the Mormons. Brigham Young had advised Colonel Kane that Cumming would be completely safe and welcome were he to make the journey unaccompanied by soldiers. So, on April 3, Governor Cumming announced to Colonel Johnston that he would accept the Mormon terms; that he intended accompanying Colonel Kane into Salt Lake City, and without military escort. The army men predicted the governor would meet violent death at the hands of the Mormons were he to pursue so foolish a course. Scorning this dire advice, and trusting to Kane's judgment, the two men, a day or so later, were on their way.

XI

IN SALT LAKE CITY, in the meantime, there had come re-evaluation of stance; a time of thinking. The changing mental attitude of the church leaders toward the tense military situation was certain to be of vast importance in the months ahead. Colonel Kane, though he may have been operating on his own altruistic impulses, and at his own expense, was accomplishing a mission of great delicacy with as much force and effect as though he were indentured as the President's own man. He may have been listened out in stony silence by Brigham Young, he may have been rebuked and insulted by Albert Sidney Johnston, still in attempting voluntarily to set up à bridge between these implacable foes, the little colonel was serving history well. His success in inducing Cumming to step into Utah, to take up his legally defined responsibilities as governor, without forcing the Mormon hand by the entry of troops, was a diplomatic move of great wisdom.

Nor had Kane's wise counsel to Brigham Young, even though spurned when given, gone completely awry. On March 18, ten days after Kane had departed Salt Lake City for Camp Scott, a council of war had been convened in the Church Historian's Office. Attending were the church's first presidency, headed by Brigham Young, eight of the twelve apostles, and thirty of the Legion's top military officers. After lengthy debate, and much

thought, it was decided to abandon the concept of armed resistance to the military forces of the United States.

The new plan evolved — a complete reversal of the belliger-
ent stance of months past — was abandonment of the Utah
settlements, and retreat into the desert. "The following Sunday
the temper of the meeting at the tabernacle was markedly different than such meetings had been. It was flight now, rather
than fight.

"The regular service of the day was converted into a special
conference. President Young 'spoke of the situation of affairs
at this crisis and presented the policy which he intended to
pursue, which was to remove the grain and the women and
children from the city and then, if needs be, burn it and lay the
country waste.' . . . It was declared to be the intention to give
those who had never before been driven from their homes the
honor of forming an advance company to lead the way into the
desert and find a suitable place of settlement. Five hundred
families were called for to form this advance company."27

In midst of the frantic efforts aimed at "flight rather than
fight," came reports on April 8, that Governor Alfred Cumming
was on his way to Salt Lake City, without escort, and to take
up the duties of his office. Next day an informal meeting was
held by Brigham Young and the leading brethren, in President
Young's office. The leader, faced now at last with actual deposition, startled his brethren by his acceptance of the situation without contest.

The Cumming entourage, with one carriage, one wagon, and
two attendants, met their first Mormon troops at Quaking Asp
Hill. From that point, with Legion escort, they were conducted
to the military encampment at the head of Echo Canyon. The
journey through the canyon, now virtually a vast Mormon fort,
was made at night. At many points the Legion had great bonfires
burning, but instead of hostility the governor found genial wel-

come and great respect. At three of the camps, Cumming was met with full military guard of honor, which left the portly dignitary both surprised and delighted.

At each of these camps Governor Cumming delivered addresses, in which he stressed the hope that the troubles of these people would soon be ended, and that the day might quickly be at hand when Mormon soldiers could return in peace to their homes and farms. "The governor himself afterwards expressed some anxiety as to these speeches, and great wonderment at his reception by the militia in Echo cañon. The illuminations there, he said, in a conversation with a number of gentlemen in Salt Lake City on the day following his arrival, 'outstripped anything he had ever expected to see.'

"Colonel Kane said he never expected to see such a sight again. 'The effect could not be described.' On finding himself in Echo cañon the governor said he did not know what to think. He was surrounded by armed soldiers, who on his arrival presented arms in honor of his coming: he said he did not know what to do: but he delivered a speech, and he did not know but what he had committed himself. Colonel Kane assured him his speech was a happy effort..."[28] In any event Governor Cumming went through the Mormon lines without facing the violent death so liberally predicted at Camp Scott.

Mormon insistence that Cumming travel the Echo Canyon route at night, ostensibly to keep hidden from his Gentile eyes the extent of military fortifications, gave Mormons also the chance to put on an impressive show. The number of fires burning were far beyond any measure of necessity, and the constant challenge of sentries, and the constant movement of troops ahead of the governor's carriage, had the desired effect of overwhelming Cumming with the strength the Legion had mounted in the field.

Colonel Kane, a consummately wise diplomat, dragged feet on Cumming's entry into Salt Lake, in order to give the Mormons time and opportunity to adjust their thinking toward what was ahead. At the mouth of Echo Canyon he dispatched an express rider to inform President Young that he and the governor expected to arrive in Salt Lake City on April 12. But at the canyon mouth, Kane detained the governor for a day of shooting. At the camp of Ben Simons, Cherokee Indian trader and interpreter, they idled another day at the sport.

Finding that the road over Big Mountain, the usual direct route into the valley, was still almost impassable with snow, it was decided by Kane and the Legion escorts to bring the new governor in through Weber Canyon, by way of the Mormon town of Farmington. This, of course, idled another day. "At the mouth of Weber cañon the Farmington Guards [segment of the Nauvoo Legion], mounted and in uniform, met him [Governor Cumming]. On his reaching the courthouse [in Farmington] the band played *The Star Spangled Banner*. Sunday evening he stopped at Judson Stoddards at Farmington. Monday morning he was visited by the Farmington band in carriages: they played *Hail Columbia, Yankee Doodle,* the *Star Spangled Banner,* and other popular airs. Cumming made a speech, remarking that he was astonished at such attachment for the national airs, he believed it could not be feigned."[29]

The surprising pleasantry of his reception had lulled Governor Cumming into a sense of complacency regarding the nature and extent of the Mormon rebellion, but next day, as his carriage and escort took him southward through Davis County toward the Mormon capital, he saw things that both surprised and shocked him. The road was clotted with people from the northern settlements, their wagons loaded with personal possessions, their men and children driving their herds of cattle, horses, sheep and pigs before them. At the call of their leader, they were abandoning homes once again, to seek a safer sanctuary in the unclaimed wilderness southward. Behind them they had left men to apply the torch to their dwellings, lay waste to their every possession, chop down every tree. The turning of Utah back to wilderness was to be their last and final protest against Johnston and his army, and the injustice of foisting upon an American commonwealth a set of officers not of their own choosing. On Cumming — by nature a kind and sensitive man — the heartache, waste and tragedy of what he was viewing, was not lost to his sensibility.

Still disturbed and silent at what he was witnessing, he and Kane rode on toward Salt Lake City, and the problems yet to be faced. At Hot Springs, three miles north of the city, the governor's party was met by the city's mayor, aldermen, and members of the city council, and officially welcomed. With the mayor, riding in the governor's carriage, Cumming was escorted to the lodgings prepared for him at the home of W. C. Staines.

No dignitary could have been treated with greater respect. In view of the reports he had heard, and the warning of the military, Cumming was completely astonished at the reception he had received — especially from a people who were reputed throughout America to be treasonable, rebellious, and blood-thirsty. There was no feigning here. The Mormon people, by nature, were kind and considerate. Probably only in the Prophet Brigham Young would he find the base anarchist of popular conception.

The day following his arrival in Salt Lake City, Governor Cumming expressed a desire to talk with Brigham Young. Without hesitance the Mormon leader made formal call on his successor, at four that very afternoon. In general the conversation was very amicable, and Brigham took the new governor on a tour of the city in his carriage. Again, instead of treasonable defiance and anger, Cumming found pleasantry, acceptance, and cooperation. Kane had promised Cumming that, if he would leave the army behind, he would find the Mormons cooperative. Cumming, relieved and happy, had found this entirely so.

Later the two governors, in closed session with only Colonel Kane present, aired their grievances one to the other. Cumming drew heat from Brigham Young when he attempted to forbid the Saints from abandoning their homes, and argued his strong disapproval of the scorched earth policy of combatting the troops. Brigham, in turn, unloaded his thoughts regarding the whole insulting travesty of the army's presence, and his conviction that the American military, by bribes and promises, had now incited the once peaceful Indians into uprising against the Saints. Brigham was indignant about a lot of things; Cumming, on the other hand, still remained concerned that burning army trains and running off army stock was rebellion and open warfare. But, as Kane had hoped, the open confrontation between the two men, with vocal interchange of ideas, was the best possible answer to the "Mormon problem."

Brigham Young and Alfred Cumming were soon measuring one another with new respect. When the heat finally dissipated from their dialogue, a spirit of friendship and cooperation emerged, which aided materially in bridging the sensitive gap between the two governorships.

It had been widely reported in the east, and in the halls of Congress, that the territorial records had been destroyed by the rebellious Saints, including the seal and official documents. In the east it was accepted as certainty that the territorial library had been completely and wantonly burned. Cumming was taken on a tour, in which he found everything pertaining to the territorial office intact and safe — the library included.

So much progress was made by Cumming in bringing order out of chaos that, as early as April 15, he was writing Johnston, at Camp Scott: "I have been everywhere recognized as the governor of Utah; and so far from having encountered insults and indignities, I am gratified in being able to state to you that in passing through the settlements, I have been universally greeted with such respectful attention as are due to the representative of the executive authority of the United States in the territory." In the same letter he voiced some of the complaints of Brigham Young, including the matter of Indian coercion by United States troops.[30] Appended, as a gesture of goodwill, was a letter signed by Brigham Young, offering Mormon food to the destitute soldiers. Cumming's report was duly filed. As to Brigham's offer of food, Johnston dismissed it with the curt answer that as commander of the Utah Expedition he would accept no help from the enemy.

Cumming, the big, florid, two hundred and forty pound Georgian, went on winning friends by his geniality and willing-ness to listen to Mormon grievances. He was distressed by the evacuation of the city, and the plans for its burning, which, in spite of his pleas and demands, went inexorably on. At request, President Young willingly allowed him to speak to the Saints in the tabernacle. On April 25, when he was formally introduced from its pulpit, there were still enough Saints left in Salt Lake City to make a large and appreciative audience for Utah's new territorial governor.

"My presence at the meeting in the tabernacle will be remembered by me as an occasion of intense interest," the governor reported. "Between three and four thousand persons were assembled for the purpose of public worship; the hall was crowded to overflowing; but the most profound quiet was observed when I appeared.

"President Young introduced me by name as the governor of Utah, and I addressed the audience from 'the stand.' I informed them that I had come among them to vindicate the national sovereignty; that it was my duty to secure the supremacy of the Constitution and the laws; that I had taken my oath of office to exact an unconditional submission on their part to the dictates of the law. I was not interrupted.

"In a discourse of about thirty minutes' duration I touched (as I thought best) boldly upon the leading questions at issue between them and the federal government. I remembered that I had to deal with men embittered by the remembrance and recital of many real, and some imaginary wrongs, but I did not think it wise to withhold from them the entire truth. They listened respectfully to all that I had to say, approvingly even, I fancied, when I explained to them what I intended should be the character of my administration; in fact, the whole manner of the people was calm, betokening no consciousness of having done wrong, but rather, as it were, indicating a conviction that they had done their duty to their religion and their country. I have observed that the Mormons profess to view the Constitution as the work of inspired men, and respond with readiness to appeals for its support."[31]

Alfred Cumming, a consummate politician, was making headway toward winning friends and establishing himself as an able and efficient governor against tremendous odds. The reports and favorable intelligence he was sending east could not fail to affect the tense situation in Utah for the better. However, no charm or logic had any deterrence whatever in changing the Mormon decision to flee the territory, and apply the torch to their leavings. The territorial capital had, long before Cumming's entry, been moved to Fillmore, far to the south. Now church headquarters had gone there with the fleeing Saints.

The Mormons, in spite of pleas and advice, were not yet ready to forget that an army was at their gates, and preparing to move on the valley. They were not forgetting that Brigham Young and many more Saints, as yet unnamed, had been cited and tried in absentia at Camp Scott. They were not yet forgetting Nauvoo and Carthage, and the mistakes they once had made in trusting governmental justice. When Johnston and his army got Utah, it would be to find it as desolate as when the Mormons had first viewed it. Governor Cumming faced the administration of a territory devoid of citizens — unless one accepted the riffraff of teamsters and camp followers at Camp Scott. Of such would be the civilian population entering with the troops. Perhaps, instead of Mormons, these would constitute the Utah citizenry of the future.

XII

THE PEACE OVERTURES initiated by Colonel Thomas L. Kane, the empassioned pacification letters being written by Governor Alfred Cumming, the determination of the Mormons to evacuate and burn, and the army's campaign rendered impotent by weather and destitution of supplies — all combined to churn Washington into a furor of confusion and criticism. The Utah Expedition, launched a year ago with excitement and breast-thumping emotion, had been farcically stopped cold in its tracks, and public support for the administration had turned into annoying and widespread public criticism. The "contractor's war," it was now being called, as its cost became ever more apparent. "Buchanan's blunder," was a term that was catching on so widely as to embarrass the President, his cabinet, and the Congress which a year ago had been so willing and anxious to make war on the Saints.

Brigham Young's gutty stand had won him many friends in the American press. Critical emphasis had shifted, during the winter stalemate, from Utah's treasonable despot, to Washington's badly fumbled military adventure. General (now promoted from colonel) Johnston's assurance that the Utah rebellion was slated for utter defeat, now sounded anticlimactic and a little silly. Realizing that Brigham Young had already won the war, without half trying, President Buchanan had been looking for a way out of the embarrassment long before Kane had escorted Cumming into Salt Lake City.

The Peace Commissioners, appointed by President Buchanan, left Fort Leavenworth April 25, 1858, by the fastest teams and army conveyance. At St. Louis five sturdy ambulances and harness had been selected and shipped to Leavenworth, to insure their speediest possible dash across the plains. To get them there, a sergeant and five dragoons were detailed to the mission, with a wagonmaster, five expert teamsters, and a guide. Each ambulance was drawn by four stout mules; with saddle horses provided as convenience to the Commissioners, should they weary of traveling by wheel. To give the expedition utmost mobility, the baggage was minimal, and the ambulances so comfortable that they were used as sleeping quarters; saving the necessity of carrying tents. So well and thoughtfully equipped were they, that they made it all the way to Salt Lake City without change or loss — something the army had utterly failed to do.

It was the President's frantic hope that his Peace Commissioners might yet stave off bloodshed, or avert another administration blunder, by arrival in Salt Lake City before the army's entry. This the Commissioners managed neatly, and with time to spare. They arrived at Camp Scott on May 29, remained there three days, while the Commissioners sopped up all that was known to date about the Mormon problem. General Johnston was warned not to move the army until after the Commissioners had completed their mission. What the Peace Commission did not know, of course, because of the time factor, was the fantastic success Colonel Kane had already achieved in seating Cumming in the governor's chair, and the complete change of attitude Mormons had assumed as to conduct of the war. Had General Johnston realized that in the Commissioners' portfolio was a pardon for Brigham Young, he would have loathed the presidential emissaries even more than he hated the meddlesome Colonel Kane.

The Commissioners were wise, able, and trustworthy men. The two, carefully selected for the delicate and confidential task were the Honorable L. W. Powell, late governor of the state of Kentucky, and now United States Senator-elect from that state; and Major Ben McCulloch, of Texas, hero of the late war with Mexico. In the name of peace at any price, President Buchanan had entrusted them with his signed "Proclamation of Pardon," bearing the date of April 6, 1858. Like Greeks lugging the torch of Olympus, they had nobly and valiantly fetched it two thousand miles, to lay it humbly before the wily victor of the still unfought war, Brigham Young.

The pardon, while listing the many offenses popularly alleged against the Latter-day Saints and their leaders, making note of their undeniable treason and rebellion, was still magnanimous and all-inclusive. "In order to save the effusion of blood, and to avoid the indiscriminate punishment of a whole people for crimes of which it is not probable that all are equally guilty," the President offered "a free pardon to all who will submit themselves to the authority of the federal government." All of which must have sounded a little academic in Salt Lake City, where Cumming already was safely functioning as territorial governor, and the entire Mormon population was leaving the territory.

On the 7th of June, 1858, Powell and McCulloch rattled into Zion, after their clean and fast trip across the plains. What astonished the two men was the great extent and beauty of the Mormon city, and the fact that it was all but deserted — the houses piled high with straw, awaiting only the torch. Even the church leaders had joined the exiting Saints and were, at the time of the Commissioners' entry, temporarily quartered at Provo and Fillmore, far to the south. The Governor and the Commissioners frantically dispatched an express rider south to inform President Young and the leaders of the arrival of the presidential emissaries, and of their desire for immediate consultation with the vanished Saints.

Upon receipt of the urgent message, Brigham Young and a large number of the leading brethren came up from Provo. On June 11, at 9 a.m., a meeting was called in the deserted Council House, for Mormons to hear out whatever President Buchanan might have to say to them. Considering the haste, and the circumstances, there was a "goodly turnout" of the brethren coming up from Provo. Governor Cumming, the new Superintendent of Indian Affairs, Jacob Forney, and the Commissioners occupied the dais of the court room hall. Brigham Young and the Mormon brethren seated themselves on the benches facing them.

President Young, at Cumming's insistence, acted as master of ceremonies, and introduced the Commissioners to the assembly. The windows of the room, carefully removed at the exodus, preparatory to the building's burning, had been hastily replaced by the Mormons especially for this meeting. And, at introduction of Powell and McCulloch, the Mormons rose to their feet and received the two men with utmost respect. Attentively they heard out the news from Washington, and the proposals in their behalf.

And then, when the peace idyll looked most promising, Brigham Young arose. His announcement had the shattering impact of a bombshell. On the way to the meeting, Brigham explained, he had been met by his trusted scout and militiaman, Orrin Porter Rockwell. As Mormon spy and observer on the army at Camp Scott, Porter had ridden madly from Fort Bridger with the positive information that Johnston "had given orders to his army to march on Monday" — the 14th of June — for Salt Lake.

Powell and McCulloch were shaken and angered by the announcement. In every way possible they attempted to assure the Mormons assembled that this could not possibly be so; that they had received assurance from the commanding officer that troops would not be moved until the Commission had reported back to Camp Scott. But Brigham Young knew better. He had no reason to question or distrust his Mormon sources of information. "Commissioner Powell assured Governor Young that it would cost Johnston his commission if he should move without authority from them."[32] But Brigham Young and his Mormons knew better. The army was coming. He could only smile bitterly at the discomfiture of the federal men.

The first day's session at the Council House ended badly. Frantically Governor Cumming wrote to General Johnston: "On the 11th and 12th of June a conference was held between the president and leaders of the Church of Latter-day Saints and the Peace Commissioners. I was present at the conference by invitation, and heard a statement made by President Young to this effect: that he had evidence of your intention to advance the army on the 14th or 15th of this month, without awaiting for communications from the Commissioners or myself.

"To this statement I gave a prompt and positive denial, alleging that General Johnston would not violate a pledge made by him to the Commissioners and myself, on the 30th of May, at Camp Scott...

"*I stated to President Young that you were pledged not to march until you had received communications from the Commissioners or myself, that you had told me that you would issue a proclamation setting forth your intentions.*"[33]

But Johnston, weary of ignominy and inactivity, and probably surfeited with civilian pussyfooting with the enemy, had indeed given the order, and the army *was* on the move, without setting forth any "intentions." In his return letter to Governor Cumming,

GEN. ALBERT SIDNEY JOHNSTON, UTAH EXPEDITION

— Courtesy of and by permission of
Henry E. Huntington Library.

[246]

he explained the reasons for his course, but made it patently clear that "The instructions of the president to the Commissioners were positive that the army should occupy the territory of Utah, and my orders do not allow the discretion of making delay, unless reasons should be offered for so doing which should appear to me sufficiently cogent."[34]

Had Johnston and his army rested but another month at Camp Scott, the burden of negotiation upon Cumming and the Peace Commission would have been infinitely easier. The pardon itself was welcome and palatable to the Saints, had not President Buchanan included in another and separate document a long-winded proclamation to the citizens of Utah Territory couched in words certain to raise the hackles of every Saint. In its dossier was echoed every accusation by press, politicians and clergy which for years had been going the rounds in the east.

"This proclamation contains *forty-two false charges,* into which he [President Buchanan] has refused, up to this time, to make the least inquiry or investigation,"[35] roared Apostle George A. Smith from the stand.

But two facts had already been established in the lonely sessions for peace, held in the empty city of Salt Lake — the army was on its way, in spite of Mormon defiance, and every good intention of Kane, Cumming, Powell and McCulloch — and the President of the United States, despite the bluster of his "proclamation," had backed down enough to forgive Brigham and his Mormons for whatever degree of treason or rebellion of which they may or may not have been guilty.

What Governor Cumming was hoping to avert was a shooting war in the territory to which he had been appointed as head, and equally important, a return of the citizenry to his commonwealth, and some desperate way to forestall the public destruction of every home, farm and business in Utah. To the credit of Cumming and the Peace Commissioners, they were tolerant and sympathetic throughout the explosive sessions of their conference. They listened well to the Mormon side of the story. Except for a few minor unpleasantries, the conference was handled ably and well.

Gradually the Mormon viewpoint moved around to facement of the inevitable. Whatever there may have been in their past which irked the Gentiles, all was forgiven. This part they could accept. The bone which still stuck in their craw, was Johnston and his army. Bloodshed may have been averted, but with Utah garrisoned by the United States troops, life in the Mormon Zion would never again be the same. The future was far more difficult to assess than the past.

But by public pledge that Johnston would not quarter his army in close proximity to the Saints, that he would march his troops through the city, and encamp them on the other side of the valley, even this concession was eventually wrung from the brethren. But the Mormons, remembering the broken promises of the past, would return none of their citizenry until every governmental pledge was carried out to the letter. A thousand Legion men, with torches ready, would make certain that flames would wipe away every vestige of Mormon accomplishment should there be least betrayal of the promise.

"But gentlemen," said Apostle George A. Smith at the meeting, "if Mr. Buchanan actually means, as he says, that the citizens of Utah should have the same privileges as other citizens of the United States, all right; but if I cock my revolver and point it desperately at your head, and say, I mean peace; my conduct looks rather suspicious; and while Mr. Buchanan points at us his artillery, minnie rifles, and bayonets, his promise of peace looks suspicious. Withdraw your armies, and that act would cry louder for peace than a thousand proclamations and promises."

The Apostle, even though his speech was well larded with bitterness and sarcasm, brought the issue to its final amicable settlement. "I propose to say to the army," he declared, "walk in gentlemen, select your camp grounds, and fulfill your orders. If we take this course, in what light will the nations view our position? The result will be that the civilized world will say, the citizens of Utah are disposed for peace ... And as to the long list of charges that have been enumerated against us by Mr. Buchanan in his 'proclamation,' the world will say, — except a few party friends, — Mr. Buchanan don't believe them true, or he would not have pardoned them all indiscriminately; or else he does not feel able to punish them; *but his mistaken policy dictated that charges grave and serious should be enumerated in his 'proclamation' to ease him down from his awkward position* ... Instead of this measure disgracing us in the eyes of intelligent men, it will lift us higher in the scale of humanity. *I say then let us not reject these overtures.*"[36]

When it came time for Brigham Young to occupy the rostrum, it is said "he spoke in the power of God; those Commissioners heard the voice and roar of the Lion." But the mighty roar apparently ended in a conciliatory purr.

"As to the gentlemen Commissioners, they have no power to investigate the past, but [are] to inquire if we will submit to the Constitution and laws of the United States. We always have and always expect to. I have ... no pride to gratify — no vanity to please. If a man comes from the moon and says he will pardon me for kicking him in the moon yesterday, I don't care about it, I'll accept his pardon. It doesn't affect me one way or the other."[37]

In answer to the Commissioners' urgent suggestion that a statement from General Johnston would do much to allay the anxiety and uncertainty of the citizens of Utah, Johnston just as quickly responded with his own proclamation:

I ... assure those citizens of the territory who, I learn, apprehend from the army ill treatment, that no person whatever will be in any wise interfered with or molested in his person or rights, or in the peaceful pursuit of his avocations; and, should protection be needed, that they will find the army (always faithful to the obligations of duty) as ready now to assist and protect them as it was to oppose them while it was believed they were resisting the laws of their government.[38]

At the close of the conference, Powell and McCulloch jubilantly reported to the Secretary of War: "We have settled the unfortunate difficulties existing between the government of the United States and the people of Utah ... They will cheerfully yield obedience to the Constitution and laws of the United States. They consent that the civil officers shall enter upon the discharge of their respective duties ... No resistance will be made to the officers, civil or military of the United States, in the exercise of their various functions in the territory of Utah."[39]

To Buchanan's proclamation, and Johnston's proclamation, Governor Cumming could now append a proclamation of his own:

Whereas, The proffered pardon was accepted, with the prescribed terms of the proclamation, by the citizens of Utah; Now, therefore, I, Alfred Cumming, governor of Utah territory, in the name of James Buchanan, president of the United States, do proclaim that all persons who submit themselves to the laws and to the authority of the federal government are by him freely and fully pardoned for all treasons and seditions heretofore committed. All criminal offenses associated with or growing out of overt acts of sedition and treason are merged in them, and are embraced in the "free and full pardon" of the president. And I exhort all persons to persevere in a faithful submission to the laws and patriotic devotion to the Constitution and government of our common country.

Peace is restored to our territory![40]

XIII

COLONEL KANE returned to Philadelphia, by way of the Expedition's trail, now fetid with the rotting carcasses of the army animals that had perished, and dotted with the heaps of iron and ashes of the wagons the Nauvoo Legion had burned. Commissioners Powell and McCulloch were free now to return to a grateful President Buchanan, and to the political laurels they had earned. And on the 26th of June, Johnston's Army entered Salt Lake City.

Not many Mormons were on hand to greet the military might of the American nation. The community still was deserted, the straw piled high, and the vigilant Legionnaires had orders to set the torch in the event the army attempted to bivouac within the sphere of any Mormon possessions. It was a grand entry, but a lonesome, haunting one.

Johnston brought his troops along South Temple Street in six divisions, but true to his promise, there was no pause. According to Johnston's own official report, the parade came in as follows:

(1) Brevet Colonel C. F. Smith's battalion, constituting the advance guard;

(2) Tenth infantry and Phelps' battery;

(3) Fifth infantry and Reno's battery;

(4) Colonel Loring's battalion of mounted riflemen;

(5) Volunteers;

(6) Colonel Cooke's second dragoons constituting the rear guard;

Each command was followed by its train and a portion of the supply train;

The headquarters were with the advance.[41]

It was the privilege of the Peace Commissioners to ride the triumphal procession with the general's staff. The bands played, and on the deserted streets there was no cheering, the music rolling back on the colums in haunting mockery. Other than the blare of brass, the clupping of horses' hoofs in the summer dust, and the clink and rattle of the wagons of the supply trains, the city was empty of noise. American journalists, traveling with the Expedition, were struck by the tormenting "stillness," so profound "that during the intervals between the passage of the columns, the *monotonous gurgle of City Creek struck on every ear.*"

The same correspondent, in recording his own impressions of Salt Lake City and the army's entry left a vivid pen portrait of that June day's conclusion to the Utah War. "It was one of the most extraordinary scenes that has occurred in American history," he accurately surmised. "All day long, from dawn till after sunset, the troops and trains poured through the city, the utter silence of the streets being broken only by the music of the military bands, the monotonous tramp of the regiments, and the rattle of the baggage wagons. Early in the morning, the Mormon guard had forced all their fellow religionists into the houses, and ordered them not to make their appearance during the day [here the reporter, of course, was grossly in error; the Mormons long before had fled their city]. The numerous flags, which had been flying from staffs on the public buildings during the previous week, were all struck. The only visible groups of spectators were on the corners near Brigham Young's residence, and consisted almost entirely of Gentile civilians."[42]

When it came turn for Colonel Philip St. George Cooke to pass through the city's center, at the head of his splendid Second Dragoons, he humbly removed his hat, and rode through Salt Lake City bareheaded — as a token of respect for the brave Mormon men he had led to California in the immortal Battalion.

By this simple gesture, at least one commander of that hated army endeared himself forever in Mormon memory.

General Johnston, while never quite lifting himself to this echelon of Mormon esteem, did acquit himself honorably this day, and at least proved to the Saints that he was a man of his word. "Not a field was encroached upon, not a house molested, not a person harmed or insulted, by troops that had been so harassed and vituperated by a people now entirely at their mercy. By their strict subordination they entitled themselves to the respect of the country as well as to the gratitude of the Mormons."[43]

To this day, Latter-day Saints make point of the fact that General Johnston, sent out by the United States Government to put down an alleged "rebellion" of the Mormons, only a few years later became a rebel himself against that same government. As a Confederate general, in the War Between the States, he died leading his troops at Shiloh.

But on this day, in the Utah War, his conduct was exemplary, and entirely as promised. "What is the present situation of affairs?" grudged Brigham Young from Provo the next day. "For us the clouds seem to be breaking. Probably many of you have already learned that General Johnston passed through Great Salt Lake City with his command under the strictest discipline. Not a house, fence, or sidewalk has been infringed upon by any of his command . . . *he has carried out his promises to the letter*."[44]

Nor did Johnston camp his army until he had reached Cedar Valley, thirty-six miles from the city, and west of Utah Lake. This permanent base was to be ever remembered by the Saints as Camp Floyd.

But now, left with no real reason to destroy Utah, the glass windows went back into the city's public buildings, the straw was removed from the dwellings, and the torch fires extinguished.

The Saints returned to their deserted homes, knowing that neither they nor the Gentiles were the victor. But, for everyone concerned, the Utah War was over. And there was still much to do in the work of the Lord.

NOTES — THE UTAH WAR

1. For Mormon success and failures in its program of evangelization of the Indian, see Paul Bailey, *Jacob Hamblin, Buckskin Apostle.*

2. *The Contributor,* IX, No. 4, p. 126.

3. See Paul Bailey, *Walkara, Hawk of the Mountains,* and *The Claws of the Hawk.*

4. *House Executive Documents,* No. 2, 35th Cong., 1st session, p. 21.

5. See *Comprehensive History of the Church,* IV, pp. 236-237; *Deseret News,* July 29, 1857.

6. *Deseret News,* July 29, 1857.

7. *Comprehensive History of the Church,* IV, p. 239.

8. This unique order of General Wells will be found *extenso* in the *Contributor,* III, p. 177.

9. *History of Brigham Young, Ms.,* entry August 23, 1857, pp. 438-439. See also *Comprehensive History of the Church,* IV, p. 249.

10. As reported in the *Deseret News,* September 23, 1857.

11. *Comprehensive History of the Church,* IV, p. 262.

12. *House Executive Documents,* 35th Congress, 1st Session, No. 71, p. 25.

13. *Comprehensive History of the Church,* IV, p. 264.

14. *Ibid.,* see pp. 265-271.

15. *House Executive Documents,* 35th Congress, 1st Session, x, No. 71, pp. 34-35. Slightly abbreviated.

16. *House Executive Documents,* 35th Congress, 1st Session, x, No. 71, p. 33.

17. A copy of the written order from which this is excerpted was found on the person of Mormon Major Joseph Taylor when he was captured by a detachment of U.S. troops. It was forwarded on to Washington by Fitz J. Porter assistant adjutant general to Colonel Johnston. It is published *extenso* in *House Executive Documents,* 35th Congress, 1st Session, x, No. 71, pp. 56-57.

18. See Lot Smith's Narrative in "Echo Canyon War," Wells, *Contributor,* III, p. 273.

19. Lot Smith's Narrative, see *Contributor,* IV, pp. 27-28.

20. *House Executive Documents,* 35th Congress, 1st Session, x, No. 71, p. 31.

21. *Congressional Globe,* 35th Congress, 1st Session, Feb. 25. 1858, p. 874. See also *Comprehensive History of the Church,* IV, pp. 294-295.

NOTES — THE UTAH WAR (Continued)

22. Johnston's Report to Major I. McDowell, Nov. 30, 1857, *House Executive Documents,* x, No. 71, pp. 77-79.

23. From *House Executive Documents,* 35th Congress, 1st Session, x, No. 71, p. 76, as summarized in *Comprehensive History of the Church,* IV, pp. 314-315.

24. *Journal of Wilford Woodruff,* entry of February 25, 1858. Quoted also in *Comprehensive History of the Church,* IV, pp. 344-345.

25. Letter of President Buchanan, *House Executive Documents,* 35th Congress, 2nd Session, 1858-59, pp. 162-163. It is interesting to note that in spite of Buchanan's disavowal of Kane as an official emissary of peace, that the President himself later appointed, and sent to Utah, his "Peace Commissioners."

26. *History of Brigham Young, Ms.,* entry for August 15, 1858, p. 927. See also *Comprehensive History of the Church,* IV, p. 349.

27. See *Comprehensive History of the Church,* IV, pp. 360-361. Young's remarks at this historic meeting are recorded also in *History of Brigham Young, Ms.,* entry for Sunday, March 21, 1858, pp. 269-272. Brigham, in advocating a wilderness withdrawal for the thousands upon thousands of Saints, seemed to have been laboring under a salubrious concept of the ability of the arid west to support and sustain a substantial population.

28. See *Comprehensive History of the Church,* IV, p. 378.

29. Report of General W. H. Kimball to President Young. *History of Brigham Young, Ms.,* entry of April 15, 1858, pp. 365-366.

30. *House Executive Documents,* 35th Congress, 2nd Session, vol. ii, part ii, pp. 72-73.

31. From a report to Honorable Lewis Cass, Secretary of State, Washington, D. C., under date of May 2, 1858. *Ibid.* pp. 91-97.

32. *History of Brigham Young, Ms.,* entry of June 11, 1858, p. 486.

33. *House Executive Documents,* 35th Congress, 2nd Session, vol. ii, pt. ii, pp. 114-116.

34. *Ibid.*

35. The speeches at the Peace sessions, as well as the Buchanan proclamation, are quoted *extenso* in *Comprehensive History of the Church,* IV, pp. 423-440.

36. *Ibid.*

37. *Ibid.*

38. *House Executive Documents,* 35th Congress, 2nd Session, vol. ii, part ii, pp. 119-121.

39. Letter of Commissioners to the Secretary of War, *Ibid.,* pp. 167-168.

40. *Ibid.,* p. 113.

41. *Ibid.,* p. 119; and Report of General Johnston to Army Headquarters of the 28th of June from camp "near Salt Lake City," *Ibid.,* p. 121.

42. *Atlantic Monthly,* April 1859, p. 490.

43. *Ibid.,* p. 491

44. Report of discourse delivered in Provo, June 27, *Deseret News,* issue of July 14, 1858.

BANNER OF THE MORMON BATTALION
CARRIED IN EARLY-DAY UTAH PARADES

— Courtesy of and by permission of
Daughters of Utah Pioneers Museum.

Perfidy, Politics
and Polygamy

I

EXCEPT for a few minor incidents, in which Governor Cumming put himself squarely on the side of the Saints, the Mormon communities of Utah learned to live with Camp Floyd (named after John B. Floyd, Secretary of War), and the rather oversize military garrison strategically and ever watchfully placed in Utah Territory. And, while General Johnston was its commandant, he strove creditably to keep the military aloof from the political and religious life of the Saints.

Alfred Cumming, accepted with such apprehension by the citizens of Utah, proved to be an exceptionally able governor. After he began to understand the peculiar people over whom he had been called upon to preside — their kindness and their goodness of heart — he grew fiercely loyal toward them. Fearlessly he took up the cudgel in their behalf, and in one Gentile at least, the Mormons felt they had a friend.

Especially did he endear himself to the Saints when, at the end of the Utah War's unpleasantries, he refused to dissolve the Nauvoo Legion. As governor, he accepted the corps as the official territorial militia, and by law, it was pledged to his use and necessity.

For the next few years, and as the national furor of the "Utah rebellion" was supplanted by national concern over other rebellious states, the Legion settled down into performance of routine duties. When it was generally indicative that the Mormons were not to be annihilated, the restive Indians calmed down. After all, "Mormonees" were more to be trusted than "Americats." So long as Johnston was in command at Camp Floyd, the United States garrisons remained watchful and aloof, and allowed the Legion to drill and parade without interference.

At the first sign of secession, however, and with the increasing imminence of war between the states, General Johnston took leave of Camp Floyd, went to San Francisco, thence back to Mississippi to put himself at the disposal of Jefferson Davis and the confederacy. And, with the opening of hostilities, the entire grand army of the Utah Expedition was hastily hauled out of Camp Floyd. Military supplies, with the exception of guns and ammunition, were sold to the thrifty Mormons at sacrificial prices. Colonel Cooke personally presented to Brigham Young, in memory of the Battalion, Camp Floyd's splendid flag staff. But the tons of guns and ammunition were burned or detonated. Nothing of military value was left to the Legion.

So, except for the memories, the scars, and a thousand Gentile camp followers dumped in Salt Lake City, Utah was as before the "rebellion." Not quite, of course, because Brigham Young was no longer territorial governor, and Utah's entire judicial system was now under the critical and unsympathetic control of eastern Gentile appointees.

Isolated and alone, with its own private thoughts regarding Washington soldiers and politicians, Utah remained comparatively aloof from the gigantic struggle now erupting in the east. Smugly, Mormons were remembering Joseph Smith's prophecy that civil war would strike the nation, and that he had accurately named the spot where the first shot would be fired. In comparison now, to a nation cleaved asunder, the trumped-up charges of "rebellion" against the Mormons looked puny and picayunish.

In spite of the fact that the Legion had a back record considered treasonable, it, in 1863, furnished two companies of United States volunteers. These were commanded by Lot Smith and R. T. Burton, both more than active against Johnston's Army in the Utah War. Both companies saw long and arduous service in guarding the mail routes west against rampaging Indians now aroused again, and regaling themselves in the absence of U.S. Regulars to garrison the posts and forts.

But Utah's breathing spell without an army of occupation was short indeed. The California Volunteers, under command of Colonel Patrick Edward Connor, had originally started for the Potomac. This thousand man army had been raised with better hopes than the policing of the west against Indians, but it never got farther east than Salt Lake City.

The men of Connor's army would have accepted any campaign assignment on earth in preference to that of Utah. In fact they voluntarily offered $30,000 in suspension of pay, if the government would order them east rather than leave them marking time in the damnable country of the Mormons. But it was in Utah they remained — their pause as great an irritant to themselves as it was to the Saints.

Ostensibly they had been ordered to the territory to guard the mail routes and telegraph lines from the Indians. This duty the Mormons, with their superb Legion, had before the Utah War, and after, done, and was willing and anxious to do. No soldiers on earth were more capable of handling this detail. It was the order for Connor to establish a military post in the vicinity of Salt Lake City that raised the fury of the Saints. They refused to believe anything other than that Mormon surveillance was the true motive of this second army's presence — especially when Connor chose the benchland, immediately east of the city, as the site for his post. Johnston had at least been sympathetic and understanding enough to establish Camp Floyd thirty miles away. Not Connor; his guns could rake Temple Square any time he saw fit.

The army's entry into Salt Lake City proved especially offensive to the Saints. Mistaking public outcry over this new encroachment of freedom and promise as rebellion, Colonel Connor vowed that he would "cross the River Jordan [the stream to the west of Salt Lake City] if hell yawned beneath him." On October 20, 1862, "with loaded rifles, fixed bayonets, and shotted cannon, Colonel Connor marched the volunteers into Salt Lake City."[1]

Entering the city from the south, by way of State Street, the army marched north to First South Street, thence eastward to the residence of Governor Stephen S. Harding [Cumming's successor], where a halt was made, the troops drawn up in two lines, and a rather bombastic speech delivered by that gentleman. The army cheered, and resumed its march through the city, to the flood of music from its bands. Two and a half miles east, on the high rise overlooking the city, Connor halted his army, and set it to work digging-in to what was to be an endless Mormon irritant — Fort Douglas.

The Saints had already discovered in Governor Harding a man as diabolically anti-Mormon as Colonel Connor. The loss of Alfred Cumming to the territory was by now being keenly felt. And this new Lincoln appointee, from the moment of his acceptance of the governor's chair, seemed to measure each Saint as an enemy to be reduced.

In July of 1862 Congress had enacted into law a measure aimed at abolishing polygamy — targeted, of course, directly at

Utah. At the opening of the Utah territorial legislature in December 1862, Governor Harding tendered special invitation for
every Gentile federal appointee in the territory, and including
Colonel Connor and the military, to attend the session, and lend
an appreciative ear to the message he had prepared for delivery.
The speech was enough to raise the fury of every Mormon in
Utah.

It was to be expected he would make some allusion to the new
law aimed at the "plural marriage" so prevalent among his constituents. In this, considering the rabidly anti-Mormon sentiments of their new governor, the Saints were not at all surprised.
What did shock them was the long and bitter harangue against
everything that motivated them as a people. He lashed out at
what he considered their lack of loyalty to the federal government. "He had heard no sentiments expressed that would lead
him to believe that much sympathy was felt by any considerable
number of the citizens of Utah in favor of the government of the
United States, then struggling for its very existence... He
attacked the whole body of their territorial laws and urged
revolutionary changes therein.

"So insulting did the legislature consider the address, both in
its matter and the manner of its delivery, that as they listened
in silence to its 'semi-dramatic' reading, they concluded to treat
it with silent contempt throughout. No copies were ordered
printed; and there appears nothing in the current impression of
the *Deseret News*, nor in the record of the legislative assembly,
to show that Governor Harding was even so much as present on
the day he read his message to the conjoint assembly."[2]

"It was written entirely for another longitude," was Apostle
George A. Smith's comment. "The neglect here [silent treatment,
and failure to get it published] may enable him to give it a
wider circulation elsewhere." That apostolic prediction proved
accurate, though probably not in the manner intended. When

Congress learned that the Utah legislature had deliberately suppressed the Governor's message, it became a matter for Senate investigation. Congress authorized a printing of the neglected speech. And the whole affair boomeranged prejudicially against the Mormon people in the far away "longitude" of Washington.

Mormons had lost the first round to Governor Harding. Triumphantly he enlisted the aid of Judges Charles B. Waite and Thomas J. Drake, associate justices of the territorial supreme court, to draft a bill which would overthrow the last semblance of popular government in Utah. The bill was amendatory to the organic act which had created the Territory of Utah in 1850. Some of its provisions included:

(a) It would strike down what had become the courts of the people — the county probate courts — by limiting them to routine clerical and administrative functions. (b) It would upset the established jury system by granting authority to the marshal to summon "any person within the district in which the court is held, that he thinks proper as jurors." (c) It aimed at immobilizing the Legion by authorizing the governor to appoint and commission *all* militia officers, including the major general, and with the power to remove them at pleasure. Also it would confer on the governor the right to set the time, day, and length of the militia's training.

The measure was forwarded to Washington with the recommendation by Governor Harding and Justices Wait and Drake that it be enacted into law. It was immediately introduced into the upper house of Congress by Senator O. H. Browning of Illinois, and referred to the committee on judiciary.

As soon as Brigham Young and the leaders were cognizant of Harding's militancy in ramming through Congress a bill threatening the rights of every citizen in Utah, a mass meeting was held in the tabernacle, and fire and fury erupted. Resolutions were drawn up, and sent to Washington — eight in all. One of them demanded that a committee be appointed to wait upon the offending officials with a request that they resign their offices and leave the territory forthwith. Another was a petition to the President of the United States to remove the three officials and appoint "good men in their stead."

A counter petition, declaring full approval of Governor Harding in his course against the Mormon people, was signed by Colonel Connor and all the commissioned officers then stationed at Camp Douglas. It never occurred to these politically-minded soldiers, apparently, that there were rules prohibiting military interference in the affairs of civil government.

So another volcano had erupted in Utah. Months later, and after the ashes and debris had settled, Governor Harding was removed from office, and James Duane Doty, who for the two years previous had served as territorial superintendent of Indian Affairs, was appointed Governor in his stead. Judges Waite and Drake, considerably subdued by the united voice of the populace, were allowed to remain as jurists.

Congress failed to pass the bill that was so patently offensive to Utah Territory, and Harding went on to a chief justiceship in Colorado, where the people were a little less militant and a little less peculiar. But again was made apparent the vast gulf and lack of understanding between Mormons and Gentiles. And, in spite of the fact that Utah could look forward to a more amicable relationship between church and state, still no appointee out of Washington ever again measured up to the stature of Alfred Cumming. The old and bitter pattern of hate, so long remembered from Missouri and Illinois, was again on the move. And the fort Connor was building on the hill had a clear sweep of its cannon on Brigham's homes and Temple Square.

Connor may have loathed Brigham Young with passion, and was acidly contemptuous of the Saints, but he was a good soldier — hard and tough. Had he been allowed to operate, with his California Column, in the eastern theater of war — his most earnest and devout wish — his army would most certainly have distinguished itself. To guard Utah, and keep a jaundiced eye on Brigham and his Saints, was as distasteful to this man of action as it was to the territorial citizens under his target of contempt.

When news of repeated Indian raids on immigrant trains, freighters and mail riders came to Colonel Connor at Camp Douglas, he moved his troops against them with speed and efficiency. The Snakes, Bannocks and Utes, emboldened by the war's withdrawal of garrisons along the overland trail, had become brazenly active in plundering the white man. Connor's brief campaign against the northern tribes ended in a decisive victory, and a lesson these tribesmen were never to forget.

Colonel Connor, with three hundred seasoned troopers, operating in the snow and cold of Bear River, found the Indians encamped in a ravine of what is now southern Idaho. The Indians put up a desperate battle, lasting four hours. But in Connor and his Californians, they met their match. When the battle was over, three hundred Bannocks lay dead, and their village, rich with the plunder of immigrant and freight wagons, burned to the ground. The loot, including seventy-five Indian ponies, were later auctioned off at Camp Douglas. This, and a few more sharp engagements, decisively convinced the tribesmen of the stupidity and futility of molesting the white man, regardless of how preoccupied he was with his great war in the east. In clearing the trails, and restoring safety to overland travel, Connor served Utah Territory well.

Connor was a hard and tough soldier, but in Brigham Young he found his match. The gutty battle between these two giants, enlivened Utah history for years. In the *Union Vedette*, published in the army camp, Brigham Young was periodically dressed down as polygamist, autocrat, Mahomet, and murderer. In the *Deseret News* was aired what Mormons in general, and Brigham Young in particular, thought of the crusty commander and the lecherous soldiers he had turned loose on a decent, god-fearing community.

There were times when the exasperated colonel threatened to march his troops into Temple Square, and take over the tacitly insurrectionist community. Especially did he loathe and publicly castigate the Nauvoo Legion — considering it as Brigham's private army, and therefore his enemy.

Between ten and eleven o'clock, on the night of March 29, 1863, Salt Lake City was alarmed by the roar of cannon fire from the military base on the hill, and the phrenetic discharge of rifles into the night. Bracing for the long expected military attack on the city, the Legion commanders frantically made their way to the arsenal. But before Salt Lake City could muster out its defense, the cause of the sudden action was made known. Over the military telegraph had come the news of Connor's promotion to the rank of brigadier general, for his brilliant and decisive campaign against the Indians. Camp Douglas was making a whooping spree of the good news. The worried Mormons went back to bed still worried.

Many were the incidents of friction in the years that followed. Brigham Young, beloved and respected leader of his people, was guiding them forward in one of the greatest religious and colonization movements of all time. All the Gentile governors, judges, and military commanders stuffed into Utah could never change the fact that President Young was the true leader of Mormondom, the prophet in the shoes of the martyred Joseph Smith. He was the Mormon "Lion of the Lord," and he never hesitated to roar back at anything that smacked of intimidation or oppression of his people. Between General Connor and Prophet Brigham there was never a soft word.

Connor had his army to back him up, but the civil appointees from Washington, in attempting to rule the territory, were exasperated and bitter when they found their power blunted by an attitude of divisive loyalty, passive resistance, and sometimes open contempt. When Brigham spoke, the word was law, and the Saints willingly and happily did whatever was bidden. When the territorial officers spoke, from the governor down, the Saints responded only if Brigham Young felt they should respond. In 1858 he had been deposed as governor of Utah Territory. Every federal appointee to the 'chair after that had reason to wonder who was the *real* governor of Utah.

Since the Saints were the constituents, in overwhelming numbers, every jury was filled with them, every mass meeting spoke their words, and, with the exception of the *Union Vedette,* and the Camp Floyd *Valley Tan* before it, the Utah newspapers, from the *Deseret News* down, spoke in chorus as the voice of the church.

Mormons were never afraid to cry out against anything they considered an encroachment of their liberties as citizens and as Christians. The same grand jury, Mormon staffed, which on April 15, 1863, castigated Governor Harding for turning loose the principals in Utah's Morrisite rebellion, labeled Camp Douglas a "common nuisance" to a large segment of citizenry in east Salt Lake City. It claimed the army base fouled the waters of Red Butte Canyon Creek, used by the said section of the city for irrigation, drinking, and culinary purposes. The number of citizens affected by the contaminated water was listed at three thousand. By establishment of the encampment, building stables and corrals along this vital water course, and diverting the flow to various parts of the camp, and back again into the main stream, the water was usurped from needful and necessary irrigation, and so contaminated as to render it useless for drink-ing and household use.

General Connor's answer to Mormon criticism and unrest was the establishment in July 1864 of a provost guard for Salt Lake City. "Having been," Connor stated in his orders, "credibly informed that there were persons within this district who while claiming and receiving protection to life and property from the government, are endeavoring to destroy and defame the prin-ciples and institutions of it," he empowered his officers to arrest and closely confine all persons guilty of uttering treasonable sentiments against the government, until they had taken the oath of allegiance, and had demonstrated the true qualities of American citizenship. "Traitors," Connor stated, "shall not utter treasonable sentiments in this district with impunity, but must seek some more genial soil, or receive the punishment they so richly merit."[3]

What rankled the Mormons was that a good deal of time had elapsed between the date the order was first issued and the sudden decision to set up the provost guard. The fact that it followed open criticism of the Saints against the governor, judges, and military, was indicative that Connor's act was one of intimidation rather than war hysteria, or any frantic search for "traitors."

The manner of his establishment of the city's guard station seemed just as unnecessary and just as insulting as the presence of Camp Douglas on the benchland to the east. It must have given Connor secret pleasure in the method by which he gained access to a house belonging to the church, directly opposite the south gates of Temple Square. "In behalf of the church," the house had been rented by Bishop John Sharp to Captain Stover, for use as a temporary military storehouse. Soon after, Captain Stover was ordered to Camp Douglas, the stores were removed, and on July 10 it blossomed out as headquarters for the provost guard.

On that same day the *Union Vedette* boasted: "As to the government, let it be distinctly understood that here or elsewhere, Uncle Sam will have what it wants — when he wants it — under all circumstances...!" The military action could not possibly have been more irritating or obnoxious. Sunday afternoon, at two o'clock, as the crowds were entering the tabernacle for worship, Mormon eyes beheld a company of United States cavalry in possession of the house, and staring contemptuously into the holiest portion of Mormondom.

Brigham Young was furious. Mayor A. O. Smoot lodged official protest, and prodded by Brigham, called out the city police, and alerted the Legion. A petition crying out against the insulting presence of the troops was drawn up and signed by thousands of irate citizens. But General Connor was not the sort of man to be intimidated or rebuffed. He dared the church to evict the tenants from its house. The provost guard remained. In the end, the only answer the church dared to give were some ranting editorials in the *Deseret News,* and the bricking up, against this eyesore, of the wide south entrance to Temple Square.

III

FROM the first Mormon entry in Utah, unswerved and unaltered by the fantastic drama being enacted in California's gold rush, Brigham Young forbade his Saints from seeking the mineral riches of the world. Up to the time of Connor's entry, the mountains and canyons of Utah had laid untouched and inviolate as to mining possibilities. In the lowlands the Mormons had built their communities to the glory of God, and the necessity of cultivating the earth. With Brigham Young's ban on seeking riches in any other fields than plowing, planting, shopkeeping and communal industries, no Mormon had dared to seriously prospect the high Rockies for gold or silver.

Coal and iron had been located, and that was important, in Mormon viewpoint, for the church-sponsored industry that was coming to Utah. Riders of the Nauvoo Legion, and the lonely missionaries among the Lamanites, had spotted rich outcroppings of other more desirable minerals in the mountain draws and canyons. Mentioning them only in their journals, the Saints turned from such discoveries to what they considered better pursuits. The great mineral wealth of Utah, for nearly two decades, lay untouched by Mormon hand.

But General Patrick Edward Connor was under no ban by Brigham. His California Volunteers, from out of a state grown rich on minerals, had been trained to look and observe. Herding and baiting Mormons, to them, was poor and unrewarding sport. Laying claim to Utah's mineral wealth was a definite plus side to soldiering in Utah, and at least made time bearable. Most of the soldiers, from General Connor down to the lowliest privates, spent their off-duty time wandering the hills and canyons of Utah. Some of the greatest mines in the world's history were located on silver, gold and copper veins dug raw by the pick-axes out of Camp Douglas. While Brigham and Connor glared and grumbled, the California Volunteers were sinking shafts and exploring ledges. What they were finding was real salve to their collective irritants.

With the inevitable news that great wealth had been discovered in Utah's mountains, many a Saint grew restive — but not Brigham. "It is a fearful deception which all the world labors under . . . that gold is wealth," he thundered from the tabernacle pulpit. "On the bare report that gold was discovered over in these west mountains, men left their thrashing machines, and

their horses at large to eat up and trample down and destroy
the precious bounties of the earth. They at once sacrificed all at
the glittering shrine of the popular idol, declaring they were
now going to be rich, and would raise wheat no more. Should
this feeling become universal on the discovery of gold mines in
our immediate vicinity, nakedness, starvation, utter destitution
and annihilation would be the inevitable lot of this people.
Instead of bringing us wealth and independence, it would weld
upon our necks the chains of slavery.

"Can you not see that gold and silver rank among the things
that we are the least in want of? We want an abundance of
wheat and fine flour, of wine and oil, and of every choice fruit
that will grow in our climate; we want silk, cotton, wool, flax
and other textile substances of which cloth can be made; we
want vegetables of various kinds to suit our constitutions and
tastes, and the products of flocks and herds; we want the coal
and the iron that are concealed in these ancient mountains, the
lumber from our sawmills, and the rock from our quarries; these
are some of the great staples to which kingdoms owe their
existence, continuance, wealth, magnificence, splendor, glory
and power; in which gold and silver serve as mere tinsel to give
the finishing touch to all this greatness. The colossal wealth of
the world is founded upon and sustained by the common staples
of life."[4]

Had gold itself been found with the comparative abundancy
of the surface wealth of California, Brigham's worst fears would
have been substantiated, and the church, its institutions, and
its high hopes would have seen a trampling asunder with the
thunderous finality of a herd of buffalo. From the days of the
Battalion, Brigham Young had been seer enough to know that
in developing God's kingdom on earth, the plow must be the
spiritual and temporal symbol above that of the gold pan and
miner's axe. He has been criticized for allowing the Gentiles to

steal the mineral wealth from under the collective nose of Zion. But Brigham Young had an earthy wisdom, and that wisdom and foresight built Utah against odds certain to have defeated lesser men. Probably what saved the church in this crisis was that Utah yielded her great mineral wealth stubbornly and slowly.

General Connor came under the scathing denunciation of Brigham Young and the Mormon people for his obsessive interest in mines and mining. To them it appeared this wealth-seeking passion too often stood in the way of his military duties. It is true that even before he and his California Volunteers took leave of Fort Douglas, he had willingly turned back to the Nauvoo Legion the task of fighting and pacifying the Indians within the territory.

He had no difficulty in inducing his fellow soldiers and California friends in setting up the first producing mines in Utah — preponderately silver. With alacrity they joined him in erecting the first smelting furnace, at Stockton, Tooele County, in 1864. Others followed.

"But the treatment of ores by smelting was a task new to these Californians, and their experience in milling the gold ores of their state was of no service to them in the task," said the *Western Galaxy*. "This disadvantage was increased by the fact that charcoal was not abundant, that rates of transportation were excessively high, and both the materials of which the furnaces were built, and those used in the daily operations were very dear. The Californians, unused to the work, failed entirely. A good deal of money was spent with no result, excepting the establishment of the fact that the ores were easy to treat... With the failure to work the mines profitably came the disbanding of the volunteer troops in the latter part of 1865-66."[5]

By that time the great Civil War was ended, the stress and strain of attitudes and loyalties laid aside for a time, and Utah mourned with the rest of the nation in the violent death of Abraham Lincoln. But Patrick Edward Connor remained on in Utah. To lay aside the sword for the miner's pick, was no problem for this mineral-seeking Irishman. To him alone goes credit for the discovery and promotion of Utah's mining industry.

The amazing thing is the gradual transformation in attitude between General Connor and Brigham Young with the passing of the years. Connor's earlier appraisal of the Mormon hierarchy as "disloyal and traitorous to the core," underwent a considerable change with time. Likewise Brigham who, in 1864, at the establishment of Connor's provost guard at the gates of Temple Square, had wrathfully ordered Mayor A. O. Smoot to summon the city police and the Legion's Life Guard to "move Connor and his men out of the city limits." Fortunately Smoot had delayed action, and by the time the preliminary arrangements for the drastic move were completed, the Mormon Prophet's temper had given way to better judgment. Had it gone on to a finish, full scale war would have erupted between the Legion and Camp Douglas. The underlying anger and belligerence of Mormonism had not been lost on General Connor.

But time worked most wondrously for these two hard-fisted Americans. After the truce, came friendship. In 1870, when Brigham Young was under federal indictment for polygamy, and facing the trial court of Chief Justice James B. McKean, it was Patrick Edward Connor who offered to go his bail in the enormous sum of $100,000. And, Captain Charles H. Hempstead, who was Salt Lake City's provost marshal in 1864, was Brigham Young's attorney and counselor during his legal battle of 1872.

IV

IN THE three years following the disbanding of Connor's California Volunteers, the military security of Utah Territory once more fell back upon the shoulders of the Nauvoo Legion. The

Indian tribes, acutely sensitive to the fighting strength of the military units opposing them, took heart when the Irishman and his soldiers melted away from the fort on the hill.

Again the Utes had grown bold and restive, and when the territorial governor appealed in vain for United States regulars to restore safety to the roads and colonies of Utah, he had no other choice than to call up the Nauvoo Legion.

Early in 1865 Black Hawk, a subordinate Ute chieftain, gathered about him a force of savage and disgruntled warriors and began attacking the exposed settlements to the south and east of the territory. Their first assault was on Manti, a Mormon frontier town where, on April 10, they killed Peter Ludwickson. Next day they were at Salina, where they killed two Saints by the names of Ward and Lambson. The nearest Legion unit was in the Sanpete military district, and commanded by Brigadier General Warren Snow. With speed and dispatch Snow mustered into service two companies of cavalry, under command of Colonel Redick N. Allred and Captain Abner Lowry respectively. Allred's cavalry pursued the hostiles through Salina Canyon, where in a narrow pass they were ambushed by the wily Utes. Two of the Mormons were killed and two wounded, before the Legionnaires decided to retreat from the hot and accurate Indian fire.

Turning back to the valley, they were joined by Lowry's company, and the two units of cavalry, numbering one hundred and seventy-five officers and men, took up pursuit of the victorious Black Hawk and his warriors. After several days, they overtook the Utes and defeated them in a heated battle. But that battle was only the starter.

On May 25, Jens Larsen was killed by the Indians, near Fairview. Next day John Givens, his wife, and four children were brutally murdered near Thistle Valley. On the 29th of that same month, the Utes returned to Fairview, killed David M. Jones, and ran off with a large herd of horses and cattle. On the 14th of July, Black Hawk and his men again rode through Salina Canyon, killed Robert Gillespie, and a man named Robinson, and gathered up another herd of Mormon stock.

Legion cavalry again pursued the hostiles for an hundred and fifty miles; overtaking them near Fish Lake. In the ensuing engagement Private Moroni York was killed, the Indians escaped, after leaving fourteen dead on the field of battle. The animals were never recovered. But while this expedition was out, another band of Utes raided Glenwood, in Sevier County, killed a man named Staley, and helped themselves to all available cattle.

After an ominously quiet August, they again appeared, this time at Ephraim, where they slaughtered five men and two women, wounded two other Mormons and made another heavy coup of horses and cattle. Again the Indians were overtaken in the vicinity of Fish Lake, and in this second battle seven hostiles were killed. General Snow, Orson Taylor, and several others were wounded.

With the approach of winter, the Utes withdrew to the Green and Colorado Rivers. In the one season they had massacred forty settlers, and stolen over two thousand head of cattle and horses. Black Hawk and his band were now as well mounted from Mormon plunder as Walkara himself had once been, and indeed the pattern of his hit-and-run operations were similar, and just as effective. And, like that great war chief of the past, they were being favorably and constantly supplied not only by the eastern Utes, but by the Navajoes.

The settlers now could only face the approaching spring with grim apprehension. Legionnaires knew from past experience how grave were the difficulties of matching forces with a foe, to whom every mile of that mountainous country was familiar and known. The Nauvoo Legion could mount guard around the communities, only to have the hostiles dart from some unfamiliar and obscure pass, wreak havoc, and disappear into the mountain fastness.

Colonel O. H. Irish, now superintendent of Indian affairs for the Territory of Utah, made application to Colonel Carroll H. Potter, who had superseded Connor as commandant at Fort Douglas, for United States troops to aid in putting down the hostiles. Carroll referred the matter to General Pope, department commander, who telegraphed back that no federal troops were available, and that the militia must bear the burden of the coming hostilities.

As expected, February opened with an attack, on Pipe Springs, on the southernmost line of Utah settlements. Two Mormons were killed, and another coup on sheep and stock. Two days later Utes were raiding Berryville, where they killed two men and a woman. General Wells, fully cognizant that this was war, called up every available unit of the Legion.

The Indians, following the line of melting snows, next attacked Marysville, in Piute County. Again they were at Salina, where they killed two more men, and escaped with two hundred head of Mormon horses. Everywhere, now, Legion cavalry was in the field, probing desperately at the cunning and victorious foe. Every community was under constant guard by Legion infantry units. Despite such precaution, the Utes struck and struck again — always calling the place to do battle; and always on their own terms.

During the year twenty more Mormons were massacred in savage attacks, large amounts of stock were stolen, and those Mormon settlements unable to "fort up," and in more exposed positions, were abandoned. Three hundred miles of the eastern frontier of Utah Territory were paralyzed. Sawmills, flour mills, and outlying ranches were deserted. Black Hawk's band, now tremendously augmented, and made bold by repeated successes, had become a fearful specter to the Mormon people.

It took three years of Legion battling to put an end to the Black Hawk War. It cost the Mormon people a million and a half dollars to equip and field their army. As many as twenty-five hundred men were under arms in the bitter and uncertain fighting — a tremendous loss of manpower to the citizenry, and an economic drain of incalculable size. In 1868 the Utah legislature memorialized Congress for the costs it had incurred in equipping and servicing the militia, and for the fact that the Superintendent of Indian Affairs had called on the United States Army to put down the rebellion, and had been refused by General Pope. Congress showed no interest in assuming any of the cost of the Black Hawk War.

V

IT WAS NOT unexpected that national money and national gratitude would be withheld the Mormon people for assuming the burden of settling the Indian strife on their borders, but it seems incomprehensible that in 1866, at the very time the Legion was fighting to protect Utah Territory, Senator Ben Wade should present a bill in Congress aimed at its dissolution. The bill, which additionally was targeted in on radically changing civil affairs in Utah, fortunately did not pass.

"After the close of the Black Hawk War, the situation in Utah grew more acrimonious," explained Richard W. Young, in the *Contributor*. "Local opposition developed; a bitter and irresponsible gentile press created prejudice at home and abroad; governors, judges, and other officials seemed to have but one object in Utah, and that was to find some means, fairly or not, it appeared to make little difference, through which prominent Mormons might be brought before the courts. Peace was not desired by the opposition; every possible aggravation seemed to be employed to bring about a conflict between Camp Douglas and the Mormons, and it was through Mormon forbearance and wisdom that trouble was avoided."[6]

A new garrison, and a new commandant, was now at Douglas. And with this new reign of hate and prejudice came J. Wilson Shaffer, of Illinois, as the appointed governor of Utah Territory. Shaffer, with his Illinois background, took a dim view of Mormonism in general, and an implacable hatred of the Nauvoo Legion in particular. His was only a brief administration, but it was long enough to accomplish the virtual abolishment of the Legion.

As commander-in-chief of the territorial militia, he appointed, wholly without warrant of law, and in flagrant disregard for Legion election protocol, Patrick Edward Connor as major general. It must have given Connor, the old Mormon-baiter and Legion hater, a wealth of satisfaction to even so belatedly hold strings on the Saints and their army.

In September 1870, Governor Shaffer issued a proclamation forbidding all musters, drills and gatherings of the militia — unless such came by his express and official order. It further enjoined the Legion to deliver up all public arms to the newly appointed assistant adjutant general. Not even a military posse could be called without approval of General Connor or the governor.

General Daniel Wells, in requesting permission to hold the usual and customary fall drills and musters, received a quick and stinging rebuff from Governor Shaffer. "You style yourself lieutenant general, yet the laws of the United States provide for only one officer of that grade. This is the first instance in which you or any of your pretended predecessors have recognized the governor as commander-in-chief, and I congratulate you on the change in your conduct. Brigham Young claims to be and is called 'President.' The militia shall not be wielded in disregard

of my authority; the musters cannot be held; I hope I am sufficiently explicit."[7] To make his point patently clear, Governor
Shaffer published his sarcastic answer to Wells in the Salt Lake
newspapers.

Wells continued the verbal tussle with an open letter, published in the *Deseret News*. "True, the United States law provides for but one lieutenant general," Wells conceded. "It likewise provides for only four major generals and limits the number of assistant adjutant generals; these offices are all filled by
United States officers. Why then do you appoint a major general
and an assistant adjutant general? If the law refers to the militia
in one case, it does in the other; but it refers to the militia in
neither case. Moreover, you appoint, where the law applicable
requires election."

The angry Legion commander continued, with irrefutable
logic: "You say this is the first instance in which I or 'any of my
pretended predecessors' have recognized the authority of the
Governor. I send you copies of letters from some of *your* predecessors which show you are mistaken. You call my office pretended. I refer you to an act approved February 5, 1852; nor
have I ever had a predecessor to my office in this Territory."[8]

But appeals to custom and logic fell uselessly on the ears of
the stubborn Gentile governor. The musters were not held. Nor
did the Nauvoo Legion ever again function in the manner for
which it was created, or effectively serve the Mormon people
or Utah Territory as an organ of civil defense. The governmental
appointee from Illinois, with one swift plunge of the knife, had
cut the heart out of the last proud Mormon army.

When the Legion's Third Regiment of the Salt Lake County
Infantry, on November 21, 1870, attempted their fall drill in spite
of the governor's proclamation, there came quick realization
that Mormon militarism was not to be further tolerated. "A
number of officers and about one hundred men and the band

of that regiment assembled on the Twentieth Ward square and proceeded to have a pleasant time drilling," Richard W. Young records in the *Contributor*. "The news of this formidable uprising was conveyed to the Acting-Governor, George A. Black [Shaffer was east, seeking further political preference], who hastened frantically to the scene with two deputies to quell (by force if necessary) this incipient rebellion.

"Black and his deputies were quite equal to the occasion, as they knew they would be, and marched triumphantly into court with eight prisoners, the officers who were present. The prisoners were arraigned before a United States judge, and as a result of the examination were held for high treason against the United States — another of those judicial farces of which the records of the Utah District Courts are so prolific. The rebels, Alexander Burt, George Ottinger, William Phillips, Charles and Archibald Livingstone, Charles R. Savage, W. C. Graham, and Charles Fennemore, being dangerous criminals were turned over to the custody of the commanding officer of Fort Douglas for safe keeping . . ."[9]

There was another occasion where Black thought he detected Mormon treason and sedition when a volunteer cavalry company attempted to join in a Fourth of July celebration. By arbitrarily staffing the Legion with anti-Mormon authority, by restriction and suspension of its activities, and by general disapproval of everything it stood for, the Nauvoo Legion was as effectively strangled as a broncho in a slip-noose. The final bitter fight against the armies of God was on — and in earnest.

The old battle cries against Mormonism — polygamy and treason — again were echoing loud and long throughout America. Denied statehood, at the mercy of federal territorial appointees, unable to get their own citizens into the high executive and judicial positions, Utah writhed at the mercy of every political caprice out of Washington. And Fort Douglas was kept staffed

MORMON BATTALION MEMBERS STILL LIVING IN 1897

— Courtesy of and by permission of Daughters of Utah Pioneers Museum.

and garrisoned — but not exactly for the purpose of hunting Indians.

The Nauvoo Legion was only one target of national reprisal. The great crusade against the plural marriages Joseph Smith so shockingly had instituted was now being carried into every town and hamlet occupied by the hated Mormons. The territorial penitentiary was enlarged and staffed. Husbands commenced being jailed, even before the congressional bills against polygamy were adequately tested as to constitutionality. Wives were threatened and intimidated, children born of plural unions were publicly branded as bastards. The non-Mormon governmental and judicial system of Utah Territory was at last having reprisal's field day against the populace they were supposed to govern and serve.

No greater ammunition could have been handed the enemies of Mormonism than the unsavory details of the Mountain Meadows Massacre, perpetrated against a Gentile wagon train in southern Utah during the "martial law" episode of the Utah War. Long kept hidden by the close-mouthed Saints, the sordid facts of this infamous affair were now at last being uncovered. The proof that units of the Nauvoo Legion had a part in the tragedy, could scarcely aid the Legion now in its fight for existence. With every added year American bitterness toward any and all Mormon institutions — including the Legion — grew in increasingly frightful proportions.

Gone now was the exuberant joy of citizen soldiery drilling on the public green. Outside of the still carefully kept muster rolls, and the overt and unpublicized membership elections, there was little remaining to indicate that the great, efficient and field-tested Nauvoo Legion could even claim existence.

The persistent enemies of Mormonism finally and completely won — when Congress, in 1887, at long last passed a law with enough teeth to bite off every writhing tentacle of the despised sect. This was the Edmunds-Tucker Act – a law aimed primarily and ostensibly at abolishing Mormon polygamy, but equally effective at wiping out the Nauvoo Legion. The price of non-compliance was complete financial and judicial liquidation of the church.

Section 27 of this vicious act stated: "That all laws passed by the so-called State of Deseret and by the legislative assembly of the Territory of Utah for the organization of the militia thereof or for the creation of Nauvoo Legion are hereby annulled, and declared of no effect . . ."

Nothing could be more explicit.

VI

In 1845 the Legion disappeared with annulment of the Nauvoo charters. In 1887 it went completely and finally down with the Edmunds-Tucker Act, which destroyed, along with polygamy, every bright and bold dream of Mormondom's State of Deseret. When finally Utah did pass into American statehood, its every tooth and fang had been pulled. It had, by then, become thoroughly safe in conformity, and a virtual carbon copy of every other state of the union.

Mormonism, born into a virile sort of life, has through the years, grown into a conservative and a most respected type of religion. Its leaders now, instead of shouting defiance, are obsessed with conformity, and with the creation by every means possible, of a chaste, peaceful and admirable public image. No longer does citizen soldiery drill on the public squares of Mormon communities. Little is said now, even among the Mormons themselves, about the military aspects of their unique creed. Polygamy, in the church, has been relegated to something unspeakable. Its armies of God, because they smack of a once bold and militant concept, are seldom mentioned. Now, above all, Mormonism wants to be well thought of.

But Mormons, from the beginning, have made good soldiers. They still serve their country when and where needed. Given their own volition and choice, however, in this matter of marching off to war — it now would likely be with a book in their hands, rather than rifle or musket. That Mormonism no longer needs or wants an army is probably tied to the fact that they have given up trying to remake the world. With military might they doubtless would have failed just as surely and just as quickly.

Still their grandfathers were handy men with a gun. And in the armies of God, they gave America a unique, daring and interesting historical chapter. And certainly, if Jackson County is ever to be redeemed as the promised site for the New Jerusalem, it will necessitate another mustering in of Zion's Camp, the Mormon Battalion, and the Nauvoo Legion.

NOTES — PERFIDY, POLITICS, AND POLYGAMY

1. Stenhouse, *Rocky Mountain Saints,* p. 603.

2. *Comprehensive History of the Church,* V, pp. 19-22. The governor's message will be found complete in Tullidge, *History of Salt Lake City,* xxxiii, pp. 291-305.

3. The order, while bearing the early date of August 6, 1862, was the basis under which Connor established his provost guard. It is published in full in *Deseret News,* August 20, 1862.

4. Discourse of Oct. 25, 1863. See *Deseret News,* Nov. 18, 1863.

5. *Western Galaxy,* "Mines of the West," March 1888, p. 2.

6. *The Contributor,* IX, No. 12, p. 452.

7. *Ibid.*

8. *Ibid.,* pp. 452-453.

9. *Ibid.,* p. 453.

Bibliography

GENERAL SOURCES

Arrington, Leonard J. *Great Basin Kingdom.* An Economic History of the Latter-day Saints, 1830-1900. Cambridge: Harvard University Press; 1958.

Bailey, L. R. *Indian Slave Trade in the Southwest.* Los Angeles: Westernlore Press, Publishers; 1966.

Bailey, Paul. *The Claws of the Hawk.* A study of Walkara the Ute. Los Angeles: Westernlore Press, Publishers; 1966.

————. *For Time and All Eternity.* A study of Mormon plural marriage and the anti-polygamy crusade of 1890. New York: Doubleday & Company; 1964.

————. *Jacob Hamblin, Buckskin Apostle.* Los Angeles: Westernlore Press, Publishers; 1948; 1955; 1961. Salt Lake City: Bookcraft, Inc.; 1961; 1965.

————. *Sam Brannan and the California Mormons.* Los Angeles: Westernlore Press, Publishers; and Salt Lake City: Bookcraft, Inc.; 1942, 1943, 1953, 1958.

————. *Walkara, Hawk of the Mountains.* Los Angeles: Westernlore Press, Publishers; 1954.

Bancroft, Hubert H. *History of Utah.* San Francisco: The History Company; 1890.

Bennett, John C. *The History of the Saints; or an Exposé of Joe Smith and Mormonism.* Boston: Leland & Whiting; 1842.

Birney, Hoffman. *Zealots of Zion.* Philadelphia: The Penn Publishing Company; 1931.

Book of Mormon, translated from the Holy Plates by Joseph Smith, the Prophet. Salt Lake City: 1949 edition.

Burton, Richard F. *The City of the Saints.* New York: Harper & Brothers, Publishers; 1862.

Brodie, Fawn M. *No Man Knows My History.* Life of Joseph Smith, Mormon Prophet. New York: Alfred A. Knopf; 1945.

Brooks, Juanita. *John Doyle Lee.* Glendale, Calif.: The Arthur H. Clark Company; 1961.

————. *The Mountain Meadows Massacre.* Stanford: Stanford University Press; 1950. Norman: University of Oklahoma Press; 1962.

Carter, Kate B. *The Mormon Battalion.* Salt Lake City: Daughters of Utah Pioneers; 1956.

Carvalho, S. N. *Incidents of Travel and Adventure in the Far West; with Col. Fremont's Last Expedition.* New York: Derby & Jackson; 1859.

Cooke, Col. P. St. George. *Conquest of New Mexico and California.* New York: G. P. Putnam & Sons; 1878.

Creer, Leland Hargrave. *The Founding of an Empire.* The Exploration and Colonization of Utah, 1776-1856. Salt Lake City: Bookcraft, Inc.; 1947.

Doctrine and Covenants of the Church of Jesus Christ of Latter-day Saints, containing Revelations Given to Joseph Smith, the Prophet. Salt Lake City: 1948 edition.

Documents, Correspondence, Orders, etc. in Relation to the Disturbances with the Mormons. Fayette, Missouri: published by order of the Missouri Legislature; 1841.

Egan, Howard. *Pioneering the West, 1846 to 1878.* Major Howard Egan's Diary. Richmond, Utah: Howard R. Egan Estate; 1917.

Evans, John Henry. *Joseph Smith, an American Prophet.* New York: The Macmillan Company; 1936.

Flanders, Robert Bruce. *Nauvoo, Kingdom on the Mississippi.* Urbana: University of Illinois Press; 1965.

Ford, Thomas. *History of Illinois.* Chicago: 1854.

Gates, Susa Young, and Leah D. Widtsoe. *The Life Story of Brigham Young.* New York: Macmillan Company; 1931.

Golder, Frank Alfred. *The March of the Mormon Battalion.* Taken from the Journal of Henry Standage. New York: The Century Co.; 1928.

Gottfredson, Peter. *History of Indian Depredations in Utah.* Salt Lake City: Skelton Publishing Company; 1919.

Gove, Captain Jesse A. *The Utah Expedition: Letters of Captain Gove to Mrs. Gove and the New York Herald.* Concord, N. H.: New Hampshire Historical Society; 1928.

Gregg, Th. *History of Hancock County, Illinois.* Chicago: Chas. C. Chapman & Co.; 1880.

Griffith, Will (Ed.). *Historic Nauvoo.* Peoria, Illinois: Quest Publishing Co.; 1941.

Hafen, LeRoy R. and Ann W. (Eds.). *The Utah Expedition, 1857-1858.* Far West and Rockies Series, VIII. Glendale, Calif.: The Arthur H. Clark Company; 1958.

Handbook of Reference to the History, Chronology, Religion and Country of the Latter-day Saints, including the Revelation on Celestial Marriage. For the use of Saints and Strangers. Salt Lake City: Juvenile Instructor Office; 1884.

Hickman, William A. *Brigham's Destroying Angel.* New York: George A. Crofutt & Co.; 1872. Salt Lake City: 1904.

History of Caldwell County. St. Louis: National Historical Company; 1886.

History of the Church of Jesus Christ of Latter-day Saints, including *History of Joseph Smith, the Prophet, by Himself.* 6 vols. Introduction and Notes by B. H. Roberts. Salt Lake City: Deseret News Press; 1902-1912.

House Executive Documents. 35th Congress, 1st and 2nd Sessions. Washington, D. C.: 1857.

Jenson, Andrew. *Church Chronology.* Salt Lake City: Deseret News Press; 1899.

Jones, Daniel W. *Forty Years Among the Indians.* Salt Lake City: Juvenile Instructor Office, 1890. Los Angeles: Westernlore Press, Publishers; 1960.

Kane, Thomas L. *The Mormons.* Philadelphia: King & Baird; 1850.

Kelly, Charles (Ed.). *Journals of John D. Lee.* Salt Lake City: The Western Printing Co.; 1938.

Lee, John D. *Mormonism Unveiled; or the Life and Confessions of the Late Mormon Bishop, John D. Lee.* St. Louis: Ryan, Rand & Co.; 1880.

Linn, William A. *The Story of the Mormons.* New York: Macmillan Company; 1902. Reprinted 1923.

Little, James A. *From Kirtland to Salt Lake City.* Salt Lake City: Juvenile Instructor Office; 1890.

Lyford, Rev. C. P. *The Mormon Problem.* New York: Phillips & Hunt; 1886.

McGavin, E. Cecil. *U. S. Soldiers Invade Utah.* Boston: Meador Publishing Co.; 1937.

McGarry, Sheridan L. *Mormon Money.* Salt Lake City: n.d.

O'Dea, Thomas F. *The Mormons.* Chicago: University of Chicago Press; 1957.

Pearl of Great Price, The. A selection from the revelations, translations, and narrations of Joseph Smith, Prophet, Seer and Revelator to the Church of Jesus Christ of Latter-day Saints. Salt Lake City: 1949 edition.

Pratt, Parley Parker. *Autobiography.* Chicago: 1888. Reprinted, Salt Lake City: Deseret Book Company; 1938.

Roberts, B. H. (author and editor). *Comprehensive History of the Church of Jesus Christ of Latter-day Saints.* 6 vols. Salt Lake City: Deseret News Press; 1930.

————. *Outlines of Ecclesiastical History.* Salt Lake City: George Q. Cannon & Sons Co.; 1895.

Schindler, Harold. *Orrin Porter Rockwell, Man of God, Son of Thunder.* Salt Lake City: University of Utah Press; 1966.

Senate Document 189. Testimony given before the Judge of the Fifth Judicial Circuit of the State of Missouri, on the Trial of Joseph Smith, Jr., and Others, for High Treason, and other crimes against that State. Feb. 15, 1841. Blair & Rives, Printers. For photomechanical reprint, see Modern Microfilm Co., Salt Lake City, Utah.

Smith, Lucy. *History of the Prophet Joseph, by His Mother.* Salt Lake City: Improvement Era; 1902. A complete and unexpurgated edition of this rare and controversial book is published by Modern Microfilm Co., Salt Lake City; 1966.

Smith, Pauline Udall. *Captain Jefferson Hunt of the Mormon Battalion.* Salt Lake City: Nicholas G. Morgan, Sr., Foundation; 1958.

Sonne, Conway B. *World of Wakara.* San Antonio: The Naylor Company; 1962.

Spencer, Clarissa Young, with Harmer, Mabel. *One Who Was Valiant.* A biography of Brigham Young. Caldwell, Idaho: The Caxton Printers, Ltd.; 1940.

Stanley, Reva. *The Archer of Paradise: A Biography of Parley P. Pratt.* Caldwell, Idaho: Caxton Printers, Ltd.; 1937.

Stegner, Wallace. *Mormon Country.* New York: Duell, Sloan & Pearce; 1942.

Stenhouse, Thomas H. B. *Rocky Mountain Saints.* New York: D. Appleton & Co.; 1873.

Tullidge, Edward W. *History of Salt Lake City.* Salt Lake City: 1866.

Tyler, Sergeant Daniel. *A Concise History of the Mormon Battalion in the Mexican War.* Salt Lake City: 1881. Chicago: Rio Grande Press; 1964.

Werner, Morris R. *Brigham Young.* New York: Harcourt, Brace & Co., Inc.; 1924.

Whitney, Orson F. *History of Utah.* 4 vols. Salt Lake City: Deseret News Press; 1892.

Wyl, Dr. W. *Joseph Smith the Prophet: His Family and His Friends.* Salt Lake City: Tribune Printing & Publishing Co.; 1886.

Young, Brigham. *Journal of Discourses.* 26 vols. Liverpool and London: 1854-1886.

Young, Otis E. *The West of Philip St. George Cooke.* Glendale, Calif.: The Arthur H. Clark Company; 1955.

PERIODICALS

Atlantic Monthly. Issue of April 1859.

Contributor, The. Salt Lake City. Monthly from 1878-1890. Vol. IX, from Nov. 1887 to Oct. 1888 contains much valuable information on the Nauvoo Legion, as recorded by R. W. Young.

Deseret News. Salt Lake City; 1852 to present.

Evening and Morning Star. Independence, Missouri and Kirtland, Ohio: 1832 to 1834.

Latter-day Saints Millennial Star. Liverpool, England: 1840 to present.

Morgan, Dale L. "The State of Deseret," *Utah Historical Quarterly,* VIII, Nos. 2-4. Salt Lake City: 1940.

Nauvoo Expositor. Nauvoo, Illinois: June 7, 1844. One issue only; suppressed as apostate.

Nauvoo Neighbor. Nauvoo, Illinois; 1843 to 1845.

Times and Seasons. Nauvoo, Illinois: 1839-1846.

Tracy, Captain Albert. "Journal of Captain Albert Tracy," *Utah Historical Quarterly,* XIII, 1-119: 1945.

Western Galaxy, "Mines of the West." Salt Lake City: issue of March 1888.

Western Monitor. Independence, Missouri. Issue of August 2, 1833.

MANUSCRIPTS

History of Brigham Young. Ms., 1844-1877. Salt Lake City: Office of the Church Historian. Reproduced by photo-mechanical process from microfilm of original.

Journal History. L.D.S. Church Historian's Office, Salt Lake City, Utah. A day-to-day manuscript history of the Latter-day Saints, from the church's inception to the present.

Whitmer, John. *History.* 1838. Reproduced in its entirety by photomechanical process, Modern Microfilm Co., Salt Lake City, Utah.

Zobell, Albert L. *Thomas L. Kane, Ambassador to the Mormons.* M.A. thesis. Salt Lake City: University of Utah.

Index